Snakecharmers in Texas

Clive James was educated at Sydney University and at Cambridge, where he was president of Footlights. In addition to his autobiographies *Unreliable Memoirs* and *Falling Towards England*, and his novels, *Brilliant Creatures* and *The Remake*, he has published four mock-epic poems, *The Fate of Felicity Park*, *Peregrine Prykke's Pilgrimage*, *Britannia Bright's Bewilderment*, and *Charles Charming's Challenges*; three books of literary criticism, *The Metropolitan Critic*, *At the Pillars of Hercules* and *From the Land of Shadows* (which is available in Picador); a book of verse letters; *Fan-Mail*, and a verse diary, *Poem of the Year*. Between 1972 and 1982 he was television critic for the *Observer*. The three volumes of selections from his column are entitled *Visions Before Midnight*, *The Crystal Bucket* and *Glued to the Box* (all of which are available in Picador, as are his collected poems, *Other Passports*). His travel writings appear in a volume *Flying Visits – Postcards from the Observer 1979–1983* (also in Picador). As a television performer he has appeared regularly in several series, most notably 'Cinema', 'Saturday Night People', 'Clive James on Television' and 'The Late Clive James'. His television documentaries include 'Paris Fashion Show' and 'Live in Las Vegas'. At the BBC, programmes with his name in the title include 'The Late Show with Clive James', a series of 'Postcards' documentaries and 'Saturday Night Clive'.

Clive James

Snakecharmers
in Texas

Published by Pan Books
in association with Jonathan Cape

To
Terence Kilmartin

A partir d'un certain âge nos souvenirs sont tellement entrecroisés les uns sur les autres que la chose à laquelle on pense, le livre qu'on lit, n'a presque plus d'importance. On a mis de soi-même partout, tout est fécond, tout est dangereux, et on peut faire d'aussi précieuses découvertes que dans les *Pensées* de Pascal dans une réclame pour un savon.

Marcel Proust, *Albertine disparue*

World is crazier and more of it than we think,
Incorrigibly plural. I peel and portion
A tangerine and spit the pips and feel
The drunkenness of things being various.

Louis MacNeice, 'Snow'

This collection first published 1988 by
Jonathan Cape Ltd

This Picador edition published 1989 by
Pan Books Ltd, Cavaye Place, London SW10 9PG

in association with Jonathan Cape Ltd
9 8 7 6 5 4 3 2 1

© Clive James 1980, 1981, 1982, 1983, 1984, 1985, 1986, 1987

Introduction copyright © Clive James 1988

ISBN 0 330 305808

Printed and bound in Great Britain by
Richard Clay Ltd, Bungay, Suffolk

Contents

v

CONTENTS

Introduction

THE ONLY unifying principle I would claim for these articles is that they are written out of real interest in their subjects. Lucky enough, in recent years, to be able to pick and choose, I might not always have chosen wisely, but at least I was never obliged to feign enthusiasm. Keenness is therefore genuine, even if misplaced.

Apart from restoring the odd short passage which was cut for production reasons, the pieces are reproduced pretty much as was – not, I hope, because I have grown lazy now, but because I was reasonably careful then. Here again, I was in a privileged position: even when I had to phone the story in, I had time to think about it first. If the reader asks how I dare presume to take lyric poetry and ice-dancing with seemingly equal seriousness, I have no short answer, beyond pointing out that *homo faber* and *homo ludens* are both members of the same species *sapiens*, and that Mozart played billiards. There is a long answer, but I will probably never get to the end of it. This book is an instalment. The activities it covers are, I believe, all creative. Not even the racing driver has any intention of smashing things up. He least of all. What drives him, while he drives the car, is the impulse to bring order out of the hurly-burly, or at least to draw a clear line.

There are patterns in the clutter. These patterns help clarify one another. Once I saw Eugenio Montale fielding questions from a crowded room full of academics whose careers were partly, and in some cases entirely, based on discussing what he had written. No matter how impertinent the enquiry, he always tried to say something of general use. Twenty years later I saw Niki Lauda give a press conference in Portugal. He spoke the same way. They were not the same man, but they were more like each other than like anyone else who might write about either. Mastery, said Montale, resides in knowing how to limit yourself. The secret, said Lauda, is to win going as slowly as possible. It was the same voice talking each time. Below their diversity was an identity. Categories are illusory. Realising this fact made me feel less guilty about loving the different forms of expression so intensely while so intensely resenting any attempt to subtract from their variety by subjecting them to an abstract synthesis. They don't need to have unity imposed on them, because underneath they already have it to start off with.

Occasionally I have added a note when something too relevant to ignore has happened since the copy was filed. Guessing wrong about the future is an occupational hazard of journalism. Rewriting would have taken care of the discrepancies but it would have conferred retroactively a power of clairvoyance which was never among my attainments, or, indeed, my aims. Seeing ahead was usually out of the question. It was hard enough to see straight, at the time. To tell what time it was, the provenance of each piece is indicated at the end. This will also help to explain fluctuations of intonation from piece to piece. One should, one must, write for the *London Review of Books* and the *TV Times* in the same voice, but in each case the voice must strike the appropriate pitch. The audience for the one publication is more specialised than the audience for the other. It is nice to be thought intelligent by the first audience, but it is essential to be found intelligible by the second. For a wide readership not necessarily privy to literary allusions, the writer is under severe pressure to achieve a certain measure of self-denial. It never hurts.

Generally, however, I was writing for the *Observer*, the *London Review of Books* or their spiritual neighbours on the other side of the Atlantic. Within wide limits I could say anything I wanted, which left me with the responsibility of finding out what I wanted to say. On the *Observer*, in particular, there was a degree of freedom which was almost embarrassing. My thanks are due to its editor, and to the editors of the *Observer Magazine*, the *London Review of Books*, *Poetry Review*, the *TV Times*, the *New Yorker*, the *New York Review of Books* and the *Atlantic Monthly*. Even when I had to fight on the telephone to save a phrase, I was grateful for their attention. Often enough they were right.

Finally, the deepest gratitude must go to the intelligent reading public, whose tolerance for this aspect of my work – they don't always say that I have done it well, but they do sometimes say that I have done well to try it – never ceases to be a comfort. The title of this book is meant to convey thanks for such a communal relationship of writer and reader. The British army officer in *The Third Man* tells the American author of westerns, Holly Martins, how much he enjoys his books, especially for the curious information they contain. The officer says he never knew that there were snake-charmers in Texas. Holly Martins looks shamefaced, but might equally have shown a certain pride. To please the officer, a good man with more important work to do than to be a literary critic, was no bad thing.

At the time of writing this introduction I am doing less journalism than I would like, mainly because of making more television programmes than sanity allows. But the desire is always present, and will be fulfilled again. The old Fleet Street has broken up and dispersed, but like Grub Street, which pulled the same trick long ago, it is somehow still there – an idea I crossed the world to grasp, and won't let go of without a struggle.

London, 1987

Part One

AUSTRALIA'S SONS

A Death in Life

**The Fatal Shore by Robert Hughes
(Collins Harvill, 1987)**

FOR THE longest part of its short history, Australia pre-
ferred to forget that it began as a penal colony. Australian
historians born under the British Empire would accentuate
the positive. When, in recent years, a new stamp of his-
torians, usually harbouring no great love for Australia's
constitutional ties with Britain, began to tell the real story of
what the formative years of the white man's Australia had
been like, it became apparent why forgetfulness had been so
nearly complete. The story was horrible. Luckily, few of
them were able to tell it with more than a modicum of
evocative power, or the result would have been hard to bear.
Now, in *The Fatal Shore*, Robert Hughes, an Australian-born
critical writer of pronounced literary gifts, has summed up
all previous efforts, exceeded them in force of expression, and
brought the whole deadly business back to life. The result *is*
hard to bear – or would be, if it were not so clearly one of
those rare achievements in the writing of history by which
the unimaginably inhumane is brought to book without
making us give up on humanity. Such redemptive work can't
be done without artistry: there are degrees of anguish which
only style can make us contemplate, since merely to recount
them would leave us cold.

Hughes might have attempted this book in his youth, and
got the story out of proportion, even if he had not skimped it.
Fortunately, he has made *The Fatal Shore* the *magnum opus* of
his maturity. By now his sense of historical scale is sound, as
for this task it needed to be. It would have been easy to call
the Australian system of penal settlements a Gulag
Archipelago before the fact. The term 'concentration camp',

3

in its full modern sense, would not have been out of place: at least one of the system's satellites, Norfolk Island, was, if not an out-and-out extermination camp, certainly designed to make its victims long for death, like Dachau in those awful years before the war when the idea was not so much to kill people as to see how much they could suffer and still want to stay alive. And, indeed, Hughes draws these parallels. The analogies are inescapable. But he doesn't let them do his thinking for him. He is able to bring out the full dimensions of the tragedy while keeping it in perspective. The penal colony surely prefigured the modern totalitarian catastrophe. Equally surely it did not. It was a unique event, with unique consequences: the chief consequence being Australia itself, which has come a long way in 200 years – a point sufficiently proved by its ability to produce a book like this. The literature of the totalitarian dystopias emerged in spite of them, and could reach only one conclusion. Australia is a more difficult subject, however damning the raw evidence.

To the penal colony, the cat-o'-nine-tails was a tool more basic than the hoe. On Norfolk Island, where the camp was commanded by a succession of sadists, there were other forms of torture as well, some of them as vile as could be conceived before the age of electricity. But flogging provided the steady rhythm of torment. What made the whipping on Norfolk Island unique was that it so often got out of hand. At Port Arthur, in Van Diemen's Land – now called Tasmania – there was less chance of the flagellator's ecstasy releasing his victim to a premature death. The idea was to impress the subject with the mechanical inexorability of his fate, even when he was being punished for nothing except the dementia or paralysis induced by previous punishment. Norfolk Island was the personal expression of whichever maniac was running the place. Port Arthur was impersonal, a research establishment where the machine that ruined you was run by technicians whose only concern was for its perfection: Kafka's penal colony, so often thought of as a harbinger, now turns out to have harked back.

But there are echoes of these things throughout history, in which the only reliable constant is the form taken by extreme

4

cruelty when it is given absolute licence. Hughes, while aware of the general considerations, declines to lose himself among them. He keeps it specific. Enough to say that Norfolk Island and Port Arthur were there to inspire terror even in those convicts who were so recalcitrant that they were not terrified already by everyday life in the penal colony proper. The outlying camps were dumps for those who were held to be unassimilable elements in the main camp, where the city of Sydney now stands. But the main camp was itself a dump. Every convict sent there was held to be unassimilable in England. Whether he had stolen a thimble or forged £1,000 was immaterial. There was no notion that poverty might have created thieves: only that thieves might create revolution. They had to go. The colony was a way of getting rid of them without hanging them. It is a nice question whether transportation was intended as an alternative more humane than hanging, or less. Everyone knew what hanging looked like. But Australia was an unknown terror. So far away that no solid news ever came out of it, it was a black hole for facts. Dreadful stories percolated back to England of what went on out there, and there was always pressure from home to ensure that what went on remained so unattractive that any potential miscreant in the British Isles would fear it more than the rope and the hulks, and think twice before breaking the law, lest the law be obliged to break him, or her. There was thus a constant dispute between the liberal persuasion, which wanted Australia to rehabilitate criminals, and the illiberal persuasion, which wanted it to scare them. The first persuasion eventually won out, but not before the second had done its worst.

There was no need to give the place a bad name. It did that well enough by itself. Female convicts were forced into concubinage on the voyage out. Their sluttishness having been thus established, on arrival they were sorted like cattle, with officers taking the first pick. There were never enough women, so sodomy was rife among the men. Boys were initiated by rape, but to become an adult convict's punk at least insured some protection against the others. Nothing except unquestioning docility could protect anyone against the lash. Male convicts on the chain gangs, flogged perpetually as they did one-tenth of the work they might have done willingly for a pittance, could have been excused for wondering if Norfolk Island could be worse. It was, because there the work was entirely pointless. Around Port Jackson and the country opening up westward towards the Blue Mountains, the road-cutting and stump-grubbing had some purpose, no matter how inefficiently it was done. Despite itself, the slave-labour camp grew into something better than that. Most of the convicts were put out to assigned labour, with the prospect of working their way to rehabilitation; the chance of freedom proved to be a carrot more powerful than the stick.

One of Hughes's best gifts is his ability to analyse the way a social order arose out of a disciplinary regime. It wasn't much of a social order to start with, because even the free settlers were not the most imaginative of people, and the convicts, far from being instinctive exemplars of the democratic spirit, were mostly so ignorant of where Australia was that they thought China was next door; escapees would set out to walk there, and eat each other on the way. Students of the American Revolution, accustomed to the mental capacities of the nascent superpower's founding citizens, will search Australia's early history in vain for a comparable group of visionaries. The Rum Corps, a cabal within the garrison, deposed the governor only because they wanted the free exercise of their monopoly in booze; it was scarcely the Boston Tea Party. Hughes is well aware that the resemblance ends almost as soon as it starts. Nevertheless, a nation emerged, and did so partly because men like Governor Macquarie – no Thomas Jefferson but no fool, either – were determined that it should.

Hughes is careful not to romanticise the convicts. The thief who stole a loaf of bread didn't always steal it from someone who had a hundred loaves. He might have stolen it from someone who had one loaf. To have grown up in the prisons and the hulks was no education for anything except crime. The few literate convicts – counterfeiters, and, later on, Chartists and Irish separatists – were cut off from home by their sentence and cut off from each other by the system. Isolated, they lost heart. Yet, on the whole, the convicts represented a lot of energy going to waste, and it was necessary only to release that energy in order for them to turn their new country, which none of them had ever wanted to come to, into a place from which most of them did not want to go home. The gold rush in the middle of the nineteenth century brought the transportation system to an end, because no incipient felon could be made to fear a place that so many free men were booking their own passage to reach, often selling all they had. The bad dream was already over – for the white man, at least.

For the black man, the disaster was unmitigated. Here again there is a parallel, but it is more with South Africa than with the United States, unless we try to keep Wounded Knee in mind and forget Harpers Ferry. The Australian aborigines were never a *casus belli* between white men, not even as a pretext. Instead, the white men united against them. The revisionist who would like to pin another mass atrocity on the occupying power, however, will get no quick help from Hughes. In Van Diemen's Land, the soldiers might have driven the aborigines like game, but on the mainland it was the convicts who posed the greater threat to the native population. The brutalised convicts had to feel superior to someone, and the aborigines were ideal casting. They toiled not, and were hated for it. When the aborigines helped the troopers track escapees, the convicts hated them even more. The troopers could offer their black collaborators no reward that did not corrode their tribal ways and make them less fit to survive. What the aborigines needed was their land, untouched. They would have had to fight for it, and for that they would have needed solidarity. But on the day in 1788 when the First Fleet arrived in Sydney Harbour the tribe on the north shore spoke a language that the tribe on the south could not understand. The aborigines were not one people. It is racism to suppose they were. There was not, and could not have been, an aboriginal general. They would have needed an Eisenhower, and couldn't produce even a Crazy Horse. There had never been any need to, until we got there.

By 'we' I mean Australians. All of us now feel the force of the plural personal pronoun. Some of us feel it so strongly that we move national self-consciousness to the forefront of the political agenda, often with tiresome results. Touchiness, however, is inevitable. Australian writers, painters, singers, actors, film directors, scientists, sportsmen, and tycoons make a disproportionate bang in the world. The outsider could be forgiven for thinking that everything must be for export. But in all these fields there is quite a lot going on at home as well. The Australian can get a bit impatient when he hears his country judged according to what its expatriates are up to, even when the judgment is praise; and when the expatriates do the judging, especially if it is dispraise, he is likely to become inflamed.

But, with due notice that the case is being put broadly, what has happened is this. Up until the late 1960s, Australia undervalued itself as a country, or anyway its intelligentsia thought it did, giving this alleged Cinderella complex the unlovely journalistic title 'the cultural cringe'. But the vogue for self-discovery, felt in those years throughout the Western world, was a passion by the time it reached Australia, rather as the Depression in the 1930s struck harder and stayed longer there than it did anywhere else. With the advent of Gough Whitlam's government, in the 1970s, Australia had begun to esteem itself at what its social commentators – an increasingly numerous and vociferous class – thought was a just valuation. Diffidence had turned to self-assertion. The change was welcome, but there was an obvious danger of hyped-up expectations, to which some of the country's more stentorian promoters duly succumbed. The cringe became a snarl. Tub-thumping was heard in areas where a reasoned tone might have been more suitable. Hughes's excellent book on Australian painting, *The Art of Australia*, adumbrated this new confidence but proved to be atypical in its tact. While analysing, appraising, and ordering the Australian painters with an authority that no indigenous critic had achieved before, Hughes was careful not to tear his country's heritage loose from its world context, and made it clear that it was only because he *had* a world

8

view, gained during his travels, that he was able to come home and see clearly what the Australian painters had achieved.

Australian defensiveness about the success of its expatriates was not to be allayed, and probably won't be by *The Fatal Shore*, either. Here again, political zeal inevitably distorts the picture. Ardent republicans would like Australia to be self-sufficient in the arts the way that it is in minerals. The idea that any one country can be culturally self-sufficient is inherently fallacious, but in the forward rush of Australian confidence during Gough Whitlam's period of government, when grants were handed out to anybody with enough creative imagination to ask for one, reason was thrown into the back seat. For the last fifteen years, Australian artists in all fields, supposedly free at last from the imposition of being judged by alien – i.e., British – standards, have been judged by their own standards, and almost invariably found to be the authors of significant works. The glut of self-approval has been most evident in literature, which in normal circumstances customarily produces a strong critical movement to accompany any period of sustained creativity but in Australia's case has largely failed to do so. The undoubted fact that some very good things have been written can't stave off the consideration that many less good things have been given the same welcome.

A consideration is all it is. Creativity can get along without criticism. When Pushkin – who was in the position of having to think what form a national culture might take – called for a dispassionate criticism, he wasn't calling for help in writing poems, which he could do by himself. He was merely stating his wish to write them in a civilised atmosphere, whose absence was reducing him to isolation, and thereby damaging his individuality. The individual needs a community. In Australia, while literature is rapidly becoming a cash crop, a literary community has been slower to emerge. Criticism is too often, in the strict sense, tendentious. Scale is duly hailed, ambition lauded, but the direction of the book – does it point the way? does it give us purpose? – is usually the basis of assessment. There are not many critics detached enough to

9

quibble over detail, and ask why so many great writers have produced so little good writing.

This is where Hughes's book will come in handy. It will be thoroughly read in the schools, whereas many of the new masterpieces are skimmed dreamily at the beach. When workaday books are well written, a culture starts to pick up: the best of the spoken language is fed back into itself, by way of writers whose ear for speech informs the content of their prose, and whose mastery of composition makes them selective. In this respect, Hughes is hard to fault. The Australian landscape has been captured like this by few painters and by no other writers at all, because anyone as vivid also gushed, and anyone as elegant was dull. Here is the entrance to Port Arthur:

> Both capes are of towering basalt pipes, flutes and rods, bound like fasces into the living rock. Their crests are spired and crenellated. Seabirds wheel, thinly crying, across the black walls and the blacker shadows. The breaking swells throw up their veils.

In the late 1950s, as an architecture student as Sydney University, Hughes was the artiest young man on the scene. His blond hair growing naturally in a thick layer cut, his lanky form Englishly decked out in lamb's wool, suede, and corduroy, he sloped forward on long-toed desert boots while aiming at you a cigarette whose startling length suggested that he was about to launch a poisoned dart. Instead, he drew you. He drew anything that caught his eye, which was almost everything; and he drew it with uncanny speed and accuracy. Eventually, he decided that his graphic work was derivative, and gave it up. Although it is true that he absorbed other people's styles one after the other, he might have arrived at this renunciation too early. When there was no one else left to absorb, the real Hughes might have emerged, as happened in his prose. In those years, you could always tell what he had been reading the day before. Even today, he is a magpie for vocables: no shimmering word he spots in any of the languages he understands, and in several more that he doesn't, is safe from being plucked loose and flown back to his nest. Omnivorous rather than eclectic, that type of curiosity is the slowest to find coherence. But his fluency was always his own, and by persistence he has arrived at a solidity to match it: a disciplined style that controls without crippling all that early virtuosity, and blessedly also contains his keen glance, getting the whole picture into a phrase the way he once got his fellow-students' faces into a single racing line. It is exactly right, as well as funny, to call a merino sheep 'a pompous ambling peruke'. Scores of such felicities could be picked out, but only on the understanding that they are not the book's decoration. They are its architecture.

There are several benefits that accrue to the Australian writer who turns himself into an expatriate. The first advantage of going away is obvious: it is the wider view he brings with him if he comes home. Hughes, a member of one of the grandest Australian Catholic families, was not very provincial even before he left, but in London in the early 1960s he was in no danger of shivering rejected in an Earl's Court bed-sit. While some of his contemporaries were doing exactly that, he had rooms in Albany, the exclusive address for gentlefolk just off Piccadilly. Hughes found his true fame later on, in America, but he would not be able to say plausibly that Britain turned down what he had to offer. Before the immigration laws toughened up in the 1970s, Australian overachievers found Britain hospitable, sometimes absurdly so. The British class system, hidebound within itself, was easily penetrated by the colonial whose accent it could not place accurately in the social scale. In London, the Australian expatriates breathed dirtier air than at home but found life more interesting. The experience did not stop some of the short-stay visitors going home as convinced republicans. But for a long voyager like Hughes it became that much harder to cast Britain as the villain, either currently or in retrospect. One of the hard issues he is prepared to face in *The Fatal Shore* is that the growth of the penal colony into a living society can't be interpreted as merely a liberal refutation of the mother country at her most repressive. England was also present at the spontaneous creation that grew out of the planned destruction. The ties with 'home' were real. The past is not to be argued away for the sake of a political programme.

The second advantage enjoyed by the expatriate Australian literary practitioner is just as obvious. Travel not only broadens the view; it sharpens the gaze. Hughes might have remained comparatively blind to the uniqueness of his native topography if he had never left it. Coming back to it, he sees it without any intervening veil of familiarity. Laudably intent on looking at what happened where it happened, he has travelled widely within his own country, to places most of his compatriots have never seen but will see now through his eyes:

> As you approach it [Macquarie Harbour, in Tasmania], sea and land curve away to port in a dazzle of white light, diffused through the haze of the incessantly beating ocean. All is sandbank and shallow; the beach that stretches to the northern horizon is dotted with wreckage, the impartial boneyard of ships and whales.

A third advantage is less talked about but ought to become more evident, now that *The Fatal Shore* has given us such a conspicuous example. The Australian expatriate, the stay-away writer, loots the world for cultural references. If he can write like Hughes, he may combine these into a macaronic, coruscating prose that would be as precious as a cento or an Anacreontic odelette if it were not so robust, vivid, and clearly concerned with defining the subject, rather than just displaying his erudition:

> The Norfolk Island birds had forgotten man had ever been there; one could pick them out of the bushes, like fruit. Even today, a walk along the cliffs – where the green meadow runs to the very brink of the drop and the bushes are distorted by the eternal Pacific wind into

humps and clawings that resemble Hokusai's *Great Wave* copied by a topiarist – is a fine cure for human adhesiveness. One sees nothing but elements: air, water, rock and the patterns wrought by their immense friction. The mornings are by Turner; the evenings, by Caspar David Friedrich, calm and beneficent, the light sifting angelically down towards the solemn horizon.

Nothing homegrown in Australia sounds quite like that, yet it is essentially Australian writing – the product of an innocent abroad who has consciously enjoyed every stage of his growing sophistication without allowing his original barbaric gusto to be diminished. Here the vexed question of what place the expatriate has in Australia's cultural history is answered in terms of intensity, as critical questions always must be. The best comparison is with that period of American prose when literary journalists were enjoying both the American idiom and the privilege of loading it with a cosmopolitan culture. The comparison should not be forced: American writers mostly had their Europe all around them at home, whereas Australians had to sail in search of it, or thought they did. (Even as early as the 1950s, the post-war immigration of European refugees had changed Australian culture profoundly, from the kitchen upwards, but those native Australians who sailed in the opposite direction were following a surer instinct than has subsequently been made out: they might have eaten baklava in Melbourne, but the Parthenon was still in Athens.)

Yet the similarity is striking. That feeling transmitted by the sheer scope of James Gibbons Huneker, which rises to a fever in the style of George Jean Nathan, is the feeling you get from the Australian expatriate writers at their most exuberant: that the world is theirs, and that they are trying to pack it all in, possessing it through the naming of its names. Barry Humphries, Australia's unchallenged genius of cabaret and intimate revue, not only wields a vast culture himself but incongruously lends it to his characters, so that his most famous creation, the housewife superstar and arch-philistine

Dame Edna Everage – who by now has taken on such an independent life that she hosts talk-shows in both Australia and Britain – turns out to know more than seems plausible about, say, German Expressionism. The poetry of the London-based expatriate Peter Porter, often thought of by even the most favourable British critics as being a showcase for his learning, sins less through calculation in that regard than through the lack of it. Porter just loves the adventure of creativity – anybody's creativity. The message of his work, far from being 'Look how much I've read', is 'Look how much there is to read.' There are lines by Porter that might be sentences by Hughes, and vice versa. Not that one suggests anything so organised as a school. (The present reviewer was at the table in the Groucho Club in London, last December, when Hughes and Porter met for the first time, Hughes having wandered the world for twenty-five years, and Porter for ten years longer than that.) But the very fact that this is not a school might be what makes it a movement: an expatriate movement in Australian writing which complements the achievement at home – without, of course, presuming to replace it.

In fact, some of the more spectacular of the Australian cultural stayaways don't seem very concerned about what happens where they come from. Germaine Greer (whose polemics are at their most effective when uttered with the kind of zest I am talking about, and at their weakest when she affects to be weary of the world) turns up in Australia mainly to stun the local talk-show hosts and harangue the feminists for so slavishly clinging to ideas she gave them in the first place. Then she takes off again. The almost dementedly clever Oxford academic Peter Conrad is nowadays ready to turn aside and sum up Australian literature – having already, in his *Everyman History of English Literature*, dealt with the old country's written heritage – but there is no doubt that his chief concern is with the world entire: his prose, like Greer's, pops and fizzes with the strain of fitting in a self-assured opinion about absolutely everything. Australia's itinerant literati, like its media entrepreneurs, are world-eaters. Perhaps it is revenge for isolation: the

Empire (among Australian expatriates the joke is old by now) strikes back.

In many respects the most damaging counterblow yet, *The Fatal Shore* is nevertheless open to criticism from several points of view. The book is dedicated to Hughes's godson, the son of a barrister who recently had the pleasure of making one of Britain's leading civil servants look ridiculous in an Australian court. The poor man had been sent out there in a misguided attempt to secure the Australian government's co-operation in repressing a book about MI5; the Australian judiciary, only lately set free from the constitutional tie by which its highest court of appeal sat in Britain, made its independence felt. But republicans pleased by the dedication might not find the book that follows wholly to their liking. If they use it to condemn the past, they will have to condemn themselves along with it, Hughes having shown how serious Sartre was when he made his apparently frivolous remark about not being able to quarrel with history, because it led up to him. Still, if the trend towards republicanism proves inexorable, Hughes will at least have helped to make the transition more intelligent, by raising the level of debate.

Professional historians will no doubt cavil about the un-academic eclecticism of Hughes's research techniques, although if they do so they will be paying him that tacit compliment of accepting him among their number, and anyway it is hard to see how his use of correspondence, in particular, could be more fastidious. If letters by convicts have been quoted from before, the job has never been done with such sympathy, so keen an ear for the telling phrase. Geoffrey Blainey's *The Tyranny of Distance* must retain the title of the most startlingly original book of Australian history, but *The Fatal Shore* runs it close, and is less like a thesis.

A more serious criticism could be made through the area in which the book most obviously excels. As a literary work, it rather tails off, as if its author had got tired of it. If Hughes plans another volume, telling the story up to Federation, at the turn of the century, it will be very welcome, though the period has already been well covered by historians. But, on the evidence of his text, his interest flags after Australia has ceased to be a paradox – a birth in death – and he interprets the approach of relative normality as a signal to pack up.

Even so, a more roundly conclusive final chapter would have been gratifying. Earlier chapters amply prove that Hughes would have been capable of it. He has that rarest ability among pictorially talented writers, of making a plain prose statement that covers the case. His television series *The Shock of the New* was good to look at but even better to hear. Giving us his view of the stack of bricks that the Tate Gallery had purchased and displayed as a work of art, Hughes made his point so simply that it didn't sound like an epigram: 'Anyone *except* a child can make such things.' (Cocteau's famous remark about the poetic prodigy Minou Drouet – 'Every child is a genius except Minou Drouet' – is funnier, but not so true.) As the art critic of *Time*, since 1970, Hughes has had the obligation of covering the world art beat in readily accessible prose most weeks of the year. Bigger stories, such as the Rothko-legacy scam, he has been able to treat at length in the *New York Review of Books*. While the typical homebound Australian literary genius veers between undisciplined newspaper articles and fictional masterpieces that grow extra chapters of self-justification if challenged, Hughes has had to perfect himself in the good journalistic practice of seeing the point and keeping to it.

For his discovery of the diligent man inside his own bohemianism ('Live like a bourgeois,' said Flaubert, 'think like a demigod') New York has rewarded Hughes well, not least with much free time. This book is what he did with it. He went home and rediscovered his country, with an eidetic intensity that recalls Sidney Nolan doing the same thing, and in a prose that adds something to Patrick White's vision of the Australian landscape – clarity, straightforwardness, a sparkling simplicity without distortion. Finally, the best thing about *The Fatal Shore* is just that: going about other business, it doesn't *try* to be a work of art. Even on a subject like this, and at such length, Hughes has managed to speak with the arresting verve that Australians of today, fancying themselves, not without reason, as natural democrats, would like to think of as their peculiar tone of voice – the breath of sanity.

New Yorker
23 March, 1987

Elaborate Brute

Christopher Brennan: A Critical Biography by Axel Clark (Melbourne University Press, 1980)

N<small>O</small> A<small>USTRALIAN</small> poet before Christopher Brennan was fully conscious of the artistic problem posed by isolation from Europe, and no Australian poet since has been fully disabled by it. Brennan's life and death dramatised the problem once and for all. It was and is a true problem, not just a difficulty. Brennan, whether he wanted to or not, lived the problem to the full, and thereby, on everybody else's behalf, got it out into the open. His messy crucifixion was all the more thorough for the degree to which he co-operated, and it doesn't have to happen again. If it does, then someone is being pretentious. Brennan spent too much of his time acting as an awful warning. That was one of the main reasons why his achievement fell so far short of his ambition: he put less energy into writing poetry than into being the poet. It was an aberration in which personality conspired with circumstances, creating a tangle which Axel Clark, in this admirably hard-headed critical biography, does much to sort out.

Brennan was a prodigy of the Australian *fin de siècle* who had pretty well given up writing by the beginning of the 1920s, thereby giving himself more time in the day to be drunk and disorderly. He went on being regarded as one of Australia's most distinguished minds even as he lay in the gutter. The local term for a falling-down drunk is a no-hoper, and it is a rare thing for a no-hoper to be so highly esteemed. For a long time before his death and for longer still afterwards, Brennan's reputation was required to bear a large part of the burden of the possibility of artistic seriousness in Australian poetry. It was aided in this task by the fact that between his death in 1932 and the publication of *The Verse of Christopher Brennan* in 1960 his work was hard to obtain. But even during this long moratorium it gradually became possible to suggest either that he never achieved what was in him or that he never had it in him in the first place.

A sensible view partakes of both possibilities. He had some talent to go with his learning, but his conception of poetry – and the conception was in too large a part a product of his learning – worked with almost complete success to ensure that his talent could not come to fruition. He is never wholly himself for more than a line or so at a time. The rest is a tortured pastiche easily mocked; a strained symbolism whose Victorian diction, Swinburne with even more water, does not even let him succeed in sounding Frenchified. Any smart critic who wanted to make a popinjay out of Brennan would have plenty to go on. But those single lines and phrases live in the memory: 'and sterile wisdom crowned his brow with power', 'under a sky of uncreated mud', 'my days of azure have forgotten me', 'beneath whose corpse-fed weeds I too shall sink', 'fire in the heavens, and fire along the hills', 'in the cicada's torture-point of song'.

No Australian writer before him gave quite that impression of concentrated, refined sensibility. No Australian poet before him *wanted* language to be so intensely organised. It is impossible not to feel that in despising the populist writers and balladeers he was missing out on the biggest intellectual adventure of all. But what he was trying for was ambitious enough, and momentarily he got there. He would be less of a discussion point, and more of an unarguable fact, if he had got there and stayed there, but literary history does not wholly consist of complete achievements, and anyway the incomplete achievements are often the more instructive. From C. J. Dennis, who knew exactly what he was up to and in *The Sentimental Bloke* did it to perfection, there is much enjoyment to be gained, but little edification about how the Australian lyric poet is to go about squaring his personal upbringing with the cultural heritage of the language in which he writes. It is easy enough now to say that Dennis did the wise thing. He set out to write popular art and he got what he was after – he was popular. But in Australia popular art, even in verse, has never been a problem. Australians have always enjoyed popular verse, much of it written to a very high standard of finish. The problem was for Brennan to know his own aims and limits in the same way that Dennis knew his. It might be too much to say that Dennis's were knowable and Brennan's weren't, but it can and should be said that Brennan was simply bound to spend a disproportionate amount of time finding out where he stood. From Brennan, in addition to those lines and fragments, you get a clear idea, as you could never get from the popular writers, of the dilemma by which Kenneth Slessor was later both impelled and inhibited, and which A. D. Hope has spent his life resolving – triumphantly, in my view – into poetry.

Brennan's background was the Irish famine. In Sydney he grew up speaking the language of the oppressor. But as a young Catholic with a failure for a father he had one conspicuous advantage among his handicaps. He was educated by the Jesuits of Riverview, who even in my time were still making sure that their pupils got plenty of learning rammed into their heads along with the dogma. Brennan lost his faith after coming up to Sydney University, but without any Joycean agonies. On his own admission, the chasubles and thuribles had been what attracted him to it. Such furniture, redolent of incense, he had subsumed under the general title of Beauty. When he became interested in modern French poetry, its propensities towards Beauty were what interested him most about it, and remained so even as his studies deepened into a life-long preoccupation. His Classical studies never did much to chasten this notion of

Beauty, which reminds you of Wilde's, except that Wilde was growing out of it even as he fashioned it into epigrams. Brennan's mind formed early and never altered its cast. His maturities are there at the start and his immaturities are still there at the end – a lack of development which gives Mr Clark a hard task to avoid monotony.

At university, Brennan deepened his scholarship but remained essentially an autodidact: a typically provincial emphasis. Similarly provincial was his determination to be a character – always, in any backwater, a promising first step towards becoming a legend. He decorated his tattered gown with jam tins. He was a terrific Classical scholar but neglected the set books 'most scandalously', as he said himself. Studying philosophy, he boasted of acknowledging no superior mind among his teachers. Against all the odds posed by his clearly superior abilities, he contrived to get second-class honours in Classics, not so much for neglecting the books as for being contemptuous of Plato. He discovered Swinburne – at that time a writer banned from the University Library – and went mad for him. So mad, really, that he never recovered. When he read Dante he said all the right things ('pure muscle, nothing superfluous') but drew no conclusions about his own use of language, which from the beginning until the end was always stiff with thou, yon, tho', ere, o'er, thro', oft and (wince-inducing even at the time, one would have thought) ween'st. Every margin was a marge and it was never murk when it could be mirk. You can't help weening that his passion for such Frenchmen as Gautier, Baudelaire and – later but most lastingly – Mallarmé was uncannily without result in his own work.

Thematically, he might have been a Symbolist, but technically, at the deeper level, that of language, he wrote as if his modern French models had never existed. More than that, he wrote as if Victor Hugo had never existed. The tightly focused language which Eliot and Pound discovered and coveted in the French moderns was simply not what attracted Brennan. The proof is in his unshaken capacity to compose with the English equivalent of the full *poncif* kit which his Gallic heroes thought of as something in the far past, back beyond the first night of *Hernani*. For Brennan such mannerisms should have been equally antediluvian. Nor can it be said that Brennan was merely echoing the London poets of the 1890s, all of whom wrote clear English compared with his. The uncomfortable conclusion – which Mr Clark bravely goes a long way towards reaching – is that Brennan's diction is a defensive system, and not just against the bourgeois reader, but against being read too closely by *any* reader. The up-to-date punctuation, with lower-case letters at the beginning of lines, might have been no more than what Stefan George, who employed such devices wholesale, was later to call barbed wire against the un-initiated (*'Stacheldraht wider Unberufene'*). But the archaic language had the more destructively alienating effect of sounding poetic while concealing meaning – or, more likely, the lack of it.

Nearly all gifted poets, however, start off by looking for spectacular ways to say not very much. When the young graduate Brennan left on a scholarship to Berlin, his admirers had every reason to believe that his precocious mind would gain weight. Yet with his travel as with his reading, the main interest resides in how little he let it alter him. He seems to have enjoyed many advantages in Berlin, not counting the love, later to prove a dubious privilege, of his landlady's beautiful daughter. He learned fluent German, but it never occurred to him to do anything else except come home. He never went to Europe again. His closeness to it was literary. Paris, the city of his modern heroes, he did not set foot in.

It could be said that he wanted to be a big fish in a small pond. But his closeness to Australia was literary too. Even in those fragments which one would like to think of as representing his characteristic voice, there is not much specific about the Australian landscape. The cicada's torture-point of song could be happening on Crete. When he says that there is snow in the north, you have to assume that he does not mean Norway. Whatever the reason why Brennan 'went in' for verse (and even his biographer seems to detect something *voulu* about Brennan's creative impulse), it was not out of the desire to register the world around him. His friend John le Gay Brereton could see the importance of Henry Lawson. Brennan couldn't. He had no interest in the bush, the Labour movement or Australian nationalism. In the Australian 1890s, a period which self-consciously but justifiably felt itself to be alive with the possibility of a new national culture, Brennan isolated himself. He took on, or was forced into, the role of the metropolitan in the colonies. But he was a metropolitan without a metropolis.

Nevertheless he might have done something to bring the nationalist impulse under an informed scrutiny, if he had really been the European artist that he was supposed by everyone, including himself, to be. His real tragedy, which precedes the tragedy of his decline and overshadows it, is that his knowledge of literature could not be brought to bear on the contemporary creation of literature, even when it was he that was doing the creating. For all that he had read whole libraries, he could tell his contemporary Australian poets nothing useful. He thought that any poetry addressed to Bill and Jim could not be worth reading. His own poetry would have to be a lot more consistently individual than it is if it were to justify such a grand assumption. He had no right to patronise Lawson, in whom he should have seen the vitality. Lawson, who wrote poems nervously defending his lack of technical polish against pedants who could talk of nothing else, might have benefited decisively – in his subsequent reputation, at any rate – from the support of a man of Brennan's stature.

Over and above what he might have done as a critic, as an artist Brennan might have given contemporary Australian poets an example of natural language composed with the rigour conferred by a mind fully aware of tradition. But it turned out that he could not give this example even to himself. Mr Clark is properly reluctant to find historically determinist reasons which might explain the whole of this failing. Clearly Brennan was glad to embrace the character, and within his own lifetime the legend, of the local man who knew as much as they did overseas. Sydney was still a small town and its circumstances undoubtedly encouraged him to waste his time playing a part. But finally the personality must be the determining factor, if only by being too complicated to explain. There was no outside reason why Brennan's learning should have remained stymied. The reason was inside. He pursued failure as if intent on achieving it at any cost and against all the odds. In 1894, his paper 'On the Manuscripts of Aeschylus' appeared in the *Journal of Philology* alongside articles by Housman and Nettleship. It should have been the beginning of a useful second career as a philologist, but in the long run the only thing that came out of it was a mention, with qualified approval, in a footnote to Sidgwick's edition of Aeschylus, and a rather more fulsome, but withal fleeting, acknowledgment from Eduard Fraenkel in his great commentary on the *Agamemnon*. Beyond that, no trace.

It was in Brennan's nature for great studies to go nowhere. The passion for Mallarmé became a discipleship but never deepened into a true influence. As Mr Clark has it, Brennan remained 'essentially a Victorian poet in his verbal habits'. The word 'essentially' is a large one and in Brennan's case essentially correct. Brennan thought Patmore was 'austere and bare'. He liked the esoteric aspects of Huysmans and Villiers de L'Isle Adam, thinking that their concern with the occult was what was interesting about them. Mr Clark rather disproportionately brings Yeats in at this point. Yeats may have concerned himself with the sacred mysteries, but they were not where he saw and heard poetry. He saw and heard poetry in real life. Mr Clark concedes that Yeats developed towards a pregnant natural speech as Brennan did not, but he could have conceded much more by using a less weighty comparison. So, after all, did Dowson – and at the time, too, not later on. Put a stanza by Dowson beside a stanza by Brennan and you can quickly see that Dowson knows exactly what he is doing, whereas Brennan is only making vague gestures.

Brennan wrote as if he thought vagueness should be the aim. The only bohemian in town, he was encouraged in the belief that he stood apart and above, a sayer of the unsayable, a seeker of the Absolute. But either he did not wish to register the ineffable precisely, or else he couldn't. Perhaps the desire and the capacity are forms of each other. At any rate, a bad marriage to his Berlin landlady's daughter kept him miserable for many years. Transported to the ends of the earth for the purpose of fulfilling Brennan's impossibly elevated ideas of spiritual companionship, she was not in an enviable position, but obviously took steps to ensure that his position was not enviable either. In Brennan's mind, carnality was a threat to purity. On the other hand, he could not do without carnality. A man does not have to be a lapsed Catholic to think like this, but it helps. Brennan's verses thus had a nameless quandary to be oblique about, but when you read them closely you find that not even the quandary is clearly seen. Dowson's poems about impossible love at least point in the right direction, so that you are not surprised, and might even be rather touched, to hear that he went potty about under-age girls. But Brennan's complaints about lack of sexual satisfaction are less than half admitted in his own mind, so that they are much less than half expressed on the page. He had nothing clear to be vague about. 'Lilith', his *magnum opus* of a poem sequence, hits its one fretful note and maintains it, with a *sostenuto* winsomeness that no amount of aestheticist decoration can make interesting. If the inspiration had been real, the out-of-date trappings would not have smothered it. The aestheticism of the English 1890s was still absorbing the iconography of Gustave Moreau, who died of old age before the century was out. D'Annunzio and Richard Strauss shamelessly employed Symbolist props and decor that had grown tatty with fifty years of constant use. But with Brennan the trappings *were* the inspiration. His nominal subject – the nominal subject never really nominated – was merely the pretext for using them. Thematically, he was all style, and all the styles were dated.

But the intensity of organisation which he admired in his model poets, and which he regarded with some justification as an achievement to be prized above the blunt speech of the balladeers, is present in his work if only as a conjured ghost, and that much of him is the reverse of dated. There are passages in 'Lilith' which, if handed out to clever students in a practical criticism seminar, might well be identified as being by Wallace Stevens.

Thick sleep, with error of the tangled wood,
and vapour from the evening marsh of sense,
and smoothness of the glide of Lethe, would
inaugurate his dullard innocence,
cool'd of his calenture, elaborate brute.

That last line, in particular, might have come straight out of 'The Comedian as the Letter C'. Sooner or later a thou, yon or ween'st gives the game away, yet for short stretches you can see that Brennan had at least the *technical* wherewithal to realise his ambitions. But technique is not inspiration. Sophistication without barbarism is the seasoning without the roast.

In 1914, Brennan took the part of England against Germany, packing his Muse off to war with shameful results from which she never quite recovered. His Irish heritage might have suggested a different course, but the determining factor seems to have been the opportunity to declare open hostilities against his wife and, even more specifically, her mother. Brennan's execrable war poetry was the continuation of household diplomacy by other means. You can tell exactly what it is about, but that is no merit. Nor, pitiably, did his great and authentic love for European literature do the least thing to make him aware of the European tragedy. Gazing without, Brennan was just as cut off from his own interior life as when he feigned to gaze within. The only difference was that he could be strident instead of stifled. With an interior life like his, however, there was good reason for staying as cut off as possible.

Even in casual retrospect, the publication of his pre-war *Poems* looks like a culmination. But as Mr Clark reveals, Brennan had in effect given up on himself much sooner. Misery wiped him out early. What should have been opportunities worked towards his destruction. As a librarian he was merely broke. When he finally got the university job he ought always to have had, he took the opportunity to become a drunken wreck, almost as if to stave off the possibility of acquiring a personal dignity befitting his mental powers. Some idea of what he must have been like as a lecturer can be gleaned from the fugitive pieces collected in *The Prose of Christopher Brennan* (Sydney, 1962, edited, like *The Verse of Christopher Brennan*, by his two old friends, A. R. Chisholm and J. J. Quinn). Christina Stead is only one of the subsequently luminous names who later said that they were inspired by his lectures, no matter how chaotically delivered. But it would have been strange if he had been anything less than inspiring. He knew a lot and was enthusiastic about it all. His enthusiasm was ungovernable. It had a mind of its own, putting Tennyson on a level with Dante and Patmore with Donne. Brighter students, especially when they as yet know little, are understandably set on fire by that kind of fervour.

But as far as his own poetry went, Brennan's pedagogy was just one more among the distractions conspiring to guarantee that he would not get much done. Another was talk. He was a lunch-club lion who spouted brilliance endlessly. The performance went on for years. You could come to him like a supplicant, push a drink in front of him, and sit down to listen. There is no reason to doubt that he spoke marvellously – no reason, that is, beyond the usual reason, which centres on the fact that anyone who sits still for somebody else's monologue is not always the best witness to its quality. But there were men of spirit who said he was marvellous. In my time he was remembered still as the most enchanting talker who never drew breath, and it is pleasing to learn from Mr Clark that in Brennan's last days the young A. D. Hope once poured the libation and heard the oracle pronounce. But legend-building is never more typically a provincial pastime than in its effect of neutralising the remarkable. The legend of Brennan the great pontificator conceals the sad story of energy running to waste. When Wilde talked, he was rehearsing what he would later write. Brennan was talking it all away.

And eventually everything was gone. He was dead long before he died. The details are here and they make grim reading. He came to terms with carnal love, but it was too late. When his mistress was killed he fell to pieces. While reading this book I was simultaneously working my way through Renate Wagner's excellent *Arthur Schnitzler: Eine Biographie* (Vienna, 1981). The comparison is instructive because the two men were contemporaries. Schnitzler's circumstances, those of a Jewish truth-teller in a society which was hypocritical when it was not anti-semitic, were truly difficult, and his personal losses, culminating in the death of his daughter, cruel. But he had control of his interior life in a way that Brennan did not. He had the necessary conceit which helps an artist to stay true to his gift. Brennan, no doubt egged on by his admirers, preened himself in every area except the one that counted. He admitted to dissatisfaction with his own work. It is a large admission for an artist to make, and should not be confused with modesty.

Locally thought to be a big name in Europe, Brennan was in fact unknown there, but the legend was fed by his notorious epistolary exchange with Mallarmé, who was kind enough to acknowledge Brennan's admiration. The admiration amounted to abject worship and went on after Mallarmé's death, which was fulsomely recorded in 'Lilith' ('as he that sleeps in hush'd Valvins hath taught') and in the dedication to 'The Forest of Night'. But one of the hazards of provincialism is the tendency for the bright young talent to be nourished by the example of a great man far away, without realising that the great man has been nourished by a whole society. An expert at long range, Brennan had a hopelessly purist notion of what literary life in Europe was actually like. And as is the way with purist notions, it got beyond the stage where he could afford to be disabused of it. When a collection of Rilke's first poems was handed to him, and he had the opportunity to see how the rarefied metaphysical experiences he had hinted at could indeed be caught and held, he handed the book back unread.

He was probably better off living and dying where he was. In the English 1890s he would have been a back-marker at best, somewhere behind Theodore Wratislaw and perhaps a bit ahead of Richard le Gallienne. Mr Clark strangely endorses Brennan's eventual disparagement of Whistler. But surely Whistler was the *Weltbürger* that Brennan could never have been. Whistler knew his origins to be a source of strength. Beyond that, he simply had a strong talent.

Nobody would now suggest that Brennan's talent was ever interesting for its strength. It was interesting for its type. His talent was married to his intellect, even if the marriage was bad. Before him, the Australian poets could write from unexamined impulse about a new world. After him, things were never so simple again. He was the timely if unfortunate reminder that the intellect would have to be part of the new world too. His *via dolorosa* of a life might have been less gruesome if there had been an Australian literary world in which he could have taken his rightful place as a man and an artist instead of as those lesser things, a character and a legend. But there was the academic world or there was down-and-out bohemia, with nothing in between, and to write literary journalism meant to be engaged in rebutting some good citizen's contention that the European philosophy of the thirteenth century had all been discredited, and that Dante was, as a consequence, no good. The provincial intellectual is doomed to arguing at low level. More than half a century later, there is still no Australian literary world, not in Sydney, Melbourne, Adelaide, Perth or Canberra. It is some consolation to realise that there is no literary world in Birmingham or Los Angeles either. I have heard that there is one in Montreal, but I don't believe it. The literary world is in London and New York, the only cities big enough to sustain magazines which can afford to reject copy.

Kenneth Slessor shared many of Brennan's civilised interests and had a far more powerful creative drive, but in time he, too, stopped writing. Once again, although in the much longer run, the difficulties of leading a literary life in a provincial community – where the artiness is as damaging as the philistinism – proved insuperable. But at least Slessor had Brennan's example, and Hope has had the examples of both of them, plus, by now, those of many more. Hope based himself on the university. When he has written prose it has usually been for the quarterlies, not the magazines. There is still no Australian literary world for him to dominate. Perhaps this is no bad thing. Perhaps he has dissipated his energies less as a teacher than he might have done as a literary journalist. Certainly he has done *something* right. Staying at home, he has done at least as good a job of reconciling himself with the European heritage as he would have been able to do by coming away. Hope's has been a fully realised career. He has been able to do good work at every stage of his life. It may distress his expatriate admirers when the smart young British critics dismiss him out of hand, but obviously it does not distress him – or if it does he is not stopped by it.

That a creative life like Hope's can now be lived in Australia is not sufficiently explained by Australia's recent, much-touted cultural self-confidence, which in many respects is just the old cringe equipped with a new snarl. It has to be explained by a far more subtle process of historical accretion. Culture builds itself like a coral reef and like a reef it entails much sacrifice. Lawson went mad because he was all talent and no intellect, so that he did not even know how to armour himself against learned taunts. Brennan was talent and intellect combined, but in a weak vessel. He was even more of a legend than Lawson and so got less done. But his failure was an invaluable act of definition. He raised the question that Australian writers must go on trying to answer, even now that the distance between their homeland and the outside world, whether because the first has grown or because the second has shrunk, is just a single day.

London Review of Books
15 July–4 August, 1982

∾

It was Professor Hugh Lloyd-Jones, in a letter, who pointed out to me that Eduard Fraenkel had paid a compliment to Brennan's scholarship. I have incorporated this information in the article, but without feeling bound to modify the conclusion that Brennan's great learning bore little fruit.

Approximately in the Vicinity of Barry Humphries

S NAILS in the letterbox. It is a surrealist image which might have been cooked up by Dali in the presence of Buñuel, by André Breton in the presence of Eluard. But the words were said by Barry Humphries in the persona of the ruminating convalescent Sandy Stone, and in the Australian context they are not surreal. They are real. Every Australian, even if he lives in Sydney's Point Piper or Melbourne's Toorak, has at some time or other found snails in the letterbox. When you step outside on a dark and dewy night, the snails crunch under your slippered feet like liqueur chocolates. Snails in Australia are thick on the ground. Nothing could be less remarkable than a cluster of them in your letterbox.

But Humphries, through Sandy's comatose vision, remarked them, and his countrymen shouted with recognition. In Australia the familiar is seen to be bizarre as soon as it is said. Or else the English language, fatigued by 12,000 miles of travel, cracks up under the strain of what it is forced to connote. There is a discrepancy between fact and phrase, a discrepancy which Humphries, linguistically more sensitive than any Australian poet before him, was the first to spot.

Laughter at his discovery was immediate, but honour came slowly. The man who makes people laugh is rarely given quick credit, even in those fully developed countries which realise that serious writing can take a comic form. In Australia, whose literary journalism has sometimes attained vigour but rarely subtlety, the possibility that Humphries might be some kind of poet has been raised more often than analysed, and most often it has been laughed out of court. Even as a man of the theatre, he has usually been put in that category where freakish spontaneity is held to outweigh

30

craft, and where the word 'effortless', if not pejorative, is not laudatory either. His popular success has served only to reinforce this early interpretation. Australia was the country in which the swimming performances of Dawn Fraser, who went faster than anybody else and with less training, were belittled on the grounds that she was a natural athlete.

Yet a detailed appreciation of Humphries's poetic gift is a prerequisite for criticism of his work. Otherwise approval becomes indiscriminate gush, and disapproval, which it is sometimes hard not to feel, degenerates quickly into the cutting down to size of someone who, beyond a certain point, can't *be* cut down to size: as a pioneer in Australia's sense of its own vernacular he must be allowed his stature even if his theatrical creations are found unsatisfactory either individually or all together. Humphries, for reasons of his own, seems determined to present at least one *alter ego* during the evening who will offend you whoever you are. As it happens, I can just stand Les Patterson even when he belches while dribbling on his loud tie, but to sit there with your eyes closed is sometimes to wonder at the price of the ticket. Other people find the trade-union con-man Lance Boyle hard to take – offended in their radical beliefs or having decided (correctly, by his creator's own confession) that Lance has set out to bore them rigid.

No matter how rebarbative the preliminary acts, Aunt Edna saves the night in the second half, but not even she has escaped worried objections or been guiltless of deliberately provoking them. There is a self-mortifying element in Humphries's theatre which is all the more striking because the selves are multiple, and which goes all the way back to the beginning of his career. But so does his extraordinary sense of language, best studied in the monologues of Sandy Stone, a character so enduring that he has proved unkillable. Like Conan Doyle precipitating Sherlock Holmes over the Reichenbach Falls, Humphries at one stage compelled Sandy to drop off the twig, but he came back from the dead more talkative than ever.

Talkative but torpid. You have to have seen the shows, or at least listened to the records, to realise that the Sandy transcripts collected in *A Nice Night's Entertainment* (London, 1982) falsify the character by moving as fast as you can read, whereas the sentences should produce themselves the way Sandy speaks, glacially. A valetudinarian Returned Serviceman – not even Humphries is sure which of the two world wars Sandy returned from – he has always been laid up. Twenty-five years ago he was tottering around the house: the famous Kia Ora, 36 Gallipoli Crescent, Glen Iris. Later on he graduated to a repatriation hospital and eventually to the beyond, back from which he rolled in the same hospital bed. On stage, he has always been mainly a face in soft limelight, thus betokening the acknowledged influence of Samuel Beckett on his creator. Combine the Beckettian talking head with the pebble-collecting word-play of Gertrude Stein's *Three Lives*, cross the result with *The Diary of a Nobody* and you've got the beginning of Sandy, but you have to slow it all down even further, not just from 45 rpm down to 33⅓, but all the way down to the rarely used 16⅔. Sandy in his own mind is a dynamo. 'I got home in time for a bit of lunch and then I had to whiz out again to the football.' But on record you can hear the effort it takes him to say the word 'whiz' and on stage you can actually see it – a little heave of the shapeless body as he evokes the memory of his dizzy speed.

On the page, it is impossible to savour Sandy's eloquent silence. 'So, Beryl and I went to bed.' On stage, his eyeballs slowly pop and then roll slightly upwards after that line, telling you all you need to know about the hectic love-life of Sandy and Beryl. (Not that a torrid romance is any longer on the cards, what with Beryl rarely feeling 100 per cent, although, as Sandy is always as quick as he can be to point out, there is nothing *organically* wrong.) But there is plenty to cherish in just reading the words, even if you have to fill in the timing and the facial movements as best you can. Sandy's slowness of speech could be the fastidiousness of the connoisseur. He fondles words like a philologist. A polysyllable is a joy to him, and with luxuriating gradualness he bursts its grape against his palate fine. His circumlocutions – 'the occasional odd glass', 'approximately in the vicinity', 'altogether it was a really nice night's entertainment for us all' – are a way of getting more to gustate into each sentence. The repetitions are not so much echolalia as a kind of epic verbal landmarking, in the same way that prepared phrases keep on coming back in Virgil and Homer. Sandy had 'a bit of strife parking the vehicle' on his first record, *Wild Life in Suburbia*, back in 1959. He has had a bit of strife parking the vehicle ever since, often several times in the same monologue, when the announcement that there was a bit of strife involved in parking the vehicle usually opens a new phase in his interminable account of a more or less recent nice night's entertainment or at any rate indicates that the previous phase is over. A recurring figure of speech is thus more a punctuation mark than a sign of impoverished vocabulary. All the evidence suggests that Sandy is lexically acquisitive. The events in his life don't leave him at a loss for words. The words are at a loss for events.

> Clive Nettleton hadn't had a real break from work since the marriage and *she* was a bundle of nerves and as thin as a rake, so seeing as they were tantamount to being friends of ours, through the Clissold girls, Beryl and I had a bit of a confab in the kitchen and we intimated to them that we were desirous to mind the youngsters for them over the Easter period while they had a bit of a breather down at her people's home.

On stage, the word 'home' would, in Sandy's mouth, die the sad death of an overparted substitute for 'house', and the duly hysterical audience might forget that the word 'tantamount' had made its struggling appearance, incongruous but naturally so, because Sandy's higher brain centre collects incongruities. Even more than Aunt Edna, Sandy is linguistically a magpie. But he is a magpie in slow motion. Edna attacks, Sandy retreats. He is consequently better qualified than she as an emblem and paradigm of Australian English, which is less fascinating for its newly created slang – Humphries, *per media* Barry McKenzie, has created a lot of that himself – than for the way old formal utterances have been strangely preserved and may be used in all innocence.

By his original sure instinct, fine ear, and the formidable scholarship with which he later reinforced them, Humphries identified the pristine quality of everyday Australian English, a language which the self-consciousness of a literary culture had not yet dulled. Not having read Shakespeare is no guarantee that you will talk like him, but vividness of expression comes most easily to those who aren't always mentally testing the way they speak against how someone else wrote. Sandy doesn't just treasure words, he treasures detail. For him, the dissociation of sensibility has not set in. He is a neo-Elizabethan whose world picture, although restricted to the radius which can be attained without strife by the slowly cruising vehicle, is dazzling in its clarity. Everything is picked out as if seen with peeled eyes.

> Beryl had cut some delicious sandwiches. Egg and lettuce. Peanut butter. Marmite and walnut. Cheese and apricot jam. And lots of bread and butter and hundreds and thousands – and one of her own specialties – a chocolate and banana log. She'd only baked it that morning and the kiddies were most intrigued. Beryl said if they promised to behave themselves at Wattle Park they could lick the beaters. We packed some of Beryl's home-made ginger beer and a Thermos for ourselves but unfortunately Beryl forgot to put the greaseproof paper round the cork appertaining to the calamine lotion bottle we used for the milk with the resultant consequence that by the time we got off the bus the milk had soaked right through the sandwiches and half-way up the log.

The appertaining cork and the resultant consequence are verbose but superficial: deeper down, there is an imagist precision that can come only out of a full submission to the phenomenal world. Sandy is Ezra Pound with the power off. You feel that Humphries himself remembers what it was like to be allowed to lick the egg-beater and bowl. To the extent that Sandy exists on the intellectual plane at all, he is the kind of dimwit who takes anti-semitism for an impressively complicated political theory. 'Personally speaking, I wouldn't have any objection if they started up their own golf club.' But Sandy would never risk the strife of translating his distaste into action, and has probably never heard about the same ideas creating a certain amount of disturbance elsewhere in the world. Hence the child-like vision, which on occasions can express itself with a purity that silences the theatre, as the audience is propelled helplessly backwards into time.

> There's a tennis club right next to the Repat outside my window and I can hear them playing right up until the light goes and the couples laughing when there's nothing particularly funny and the sprinkler on the spare court and the couples saying thank you to the kiddies when a ball lobs over the fence and I can hear them shut the cyclone gate and the cicadas and the different cars going off into the distance.

The accepted wisdom is that Sandy Stone is Humphries's most rounded character. If he is, it is partly because of his physical immobility: Humphries is a hypomanically physical actor who with his other characters gets a lot of effects from stage business, so with the catatonic Sandy he is obliged to put more into the writing. But the main reason for Sandy's satisfying density of texture is that Humphries is not taking revenge on him. Humphries, for once feeling more complicity than contempt, is at his most poetic with Sandy because he is at his least satirical. To Sandy, and to Sandy alone, he is fair – and as Kurt Tucholsky once memorably insisted (in his 1919 essay 'Was darf die Satire?'), satire is unfair in its deepest being: in satire the just shall suffer along with the unjust, as the Bible says.

Driven to death by the Nazis, Tucholsky perhaps had occasion during his last days to wonder whether satirising bourgeois democracy, as opposed to merely criticising it, had ever been a particularly good idea. Golo Mann, writing after the Second World War, usefully dared to suggest that post-First World War society in Germany and Austria got far more satire than it needed. This suspicion is not necessarily dispelled by an extended study of Karl Kraus, who in my experience becomes more disheartening as you read on through *Die Fackel* and its attendant works. His aggressive sensitivity to journalistic and political clichés – a critical propensity of which Humphries is a latterday incarnation – remains a thing for wonder, but we can legitimately doubt whether he had a proper estimation of the forces which held the society he castigated together. Other products of the Viennese cabaret world, most notably the polymath Egon Friedell and the essayist Alfred Polgar, seem in retrospect to have the deeper insight which comes from a greater range of sympathy. Their *Kleinkunst*, the little art of cabaret and intimate revue, gave rise to a thorough understanding of the modern world, but in the process they left satire behind them, having embraced fairness as a principle. Polgar, indeed, however toughened by the bitterness of exile, is the most heartening example imaginable of just how sweet reason can be.

The rich, doomed Vienna of these brilliant men might seem to constitute an over-mighty standard of comparison, but there can be no doubt that Humphries, by world standards already a master of *Kleinkunst*, also has a conscious mission to correct taste and criticise morals in the society of his birth. He would be the first to point out that Moonee Ponds is not Vienna. To disabuse the allegedly burgeoning Australia of its notions about a New Renaissance is one of his aims in life. But equally one of his aims in life is to mount a full-scale satirical critique of a whole culture, even if, especially if, it is a culture in which Beryl's chocolate log counts as a work of art.

He has the required range of talents. As a writer-performer of one-man cabaret the natural figure to compare him with would have to be adduced not from Vienna but from Munich – Karl Valentin. Humphries's own choice of an informing background would no doubt be Paris. In real life he dresses expensively as an English gentleman, but that broad-brimmed trilby, tending towards a sombrero, is worn at an angle reminiscent of Aristide Bruant. One night during the filming of the Paris location scenes for the second Barry McKenzie film – directed, like the first, by Bruce Beresford – Humphries led a party to see the cabaret at the Alcazar, which was then still in its full glory. As a bit player in the film, I was along for the ride. The Alcazar cabaret had visual effects which I had never known were even possible. There was a Zizi Jeanmaire impersonation in which Zizi's head appeared from the top of an enormous feather boa while her feet pounded out a frantic flamenco underneath. Half-way through the number the boa underwent a sudden meiosis and there were two Zizis half the original size. One midget girl had been riding on the other's shoulders.

Humphries drank the spectacle in as if he were lapping fresh water from the source. He is a dandy who has studied Europe's history of style more intensely than any of its own dandies. But his hunger for this kind of knowledge has never been slavish. Grub Street literary reviewers who find something risible about how the Australian expatriates gulp at Europe often neglect the possibility that there is such a thing as an unjaded appetite. Humphries is among the most adventurously well-read people I have ever met. He has also spent a quarter of a century assiduously collecting Symbolist paintings. He was a pioneer in re-establishing the reputation of Charles Conder and at one time, before a divorce intervened, he had the most important collection of Conder's paintings in private hands. He is so learned in the more arcane regions of late nineteenth and early twentieth-century culture that there is scarcely anyone he can talk to about more than a part of what he has in his head. Most of us know of Marmaduke Pickthall, for example, only as someone who collaborated with Christopher Isherwood in the translation of the Upanishads. But Humphries has read all the works of Marmaduke Pickthall. And the name Marmaduke Pickthall – I thought Humphries was making it up when I first heard him mention it – is a blazing light compared with the names of some of the composers whose complete recorded works probably exist nowhere else except on his shelves.

As so often happens with the Australian expatriates,

however, Humphries discovered his Europe before he got there. When an undergraduate in Melbourne in the early 1950s, he was already a Dadaist – the first Dadaist Australia had ever had, and the last thing it knew how to handle. The story has often been told of how in his first revue, *Call Me Madman*, the curtain went up only so that the cast could pelt the audience with fruit and vegetables, after which it went down again. Humphries also staged the first-ever Australian exhibition of Dadaist art works, all of them confected by himself. They included a pair of wellingtons full of custard ('Pus in Boots') and a large canvas empty except for three tiny newspaper clippings of the word 'big' centrally arranged ('The Three Little Bigs'). If this came a long way after Tristan Tzara, it came a long way before Yoko Ono and was much funnier than either, but more prophetic was his knack for street theatre. Still a schoolboy in Sydney, I heard about these daring adventures only later, but everybody in Australia got to hear about them eventually. Apparently there was a progressive breakfast, in which Humphries, riding towards Melbourne University on a train, was handed a new course through the carriage window at each station by an accomplice. He particularly favoured public transport because of the captive audience. Having had his right leg specially immobilised in a large white plaster cast (the immense trouble he will take to get an effect has been a trademark throughout his career), he would sit in a crowded railway carriage with the glaringly encased leg sticking out into the aisle until everyone on board was aware of nothing else. Then an accomplice would come along and jump on it. Women accomplices were known as hoydens and doxies. He would dress them up as schoolgirls and passionately kiss them in the street until the police arrived whereupon birth certificates would be produced.

The theatrical gift inspiring all this was unmistakable from an early date. So was the desire to shock. Humphries sprang from the bourgeoisie himself but never seems to have doubted the validity of his mission to shock it. Those of us who think that everyday life in the modern world can be relied upon to be unsettling enough on its own account sometimes find it hard to see why the bourgeoisie needs to be shocked in the theatre as well, but no doubt this attitude is complacent, not to say squeamish. Humphries has always had a strong stomach. One of his tricks as a junior Dadaist was to plant a chicken dinner in a public garbage bin during the night so that he could come along dressed as a tramp in the morning, search the bin and dine gluttonously off what he found. At a later stage, when he started commuting between Australia and Britain on the jet airliners, he would stuff the sick-bag with potoato salad early in the flight so that he could conspicuously eat from it with a spoon later. Even today he is likely to fall with glee upon any medical textbook featuring deformities, abortions and disfiguring maladies. His first book, *Bizarre*, was a freak show that you had to be a pathologist to find funny.

Although this Ubu-esque taste for the manufactured atrocity gradually faded as he uncovered more of the truly grotesque in everyday Australian life, nevertheless his scope of apprehension has remained either bravely comprehensive or morbid, perhaps both. Perhaps he thinks we are not really revolted, just pretending to be. But there can be no question that in the theatre one of his ambitions is to put you off. Les Patterson is hard to watch even from a distance and in the front row you need a mackintosh. He is so excessive a reaction that you wonder at the provocation. Surely the worst thing about Australian official spokesmen for the Yartz since the Whitlam era has been not that they are totally ignorant, but that they do know all the right names yet push them like commodities. I once heard Humphries fondly reminiscing about a mayor of Armidale, NSW, who shook hands, called him Brian and apologised for not having met him at the railway station 'owing to the pressure of affairs of state'. Probably Les began from moments like that, but in the course of time he has grown into an ogre so colossal as to have lost his outline. Lance Boyle the careerist shop steward is perhaps closer to identifiable reality. One looks in vain for a redeeming feature, but no doubt one would have done the same with the original. Seeing, however, that Lance establishes himself as an unmitigated horror in the first five minutes on stage, when he goes on being horrible for twenty-five minutes more you can be excused for wondering about a point so obsessively made, even if his self-revealing speech patterns are never less than well caught. The same applies to Neil Singleton, the pretentious and vindictive grant-subsidised intellectual. He is accurately observed in detail, but he is a perfect monster rather than that more edifying occurrence, a human being gone wrong.

Humphries impersonates these incubi in solo playlets which are astonishing for their stagecraft. As a combination of writer, actor, singer and self-producer he is more plausibly compared with Noël Coward than with any of the cabaret stars. But Humphries, along with the right to shock, claims the right to bore. The originals of his satirised characters bore him, and he takes his revenge by making their simulacra boring in turn. They go on until the audience squirms. On the first night of one of his London shows I saw him nearly lose the audience by giving Les, Neil and a record-breakingly long-winded Lance one after the other in the first half. The second half belonged entirely to Edna but by the time she got on stage to save the night there wasn't much of the night left – it was almost dawn. The remarkable thing was that Humphries, with his radar antennae for audience reaction, must have been well aware of the risk he was running. The Devil gets into him, and he seems to welcome the invasion.

Certainly Edna welcomes the invasion. She would, being a witch. Edna incarnates everything Humphries finds frightening about his homeland – which includes its raw energy. At her most philistine when she is interested in art, she breaks the balls of the whole world. She knackers Kerry Packer and she bollocks Jackson Pollock. She has a Balzacian *gourmandise*. She is a tiger shark wearing Opera House glasses. She is also the active principle in her author's creative personality, just as Sandy is the passive principle. While Sandy Stone lies contemplatively stationary, Dame Edna Everage, Housewife Superstar, indulges that part of her creator's nature which craves world fame. Once Humphries searched Australia for a town called Carnegie so that he could stand in front of its town hall with his body obliterating the word TOWN and be photographed for the cover of his album BARRY HUMPHRIES AT CARNEGIE HALL. Nowadays Edna satisfies that urge on his behalf. She punishes Australia for its vulgarity by personifying it for a startled world, and especially a startled Britain, where she is a bigger star than her inventor. But she could never have been so terrifying if the docile Sandy had not first gathered the banal information she purveys, and Sandy would not have had such a finely calibrated ear if the young Humphries had not first embraced the culture of far-off Europe in its most refined, preferably decadent, forms. When Humphries writes *in propria persona* his prose can scarcely contain its freight of cultivated allusions. He writes the most nutritiously rococo English in Australia today, but nobody will be able to inherit it. To know him would not be enough. You would have to know what he knows.

In London during the early 1960s, he stayed alive as an actor. Visiting Australians who knew his legend would go to see him improvising his way through Christmas pantomimes. (Bruce Beresford, who saw him as Captain Hook, once told me that his catch-phrase was 'I'm going to take a peep around the poop' and there were children saying it in the foyer during the interval.) His memory sharpened by absence and new experience, he became more conscious than ever of the all-pervading oddness into which he had been born. On every voyage home his ears were tuned more keenly, his eyes skinned another layer. If he had not had his Europe, he would never have completed his rediscovery of Australia. That is the saving grace to remember when his less sympathetic characters punish their birthplace by representing its pretensions and ignorance to the world, or when Edna shows an unlikely knowledge of minor Belgian pointilliste painters. By bringing his country more understanding than it understands, he is acting out a conflict, living a problem. A thoroughly introspective artist, he is well aware of the anomaly.

The anomaly is resolved nowhere else but in language. Audiences will always leave the theatre wondering where

Humphries stands, because to raise such questions and leave them unanswered is part of his purpose, which is in its turn a complex mixture of the worthy desire to raise consciousness and the incurably Mephistophelean urge to raise Hell. At school, so they say, when forced to attend a rugby match he sat facing away from the field, knitting; and as an army cadet he turned up on parade in immaculately blancoed webbing and polished brass, except that it was all put on over his pyjamas. He would have been a handful in any society. He is a misfit and fully conscious of it. The punctilio of his old-world manners, the dandified scrupulosity of his Savile Row suits, are compelled by an unsleeping awareness that he has no more business among ordinary human beings than a Venusian. But his language, at its best, is the language of unfeigned delight. As all his characters, but especially as Sandy, he makes long nominative lists in the way of those writers who are in on the historic moment of discovering the verbal tradition of their young country. Sandy's diction, if not his aphasic voice, was heard before in the glossaries and prose poems which H. L. Mencken composed after the First World War. 'Pale druggists in remote towns of the hog and Christian Endeavour belts, endlessly wrapping up bottles of Peruna . . .'

The rest of it is in Mencken's little *Book of Burlesques*, published by Knopf in 1924. It is a chrestomathy of essays, sketches and wisecracks rather along the lines of the Peter Altenberg scrapbooks popular in the German-speaking countries right through the First World War. *A Nice Night's Entertainment* would have been more digestible if it had been compiled in the same way, with a few more of Humphries's adroit lyrics and some of the captions, usually signed by Aunt Edna, which he throws away in soft-covered photo books – a bad genre because nobody reads them twice, whoever writes them. The tradition of the catch-all cabaret book sorely needs to be revived. But the mention of Mencken is a reminder to get things in proportion. He brought a cutting wit, hard sense and tireless word-collecting diligence to the business of educating a world power. Australia is, and is likely to remain, a less important place.

One of the most successful representatives of the new energy conferred by an immature country, Humphries has never lost sight of its immaturity. Instead of empty boosting, he has given it a sharp tongue. Australia has allegedly progressed from an inferiority complex to a sense of its own worth. Humphries is inclined by nature to question complacency of any kind but in this instance he has had special reason to be scathing, since so much of the new confidence has proved simple-minded. As a notable contributor to the resurgent Australian film industry he has a right to be sceptical about some aspects of the strong sense of story which is supposed to be its peculiar virtue. Some of the strong stories are simplifications: *Gallipoli*, for example, contributes seductively to the euphoria of the Australian present but denigrates Britain in a way that disowns the past. Sandy Stone lived and died at Gallipoli Crescent without ever being so cocksure on the subject either way. Humphries has the right idea about that sort of unearned assertiveness.

Beyond that, he has the right idea about popular culture. His instinct led him away from a respectable literary career and towards the people. Earlier, in the 1930s, Kenneth Slessor had felt and responded to the same compulsion, having realised that high art was a watched pot. Slessor's popular lyrics for *Smith's Weekly*, later collected in *Darling-hurst Nights* and *Backless Betty from Bondi*, were an important step in his own work, and in the brief history of Australian poetry should be regarded as one of those moments when an individual talent breaks through to a new set of possibilities that lie so close at hand they are hard to see. Humphries is another such talent, but with him the effort looks set to last a lifetime.

A difficult lifetime. For someone so clever there are no days off. Being him is obviously not easy. Like many people who know them both, I have always got on better with Edna. I suspect she is happier than he is. But peace of mind could never have produced such a quality of perception. Barry Humphries is original, not just for what he has created, but for how he has attuned himself to what created him. Hence the feeling of community which he arouses in his countrymen even when the night's entertainment turns out to be not so nice. Bringing out the familiar in its full strangeness, he helps make them proud of their country in the only way that counts – by joining it to the world.

London Review of Books
6–19 October, 1983

The Boy from Brisbane

THERE IS a touching moment somewhere among the later work of F. R. Leavis when the good doctor suggests that it is possible to love music too much. The most likely sub-text is that an enemy, or more probably a colleague, had shown signs of ascribing transcendental genius to Beethoven rather than to D. H. Lawrence, or had adduced, as a paradigm of Felt Life, a piano concerto by Mozart rather than a chapter of *Revaluation*. But you don't have to delve deep to get at the essential mania. It is right there on the surface, in the suggestion that music is something you can be too passionate about, at literature's expense.

Peter Porter loves music. He loves all the other arts too, including literature, this latter being a rare proclivity for a man who makes his living at it. His unembarrassed admiration for the historic over-achievers in all artistic fields is one of the driving forces of his poetry as well as one of the delights of his conversation. But music comes first and includes everything else under its divine protection. From even the most superficial reading of his books of poems, it would be a dull student who did not see how, in their author's mind, it is through music that Heaven makes its only clean contact with Earth. I once heard him say that as far as he was concerned, without music there would not be enough felicity in life.

But part of his stance is to undervalue himself. The evidence of his wide and undiluted appreciativeness suggests that if there were no Donizetti then he would feel the same way about Delacroix. Luckily the question is a phantom: without music there would be no life at all, or at any rate no Europe – a word which in Porter's verse always seems to have an oversized capital letter, an intruder from a larger font. Porter's Europe is a place transformed by time into an idea. In 'The Widow's Story' from *The Last of England* it is like a bottle committed to the deep, fetching up in Los Angeles as a 'club of those that got out'. Europe goes to Australia, gets reborn as Peter Porter, and sails back to where it came from. Europe is everything from a Salzkammergut salt-mine at the time of Martial to a King's Road coffee-bar from the age when winkle-pickers were still sharp. The typical Porter poem is the metamorphosis of one piece of Europe into another piece. Above all else, though, Europe is music, The fastest way for the poet to become humble is to remember that it took Bach to compose the oboe ritornello of the soprano aria from Cantata 187.

This is the true humility of Peter Porter, all other humilities being open to question. In his poetry he complains of a condition called 'plainness in the mind' but in real life he is an attractive man, dapper in the T. S. Eliot-Wallace Stevens-Roy Fuller executive tradition, rather than flakily bardic. In real life he complains of bad health but seems to be in better shape than most poets a generation younger. Sorting out how much of his artistic personality is real, and how much of his real personality is *künstlich* (German, his artistic personality claims, is the only language he likes to quote from) is probably a task beyond even him. Dr Johnson was only half right when he said that any man who impugns his own virtue is just telling you he has a lot of it to spare. Some people simply judge themselves by an unreal standard, as if Christ had died in vain. I have several times heard Porter convict himself of the sin of envy, yet of all the poets I know, he is the one who least suffers from that particular occupational disease. That he should accuse himself of it is probably the mark of his relative immunity.

In most respects, however, it is typical of him not just to be very aware of the questions raised by the relationship of art to biography, but to make a subject of them. His opinions on the topic received their prose summary in a contribution to the *Sydney Morning Herald* for 9 August, 1975 – an article which his prospective academic students, urged on by the anathema he has pronounced against them in advance, have no doubt already got on file. The gist of the piece is that a true lover of a work of art does not want to be told too much about the biography behind it. But here as elsewhere, Porter takes the naive view only after fully informing himself. The example he chooses is Auden's 'Lay your sleeping head'. Porter says that he does not really want to know which man it was written for, or even that it was written for a man at all. He knows that Auden took roughly the same view as he does about the irrelevance of biographical fact. But he also knows that Auden could not refrain from gossipy curiosity, and knows, on top of that, that these facts about Auden are biographical ones.

When the same vexed topic gets aired in the poetry it is always treated as a problem without any solution except art. In 'Homage to Gaetano Donizetti' (from *Poems, Ancient and Modern*) the poet knows all there is to know about Donizetti's life. The poet is unable to stop the historical process of intellectualising about art but at least he can make that a subject too, like ploughing cut weeds back into the earth – making it a part, that is, of 'all we use', as he says in his beautiful poem for Philip Larkin's sixtieth birthday, 'To make art of a life we didn't choose'. Awareness is reconstituted as experience. The most striking instance is the poetry he has written about the death of his wife. Nothing can save the artist from the effrontery of reducing a loved one's suffering to material, but the effrontery is offset, or at least enriched, by being seen for what it is and made a subject in its turn. There is a traditional sanction for the threnody so sumptuous that the subject's death is put into an even deeper shade. Even Ben Jonson's little son, let alone Milton's

Lycidas, can't help but seem a pretext, and Verdi's *Requiem* was written for two different occasions. But Porter is aware of all this and gets it into the poetry, so that the plangency, instead of settling into its own automatic rhythm, worries about itself, always a lament and never a lullaby. Catullus set the tone when he addressed the ashes of his brother *nequiquam* – uselessly. To the poet but not to us.

The question of honesty in poetry is not much more interesting than the question of honesty in architecture, if honesty is interpreted as fidelity to facts. But if honesty is interpreted as fidelity to feelings then the question will always be important. The way Peter Porter has faced the likelihood that a professional artist's feelings will be tainted with professionalism even at – especially at – the moment of their greatest intensity is supremely honest. It is a measure of his critical intellect and historic view that he should realise such a thing might happen, although it might be hard to persuade him that it probably happens less to him than to anybody else. Here again, only the humble accuse themselves of that kind of conceit. The conceited are too busy looking sincere.

But suppose there were facts to prove that the egocentricity the poet accuses himself of were truly so; there would still be, as proof of his capacity for the opposite, his constant recognition and celebration of music. Merely as a poetic strategy, music would be good shorthand for Europe. Clearly, however, the matter goes beyond strategy, into the passion which the worthy doctor thought you could have too much of, as if there could be such a thing as an excess of saving grace. The secret of how Porter's poetry can be concerned with self without becoming cloyed lies in its admiration for what exists beyond the self. The relief you feel when reading Porter's poetry is from the absence of solipsism. All that self-examination is taking place within a soul which genuinely feels its own insignificance and has a measure for it.

The contribution of Porter's work to the contemporary artistic output of Europe is undoubted but inherently problematic, not because of the work but because of Europe, which probably thrives, or at any rate survives, as much on discontinuity as continuity. The writer of my own ideal imaginings would have read one book, like Rembrandt, although since he would have had to have read it the way Rembrandt read it, perhaps it would be better to make the point differently, and contend that all the reading in the world doesn't absolve us from the obligation to write simply. Some of Porter's poems are so freighted with learned references that I can't even tell if I don't know what they mean. For someone with his authentic and well-justified fear of being academically estimated, he positively invites academic estimation. Dürrenmatt, I think, was closer to the mark when he said that the aim should be to produce works of art which will weigh nothing in the scales of respectability. That would be my own aim if I had the courage.

Porter's role in Australian literature is clear. He is one of the necessary exiles. It is a matter for regret that he has said so little in praise of A. D. Hope, since Australian poetry, if we want such a thing to exist as a special category of poetry in the English language, has benefited as much from Hope staying as from Porter going. The staying and the going have produced their different visions of Europe, a word which is, after all, only shorthand for the past history of the world entire. Hope has produced one kind of quality, Porter another; and that is all art is, although it is no less – a festival of the qualities. But here again, Porter's generous instinct has a sure grip on reality, setting out to cry over the last things, and sounding like a carnival.

Poetry Review
1983

Les Is More

The Vernacular Republic: Selected Poems by
Les A. Murray (Canongate, 1982)

AUSTRALIA is still a foreign country for everyone including
Australians, most of whom live in the cities and rarely
penetrate into the hinterland, although in the last quarter-
century or so there has been a determined attempt at cultural
self-discovery. But most of the discovering has had to be
done in the first instance by artists of various kinds, first
mainly the painters and later mainly the writers. Austra-
lians, inhabiting a stretch of ancient geology on which
modern civilisation sits conspicuously even when it does not
look awkward, rely on having their surroundings described
for them, so that the strangeness can acquire familiarity and
the vastness a set of names. The job was done badly before it
was done well. In this century it began to be done very well,
and by now there are subtleties forming which should in-
terest anybody anywhere. Les A. Murray's fine book of
poems is certainly one of them.

Murray, among the most original of the new generation of
Australian poets who came to prominence in the 1960s,
brings the landscape into sharp focus, detail by detail,
without urgency but with a special fastidiousness, as if his
spiritual life depended on it. He takes his city-educated
sensibility back out into the countryside. When he writes
about the cities, it is with the reinforced self-definition gained
by having submitted himself to a geography without history,
a panorama in which aboriginal totems have the status of the
Domesday Book and white civilisation is only a few gener-
ations deep. Confessedly a member of the awkward squad,
yet determined to achieve personal equilibrium by getting
back to nature, he is like a latter-day, antipodean Leopardi,

tubby instead of hunched. But his language has abundant reserves of grace, equal to what it describes. Australia, he suggests, is waiting to be found by anyone with the nerve to stop looking for Europe or America.

His mudguards still wet from mountain cloud, the narrator of 'Driving Through Sawmill Towns' drives slowly through a town in New South Wales and listens.

> The half-heard radio sings
> its song of sidewalks.

For the American reader, the word 'sidewalk' will need interpretation, precisely because he understands it. The Australian word for 'sidewalk' is 'footpath'. So by saying that the radio is singing about sidewalks, the narrator is saying that it is singing an American song. The British reader, for whom the usual word is most likely to be 'pavement', might also get the idea that the Australians use the same word as the Americans. But Murray's writing elsewhere in the book is too vivid to allow the possibility that he has written a flat line here, so even the American or British reader who knows nothing at all about Australia will be able to guess that something is being implied, although he might not be able, through the barrier of a common language, to tell quite what.

What Murray implies is that Australia is not yet fully in possession of its own culture. He is also implying, throughout the book, that the Australian poets of his generation have a duty to do something about this, and should forgive themselves a certain inescapable measure of self-consciousness as they set about the task. It could be argued that this is a greater burden of implication than a single book of poems should be asked to bear. But in fact the question does not arise in that form, because the first thing that strikes you is how successful Murray is in speaking a version of English that should not only be understood wherever that language is spoken, but also immediately apprehensible as poetry. He has an enviable way of putting things:

the snake rose like a Viking ship
signed mud with a scattering flourish and
was into the wale of potato ground
like a whip withdrawn . . .

In Britain at the moment there is a school of poets, called the Martians, who are composing poems exclusively of such startling verbal effects, but rarely do they make it look that easy. Ted Hughes would make it look natural but not sound so detached. In Australia I never heard the word 'wale' used, but then, like most of Murray's fellow students at Sydney University in the late 1950s, I was an urban boy, and not even Murray realised until much later that the really interesting subject matter was back up-country where he had come from. Perhaps they said 'wale' around the potato patches of northern New South Wales, but more probably Murray got it from the OED, where it turns out to mean 'ridge' and date from the Old English. But even were 'wale' a specifically Australian word, there is nothing about this confluence of imagery that could not be instantly understood and appreciated in Durham, Dublin, or Dubuque. And any reader, while being properly wary of the enactment fallacy, can appreciate how the movement of his eye between 'ground' and 'like' reproduces the way his eye would move if he were watching the whip being withdrawn.

But poets get even their calculations from instinct. They make happy discoveries. It is their mark to be *unfairly* interesting, as if they didn't deserve to get so much said in such a short space. When Keats read Shakespeare he made notes in the margins about the quality of the 'bye-writing', by which he meant the wanton number of instances in which the poetry was good when it didn't need to be. It isn't possible to be Shakespeare again, and least of all in an ex-colonial country, but that original capacity to surprise himself is still the poet's insurance against sophistication.

. . . The severed trunk
slips off its stump and drops along its shadow.

Not only do you wonder how he thought of that, you imagine him wondering too. Such flourishes are hearteningly numerous in Murray's poems. Here is an example of a prepared phrase coming back to life:

> Dead men in the fathoms of fields
> sustain without effort millennial dark columns . . .

He could have read 'sustain without effort' in a ballet review or cricket-match report, but placed six feet below the ground the same idea seems very different – and yet even more unstrained, as if, beyond the relaxation of cliché, there were a further carelessness where meaning bubbled up whatever stock phrase you wrote down. Or try some of the beans from 'The Broad Bean Sermon'. Admirers of Richard Wilbur's poems about such staple foods as the potato will find the same easy-seeming accuracy.

> beans knuckled and single-bulged, minute green
>   dolphins at suck,
>
> beans upright like lecturing, outstretched like blessing
>   fingers
> in the incident light, and more still, oblique to your
>   notice
> that the noon glare or cloud-light or afternoon slants will
>   uncover
>
> till you ask yourself Could I have overlooked so many, or
>   do they form in an hour? unfolding into reality
> like templates for subtly broad grins, like unique caught
>   expressions . . .

This is all alive, and none of it fails to count as good noticing, but the hemistich 'like templates for subtly broad grins' is the lucky strike. There is another good example in 'The Power-line Incarnation', a poem about how it feels to clear fallen power-lines off the roof of your house and find them to be still transmitting their full load of electricity.

> When I ran to snatch the wires off our roof
> hands bloomed teeth shouted I was almost seized
> held back from this life
>   O flumes O chariot reins
> you cover me with lurids deck me with gaudies . . .

The non-Australian reader need not think that there are outback Australians who call wires flumes. 'Flume', meaning an artificial channel, is Middle English following Old French, and comes out of the dictionary, not out of colonial usage. But the flumes, lurids, and gaudies seem appropriate here because the shock has sent the narrator back to the roots, of language as of life; the voltage has impelled a Jungian power-dive into the collective unconscious.

At such moments Murray's copious vocabulary is powerfully put to use. It only sounds like a paradox to say that a poet does not always gain from being interested in words as such. In Auden's later volumes you could guess when he had been reading the OED, because his use of what he discovered in it tended towards the mechanical. But Murray, on his smaller scale, has absorbed several different European dictionaries by a purer instinct, as a way of getting Australian English back in touch with the variety of languages from which it grew. This is an opportunity open to the colonial writer, because of the way that the usages of the old country get trapped by time pockets in the new land. But to seize the opportunity takes a sure nose for lexical wealth.

And indeed Murray, in this regard, goes better by touch than he does by thought. The question of where a unique Australian literature is to come from, like the question of where a unique American literature is to come from, was answering itself before it was posed. There can be no such thing as a unique Australian or American literature. But the question of a unique Australian culture is something else. To begin with, it is not just a question but a problem. The example of America has not yet been sufficient to teach many Australian writers that such a problem has to be lived through. It can't be hectored away.

Culture is a much more inclusive affair than literature.

Among other things, it includes discussions about itself. There is a lot of discussion about Australian culture in Murray's poetry and rather too much hectoring on top of it. A poem about the allegedly oppressive British connection, called 'The Swarm', will do to exemplify the hectoring.

> On a stone wall, adrift from their hive
> seeking shelter away from the wind
> of a bitter blue day, this tight swarm
> of brown English bees is adhering.

> Poor monarchists, clumped around their queen,
> they look like a furry, half-risen
> loaf of gingerbread dough, with transparent
> mica scales crusted on it: worn wings.

This poem has gained resonance in the aftermath of Gough Whitlam's fall. You did not have to be a republican to be annoyed that the British government, acting through Governor-General Sir John Kerr, helped to push him. But even though the narrator's passions are screwed well down, the ironic tone is still bombastic. It could be said that those Australians – the majority – who want to retain the connection with the British monarchy, or anyway don't want the fuss of getting rid of it, lack sufficient political acumen to see that Whitehall still has altogether too many powers of interference in Australian affairs. But to say that they are seeking shelter away from the wind of a bitter blue day is the merest rhetoric. It implies that only the republicans have courage and imaginative grasp. Yet in fact even the republicans are proud of the courage which Australians have shown in wars that the British helped to get them into: often the loudest critics of imperialism are the most dewy-eyed about the Dardenelles. Nor, more seriously, is it at all certain that there is anything unimaginative about a wish to keep the monarchist tradition.

Monarchism at least provides a substantial object for the mythologising impulse, which the Australian republicans who became vocal during the 1960s showed immediate signs of redirecting towards one another. Murray's verse is at its weakest when his friends, some of them rather less accomplished writers than his hagiographical treatment of them suggests, get talked about as if they were members of some revolutionary movement. Germaine Greer is referred to as just 'Germaine' – a provincial piece of name-dropping which the beneficiary would be the first to mock by pointing out the existence of Germaine de Staël. But these are examples of Murray's poetry being invaded by the characteristically bad prose of Australian literary journalism, where it is rarely conceded, or even perceived, that the putative issue of a uniquely Australian culture is not one on which a writer, or any other kind of artist, can realistically take sides.

Murray, however, can hardly be blamed for not rising above Australia's prevailing standard of debate, and usually his poetic instinct is sure enough to keep bad prose at a distance. When working by touch, his verse sinks no lower than a sort of warmed-over Frost ('I'll get up soon, and leave my bed unmade. / I'll go outside and split off kindling wood'), with the occasional intervention of an unqualified bromide ('a landscape wide as all forgiveness'). Most of the time, though, his acute sense of what is alive about language, allied to his sharp eye for nature, ensures continuous small pleasures of the kind that recall the bye-writing of Marianne Moore and Elizabeth Bishop, as well as a long British tradition extending back from Andrew Young to Clare and beyond.

But the larger excitement conferred by form has been given up. That Murray is capable of it was proved when he was starting out. One of his poems was among the first by any of my contemporaries that I knew by heart.

> In my secret garden
> I kept three starlings.
> In my secret locket
> Three copper farthings.

The poem appeared in the Sydney University newspaper *honi soit*. I didn't yet take Murray seriously as a poet, but still could recall the lines when I left for England.

> One zinc-grey evening
> The birds escaped me
> And a crippled man stole
> My shining money.

Twenty years later I can still remember all three stanzas and am certain that the memory is exact.

> The starlings wandered
> Till three hawks took them,
> And now my agents
> Have caught the cripple.

At this distance the poet might well say that the secret garden is too secret at the beginning, no matter how the imagery toughens up later. But the lasting impression is of a rhythmic force which the poems in this book do not possess. Murray's poetry, along with the poetry of many of his best contemporaries as well as all the worst, has renounced all vestiges of set forms. This seems a kind of political gesture – the striking of fetters forged in England. But aside from the distinct likelihood that one imperialism has merely been exchanged for another, there is also the certainty that a range of poetic qualities has wilfully been ruled out.

As is often the way with cultural upsurges, the 1960s made more commotion in the backwaters than they did in the mainstream. Australia was particularly hard hit. One of the benefits was a disinclination to go on accepting the status of a second-hand country, but the new concern with rediscovering Australia's past did not always entail a proper estimate of what had already been achieved by Australian artists supposedly in thrall to an imported élitism. The young poets got back to nature, but the Australian landscape had already been carefully registered by Douglas Stewart, who had all of their open curiosity and a highly trained formal ability as well, so that his best poems were memorable entire and not just from moment to moment. And in the poetry of A. D. Hope there was an exhilaration, largely thanks to his range of metrical patterning and dramatic strategy, which left you wondering whether the younger generation of poets were not fooling themselves about having made a step forward. It looked more like a step back, or at any rate no more than a new phase of self-consciousness, mitigated by calling itself self-conscious but not fully aware of just how parochial it threatened to become.

The generation of Hope, Stewart, James McAuley and Judith Wright did at least as good a job of seeding the ground as their successors have done of reaping the crop, and certainly they were more capable of critical argument. By comparison, literary criticism among the writers of Murray's generation can scarcely be said to exist. But art, for a while at least, can get along without criticism, which can always be done later, or somewhere else. Murray's poems might be formally uncertain but his language is alert, so there is always a case for saying that he has stumbled on something better than symmetry. These are the luminous fabrications of a gifted yarn-spinner. As the Australians have it, you will be sucked in. Finally what counts is the magic sentence, and this is a book full of them.

New York Review of Books
14 April, 1983

A Dream of Zinc Cream

EVERY summer Michael Blakemore and I go surfing at Biarritz, because on the right day the Atlantic waves remind us of Bondi. Despite the erstwhile glamour of its name, the faded old French resort is nowadays a place where it is possible to live modestly if you don't mind one-star hotels, but even if we were forced to put up at the Palais it would still be cheaper than Bondi, because Sydney is twenty-six hours away by Boeing 747 and Biarritz is just an hour down the road by Fokker Friendship. So at Biarritz, instead of Bondi, we first settled down to collaborate.

Somehow we never wrote anything together, but to make up for our collective sloth we wrote a lot of things separately. Sitting on the beach writing, or preparing to write, we could dab zinc cream on our peeling noses and pretend that we had just climbed off a Bondi tram. (The last Bondi tram had run twenty years before, but we had been a long time away from home.) The year that I showed Blakemore the finished manuscript of my book *Unreliable Memoirs*, he showed me the draft script for his projected short film *A Personal History of the Australian Surf*. I thought straight away that it was dauntingly good: evocative, economical, spot on. You could see the pictures when you read the words.

Blakemore was such an accomplished theatre director that it seemed a bit unfair he should be a good writer too. Of course one already knew that: his novel *Next Season*, which came out in the 1960s, is one of the best ever written about the theatre. (Some publisher should do himself a favour and bring it out again in paperback.) But here was another reminder that he could write very well. He is far too modest to say that about himself, but his style says it for him. The same should apply to another of his abilities, the ability to surf. As the finished film demonstrates, he makes surfing with the bare body seem effortless. So it is, for him. Somebody in a position to know, however, should point out that for the rest of us there is nothing effortless about it.

Nowadays the young Australian surfers are lightly muscled creatures who balance elegantly on top of featherweight twin-fin potato-chip boards while riding through the translucent tunnel of a tubular wave. Some of them have evolved to the point where they can breathe white water by straining it through pursed lips as they fight their way upwards after being wiped out by a cliff-sized wave in the Banzai Pipeline. They talk incomprehensible dialogue to each other while waiting for waves. Their beautiful girlfriends are on the beach keeping their towels warm by sitting on them. Mobility is the key concept. A surfing contest, which they call a conness, may take place anywhere in the warm-water world. To go there, they slip the precious board into a carry-case and leave the girlfriend in storage. Everyone travels light and there is only one country, the sea. Everyone you know can ride a board. You don't want to know anyone who can't: life, or at any rate youth, is too short.

But for the previous generation, to which Blakemore and I belong, it wasn't quite like that. Back in the 1950s, air travel was still expensive, so the Sydney beaches were the whole surfing world, stretching from Palm Beach in the north to Cronulla in the south. Most of the surfing was done with the body, and comparatively few aspirants became really good at it, no matter how hard they tried. What Blakemore forgets to say in his film is that he had an exceptional talent for the sport. He was, and is, the kind of surfer who can catch a giant wave from the third line of breakers on a stormy day, when the average rabbit like myself is sheltering up among the rocks with a rain-soaked towel over his head. His style has a sound classical foundation, with the open hands placed together far out in front so as to form a hydrofoil, meaning that his chest, which functions as the hull, lifts further and goes faster. Even when no longer in his first youth, a surfer who commands that technique can stay with the wave for as long as it lasts. Particularly noteworthy in the film is the way that he pulls himself on to the wave in two or three strokes, so that it is already carrying him before it breaks. In my own technique, quickly learned but flashily unsound, the hands are back beside the body so that the head and shoulders hang out of the front wall of the wave like a gargoyle. Even when I was young enough to have a strong kick in my leg, I couldn't go fifty yards that way without the wave running on and leaving me behind. Also there was a strong chance of getting dumped.

Surfing vocabulary was limited in those times. A wave was called a greenie before it broke. After it broke it might turn into a dumper. A dumper, instead of breaking smoothly and carrying you along, collapsed vertically, pounding you into the depths of an underwater sandstorm. Star surfers like

Blakemore either bounced safely out in front of the mayhem or else never got on to the dumper in the first place, being blessed with the connoisseur's eye for a wave. Rabbits went home bruised, if they went home at all. But they came limping back next day in the hope of getting lucky, because riding a wave with the bare skin was pretty well the most sensual thing a human being could do on his own. A good body-surfer got all he wanted out of the ocean just by lying on top of its fraying edge. There was not much of an urge to ride boards, which was lucky, because the boards in those days were terrifying objects.

The Malibu lightweight board having not yet been perfected, the standard surfboard was a wooden, waterlogged, boat-built behemoth about as long as a city block. Just to carry it was already an athletic feat. Getting it out through the breakers could take half the morning. When riding it, there was no question of doing any complicated manoeuvres. It went in a straight line and it was up to any body-surfers in the area to get out of the way, because if the thing hit you it would kill you outright. When a big wave dumped at a late stage it was carnage. You would see the surf boat disgorging life-savers like Gericault's *Raft of the Medusa*, while surfboards which had gone spearing in would pop out again and go straight up in the air spinning. All the people involved in the catastrophe, even the life-savers in their caps and Speedo costumes with the coloured zigzags, were basically body-surfers. You could ride a board or row in the boat for part of the day, but only on the understanding that when it came down to bedrock your bare body was the essential instrument. If you couldn't ride on that, you couldn't ride on anything else. It wasn't a matter of strength, as was proved by the relatively high proportion of gifted women surfers, who came diving at you out of clouds of white water like playful angels in electric-blue satinised latex Jantzen one-piece costumes bleached to azure by the sun and salt. It was a skill.

Today's board-riders, needless to say, are skilled too: more skilled than the old body-surfers used to be, more skilled than it is sometimes possible to believe – skilled like a

Space Invaders fanatic, dedicated, obsessed, monomaniacal. They are also very specialised. Some of them can hardly even swim. When they aren't out in the water doing all those marvellous things on surfboards they are on the esplanade doing them on skateboards. The sea is just their dance-floor. If they had their way they wouldn't even get wet.

Perhaps I am carping. We only get one chance of being young, and it is never very pleasant to think that the next generation is having a better time. People who grew up dancing to Doris Day found it hard to admit that it was much more fun dancing to the Beatles. But in any age the true champions manage to fulfil themselves, no matter how cramped the prevailing style. The young Michael Blakemore went into the maelstrom and found himself. It was his first means of artistic expression. Today, when he directs a new farce by Michael Frayn, or a film script by Peter Nichols, he employs a sense of gracefully effective movement which he learned when sorting out the greenies, letting the dumpers go crunching by, and catching, with a couple of easy but perfectly timed strokes, the big smooth comber that would crumble gently and take him all the way to the beach, so that when the thin water ran out again it would leave him lying there on the sand.

TV Times
20–26 November, 1982

Part Two

WONDERS OF THE MODERN WORLD

The First Iron Lady

S TILL lifting her lamp beside the golden door – if not nowadays quite so eager to receive your tired, your poor, your huddled masses, wretched refuse and tempest-tost homeless – the Statue of Liberty is coming up to the 100th anniversary of her dedication. On her star-fort island site off the tip of Manhattan, the finishing touches were put to her in 1886. But in order to ensure that her kit of parts fitted together, she had already been fully assembled on a try-out basis in Paris two years previously, so really, as of now, she is 100 years old if she's a day.

The first thing to say about her, however, is that she carries the years well. Her status as triumph of engineering was never in doubt, but it has become steadily clearer that she is a work of art as well. Frédéric-Auguste Bartholdi was a formidable sculptor. It was just that he sculpted on such a grand scale it took about a century to assess the results without prejudice. By now, though, as you board the launch at the Battery pier and head out towards Liberty Island in a downstream curve that shows you the great lady from both sides, it is possible to cherish her unashamedly for what she is. She is not kitsch. She is class, in the American sense of being classless with poise. Her only drawback is that she is a trifle large. In our time the most sophisticated sculptor will have difficulty carving a woman three feet high without getting her wrong: too much thought cramps perception. In those days a fizzing enthusiast like Bartholdi could carve a woman with her head 300 feet off the ground and get her exactly right.

As the tugs keep pulling the garbage scows down and out to sea, your boat curves round to the far side of the island so that when you debark you see Liberty striding away from you, her back foot showing its heel as it trails a broken shackle. The pose, with the torch arm thrust straight up, is slightly reminiscent of John Travolta in a disco, but without the pimples. For the first thirteen years after she was assembled on Bedloe's Island – its name was later officially changed, which was tough on Bedloe – she was the world's tallest structure. Nowadays, if she were placed somewhere in Manhattan, she would be dwarfed by the merest department store. But on her own island she retains her monumentality unchallenged. The Trade Center and the Empire State Building are duly overawed by an edifice which was there a long time before they were. The Statue of Liberty was, after all, the first skyscraper.

If a skyscraper is defined as a building whose steel frame carries the load and whose curtain walls bear only their own weight, then Liberty fills the bill exactly. Hence the unique opportunity she affords – if the indelicacy can be excused – to get all the way up inside a woman. The elevator, which was designed in as an original feature even though it took several years more to finish inventing it, rises through a steel armature which is sunk into the concrete-cored pedestal and supports the entire structure. Iron branch supports for the individual sections of skin are cantilevered out from the armature. Bolted to these ribs, each section of the copper sheeting which forms her surface carries only its own weight. The copper sheeting is only 3/32 in. thick. The lady is practically transparent. Weight for weight and height for height, she has a skin like Meryl Streep.

In other words she is just floating there. Like a dolphin adapting its epidermis to the speed of the passing sea, she ripples and flexes in the wind, redistributing the air pressure so that it can never push her over. Only the Park Service personnel are allowed up her right arm into the torch, which they say is the best place to experience how she can shimmy like your sister Kate. She is strong because she is not solid. If she had been solid, she would not only never have got across the Atlantic, she would have cracked under her own weight without even leaving Paris.

While the big statue was still a gleam in his eye, Bartholdi crossed the Atlantic to take a look at the New World. He had already tried to build a giant lady for the Suez Canal – a metallic Aida which was to have been called 'Egypt Carrying Light into Asia' and which would have doubled as the canal's lighthouse. But when the deal fell through he switched his pretext to America, in roughly the same way that Verdi's *Requiem* had to commemorate two different deaths before it got finished.

Bartholdi, however, was celebrating a birth, and the birth of America was an even bigger and better object for elation than the joining of Africa and Asia, two continents which were comparatively old hat. Under the Second Empire there was a lot of Republican feeling in France which found its outlet in the Union Franco-Américaine, a friendship society by which Frenchmen smarting under the royalist order could daydream openly of freedom. After the declaration of the Third Republic in 1871 the fondness for America sought practical expression through Bartholdi's great project, which nobody concerned thought was mad, although clearly it would take a lot of money to get it off the ground.

In the beginning the statue, or bits of it, stayed on the ground, where the public could inspect the work in progress and be enthused to the donation of cash. The statue's head was in the Paris Universal Exposition of 1878. Her right arm plus torch had already been at the Centennial Exhibition in Philadelphia in 1876, whence it had to go all the way back to Paris for the try-out. A campaign in the Pulitzer newspapers raised a lot of money in America. Fuelled by popular donations, the entire lady took shape in Paris. There the giant moulds were formed into which the copper sheeting was placed and beaten into shape from the inside out. The statue is the world's biggest *repoussé* bauble, made the same way as an alloy bangle you might buy in the Paris flea-market, except that the copper is pure, no additives. The armature was designed by Gustave Eiffel, of tower fame. When all the bits had clicked together and been checked for fit, the whole thing was taken apart, numbered, crated and shipped.

When you get out of the elevator at about the level of the lady's clavicle, there are still 160 steps leading up to the diadem, but before you start the climb it is wise to allow the party of Japanese tourists with whom you have shared the ride upwards to get well ahead. The up and down staircases are a tight double helix, the ladies are in national dress and each of the gentlemen is carrying a Fujica ZXM-500 minicam with a wind-gagged mike. Instead of getting trapped among the kimonos and the cables, look around you. Those strangely sweet metal curves are Liberty's thin skin from the inside. Over there is the interior of her left breast, a flea's-eye view of a modestly ample C-cup from within. That tunnel entrance up there to the right is a shaved armpit. All the angled struts and bolted fishplates are there only to hold a surface out into the atmosphere. Here and there the hole left by a popped rivet reveals a pinpoint of blue. It is the sky.

Spiralling upwards on the metal stairs, you can identify various components of the lady's face. There is her mouth, ten feet across, and that tall tapering indentation is the inside of her classical nose. Once up in the diadem it is possible, by squeezing between Madam Butterfly and a man with a small Tokyo televison station on his back, to squint leftwards through one of the little windows and see Manhattan. The torch would be a better vantage point but the public isn't allowed up there, not because one of Hitchcock's villains fell off it but because nothing except a small ladder leads through the arm and it would be impossible for people to crawl in two directions at once if one or more of them wanted to quit early. Some visitors don't even make it up the spiral staircase but there are way-stations built in so that they can shyly cross from the up-spiral to the down-spiral and thus descend to meet the elevator, whereupon, after a quick ride downwards, pride can be recovered during a tour of the Immigration Museum.

The Immigration Museum is built against the base of the pedestal. It shows, mainly through photographs, the story of the huddled masses being made welcome. Many of the immigrants were Jewish refugees from Tsarist terror and their descendants have been generous with donations. They have also been generous in not mentioning that the open door swung closed during an even darker hour of Jewish history, so that many hundreds of thousands of innocent people died unspeakably at Hitler's hands who might have sailed past the Statue of Liberty and into the previously hospitable America. But America, the last fertile place in the world to fill up, had decided it was full up.

Ellis Island, only a seagull's cry from Liberty's sweeping skirts, had once admitted 98 per cent of all immigrants, usually after asking them nothing more taxing than whether they had ever practised polygamy or espoused anarchy. The buildings on Ellis Island are now restored, after threatening to fall apart. The widespread impression that droves of helpless people were retained there for long periods is mainly incorrect. On the other hand, the impression that the Statue of Liberty represents a hymn to freedom, a New World Symphony in imperishable metal, is mainly correct. The French Revolution favoured gigantism in architecture. Most of the grand schemes did not flourish, partly because *Égalité* and *Fraternité* are abstract concepts which are hard to agree on. But *Liberté* is a real thing. Bartholdi felt it like love and produced an object of adoration.

As the launch chugged back to the Battery leaving Liberty behind, I looked up to her in the gathering dusk. Soon the floodlights would be switched on, along with the lamps in the Tiffany torch-flame, whose electrics and fenestration took decades to get right. (The man who finally made the torch into the lighthouse of Bartholdi's dreams was the memorably named Gutzon Boglum, who went on to transform Mount Rushmore.) Her face is a Neo-Classical ideal of the classic, rather like Marlon Brando's. The main inspiration was probably Delacroix's painting 'La Liberté guidant le peuple', but you will recognise many of Michelangelo's faces too, including several of the Sibyls in the Sistine ceiling. It is a stylised face. She is a simplified figure. But that was what Bartholdi was after. Liberty, after all, is a simple thing. Hard to achieve, easily lost, but recognisable instantly by all.

Hegel defined history as the story of liberty becoming conscious of itself. In America it became self-conscious and eventually proud. But there is a lot to be proud of and if the statue boasts, it does so with some style. Indeed, the lady grows more elegant with time. The original shine of the

untarnished copper was gradually overcome by a pale ver-
digris which protects the metal and makes her look soft
against the sky, maternal for all her power. Though firmly
anchored she is flexible, though stronger than all the forces
ranged against her she is light to the spirit – America as it
would like to be, and at its best is. When night falls the big
lights grouped around the eleven-pointed star-fort send up
their coned beams to illuminate her as she strides seaward
carrying her Declaration of Independence – the woman of
liberation, *éclairant le monde* in a spiked hat. Tricky to deal
with but not unattractive if you like them tall.

Observer Magazine
16 October, 1983

Ruins Without Value

S oon it will be fifty years since the Zeppelinfeld outside
Nuremberg played host to its first full-scale Nazi rally
with décor and choreography by Albert Speer. There is
enough left of the tribunes and stands around the parade
area to give you some idea of its original proportions, even
though the great stone swastikas, eagles and colonnades and
their marble veneers were all blown up in 1945. The place
looks a bit like Stonehenge, except the circle has been
squared, and, thankfully, flattened.

If you take the No. 6 tram out of Nuremberg, change at the
Meistersingerhalle to a No. 55 bus and get off at the next stop
after a very large totalitarian-looking horseshoe-shaped
building which nobody will say was once the Kongresshalle,
you can walk back 100 yards, make a dog-leg to the left and
be standing alone where 90,000 Nazis used to stand in line

yelling while another 150,000 Nazis in the grandstands yelled back at them, and Hitler himself, on the podium which is still intact, yelled louder than anybody. It was an amplified uproar in a blaze of light. But nothing happens now except a few lonely madmen scrawling graffiti by night, the inevitable Japanese tourists taking photographs of one another, American service personnel playing football, and the quiet, the blessedly quiet, passing of time.

The place used to attain its full evil glory after dark, Nazism being essentially a thing of night-time and the forest. Walled in by giant swastika banners, the square was open at the top to the night sky. Then the searchlights would be switched on. Spaced closely and evenly right around the outside of the ramparts and pointing vertically, they sent their beams straight up to form a *Lichtdom*, a cathedral of light five miles high. In his memoirs Speer says he got the idea just before the 1934 *Parteitag*, but typically he is re-arranging the facts. He pioneered the notion at the Hamelin rally the year before. At Hamelin, however, he had only ordinary theatrical floodlights to play with: it was the search-lights which gave a Nuremberg rally its dubious title to being the apotheosis of *Versammlungsarchitektur* – Speer's term for the architecture that brought people together.

When the Nazis got together on the Zeppelinfeld, Hitler appeared on the podium so that they could all aim their right armpits at him. I appeared on the same podium and tried to imagine how it must have felt. Like most television per-formers I am accustomed to being told by confident pundits that I am engaged in a form of demagoguery, with a mass audience as the more or less willing victim. But in fact the mass audience is confined to the studio and usually consists of four cameramen plus two floor-managers and a group of scene-shifters reading *Penthouse*.

The television audience sits at home and consists of a lot of individuals. A mass is the last thing it is. At Nuremberg, Hitler's audience was all there together in one lump – a mass was the first thing it was. I did not feel inclined to address its phantom. There was nothing out there on the wet grass except crows feeding on the scraps left after a football game.

Beyond the back entrance at the other end of the arena, the pine forest still stretches away, the dark green trees out of which the brown poison seeped and into which it was eventually driven back. The thought of all those brick-red yelling faces is chilling even when you consider that a rally was the only time when the Nazis weren't actually engaged in hurting anybody. Besides, the consideration would be not quite true. Nuremberg was Streicher's personal city and even while he was playing host to the Führer his standover men were active all over town, kicking, whipping, torturing and always shouting, shouting, shouting.

In his monograph about his own architecture, published in Frankfurt in 1978, Speer makes great play with the idea that the buildings he designed for Hitler arose out of practical politics rather than ideology. The Nazis spent a lot of time getting together, so a Nazi building had to be a gathering place. Paraphrasing Goethe's remarks about the lay-out of a Roman amphitheatre, Speer said that an assembly building must be so constructed that a whole people could become 'impressed with itself'. When it came to ideology, Speer after the war was always ready – although never, cannily, eager – to pass Hitler the buck, or in this case the *Reichsmark*. The sheer size of the Nazi building schemes, according to Speer, came out of Hitler's imagination.

In January 1934, Hitler's favourite architect Paul Ludwig Troost – author of the extremely ugly Haus der Kunst and several other limestone horrors still standing in Munich – cashed in his chips. Speer took over top spot at the age of thirty-one. Between him and Hitler there instantly blossomed such a friendship as is possible only between two closed men who have a passion in common. In their case it was architecture. Hitler, by his own estimation, was a great artist who had been deflected by political necessity from what would have been a brilliant career. In Speer he saw the personification of his young life's dream. He not only loved Speer, he said so – the only man he ever said that about in public. Through Speer he would become an immortal Maecenas. Immortality was a word that received much stress. The buildings would be there for thousands of years.

The first big job would be the Zeppelinfeld, which Speer had only a few months to transform.

At first sight it was an uninspiring brief. The rally was not for the army or the well-drilled squads of the paramilitary élite formations, but for party functionaries with large bottoms who would not look too impressive all lined up, although the darkness would help. Yet Speer, intuitively responding to the Assembly-style of the Movement, thought big. For the Haupttribune, the main tribune, he sketched out a design twice the length of the baths of Caracalla. 'I was worried,' he says in his memoirs, 'because the design went far beyond the scope of my assignment.' To the end of his life, Speer was pleased that Hitler accepted these grandiloquent ideas without demur. But the pretence that he was merely fulfilling Hitler's dreams is, like so many other points in the memoirs, clearly contradicted on his own evidence. As often as Speer refers to 'Hitler's demand for huge dimensions', he reveals that he, Speer, was thinking on a scale to which not even Hitler could aspire, at night in bed after a lobster dinner. If Hitler's was the megalomania, Speer's was the gigantism. Speer made Hitler's vague ideas concrete. Better than that, he made them masonry with marble facings, a Neo-Classical power station for the searchlights, and toilets in every second bastion for the party functionaries caught short after a hard afternoon in the beer cellar.

Budget was no object. Speer was given the contract for the whole of the Reichsparteitaggelände, or Party Day Grounds, a 6½-square-mile complex of which the Zeppelinfeld would be only a part, and which would have no other use except for the Nazis to rally in for one week every September until Hell froze over. The Kongresshalle had already been built, to the suitably glowering but otherwise pedestrian designs of Ludwig Ruff. (Today it has a music school at the front and a plastic bag factory at the back, but if you can get inside you will find the walls of the old refectory still decorated with the kind of fake peasant murals that the Nazis, many of them farm boys, thought were great art.) Everything else was to be the work of Speer.

Along an axis lined up with the old city in the distance, he designed an enormous Paradestrasse, or parade street, which would run from the SA and SS stamping-ground in front of the Luitpoldhall, across the lake called the Dutzendteich, and past the Zeppelinfeld to culminate in the Märzfeld, an unprecedentedly gargantuan assembly area in which the Wehrmacht, under a statue of a woman forty-six feet higher than the Statue of Liberty, would manoeuvre on a scale that would leave the Zeppelinfeld looking like a sandtray. On the other side of the Paradestrasse from the Zeppelinfeld would be the Stadion, a giant stadium three times the size of the Circus Maximus, with three times the volume of the pyramid of Cheops. (The rules of the Olympic Games would be rewritten to fit – no problem, because after the war the Olympics would always take place in Germany.) The whole deal would be all set to go for the Party Rally in 1945.

Not much of it got built, but there is enough of it still lying around to make you think. The Paradestrasse is there, with its specially roughened flagstones so that men might goose-step in ranks 150 feet wide without risk of injury. At the SS end of the axis, the Kulturhalle, from which Hitler was to have addressed the world on cultural subjects, luckily didn't get built. The stadium, which was to have had a pink granite exterior, for a mercy didn't get built either: it would have been a bathroom suite the size of a mountain. But a start was made on the Märzfeld, and the work in progress, suspended in 1939, was lovingly photographed for Nazi publications throughout the war, with assurances that after the inevitable victory the aggregation of colossal edifices would be completed, thenceforth to stay open for ever.

But it wasn't just the war that slowed things down. Speer's attention had been diverted towards what was for Hitler a more important object – Berlin. Speer got quite a lot done in Berlin and if hostilities had not started early he would have transformed it utterly, with consequences far more hideous than anything achieved by the RAF. The city would have acquired, grouped around a new axis, a complex of buildings exceeding – and these are Speer's own terms of measurement – the Tower of Babel, the Pyramids, the cathedrals of Ulm and Beauvais, Karnak, the Colosseum and all seven

Wonders of the World. Topped off by the Kuppelhalle, a green copper-clad dome 300 feet high with room for 180,000 screaming Nazis to assemble underneath, this architectural extravaganza would also have been, Speer forgot to mention, the single most horrible group of buildings ever conceived by man. Merely to look at the drawings and models is enough to give you a white migraine. Beside them, Stalin's skyscrapers are as relaxed as a toolshed on an allotment.

And that's really the first thing to say about Speer's architecture. It was just awful. A genius without talent, he was essentially a theatrical personality, with enough gumption to be quiet about it. When he says in his memoirs that it shocked him when the Nazi hierarchs acted so well in the retakes for Leni Riefenstahl's movie, *Triumph of the Will*, he is concealing, with typical self-deception, the fact that he himself was histrionic through and through. In this he and Hitler were as one. When Speer advanced his Theory of Ruin Value, he knew that Hitler would not be shocked. Part of the Zeppelinfeld area was an old tram depot before the Nazis moved in. Speer was not impressed by how the tram depot's ruins looked after its demolition. He told Hitler that when the time came, Nazi remains should look more impressive, and that the buildings they designed together should be so constructed that when they were in ruins thousands of years from now, they would still transmit a sense of grandeur, like the great shards of the far past. The other leaders were horrified at the very idea of suggesting to Hitler that the Nazi era might ever be over, but Hitler saw the point immediately and told Speer not to stint with the marble. Hitler knew that a theatrical event must have a last act. What neither he nor Speer could guess was that it would come not in 1,000 years or even 100, but a mere twelve.

Nor did the Theory of Ruin Value quite work out. The Zeppelinfeld is not very impressive. It is just sad. Don't imagine that you will hear the ghostly roar of a mass *Sieg heil!* from the past. That happens only in movies. Nor will you hear, unless you are a saint, that much more lastingly characteristic sound of the Nazi epoch, the despairing cries of the tormented. All you will hear is the grass growing under your feet, where the flagstones used to be. The graffiti on the back walls of the tribunes feature ill-drawn stars of David and not very bold assurances that Hitler lives. In the dirt-filled bastions there are buckled Fanta cans and the discarded plastic webbing for six-packs. *Ballspielen verboten.* US ARMY: KEEP OUT. The football scoreboard tells you to have a Coke and smile. But the glory has not departed. It was never really there. Mostly it was made of cheap white light, and the free people came to turn off the power.

Observer Magazine
2 October, 1983

Ground-Level Entrance

J UST WEST from Titusville in central Florida the road to the coast runs into an indeterminate flat lowland of boondocks and lagoons. If a white convertible driven by Morgan Fairchild were to overtake you it would not be surprising. On the other hand it would be surprising, unless you had been forewarned, to see a big rocket pull a ball of light out of the flat landscape and go all the way up to space. It doesn't seem a very likely spot for a space centre. But Baikonur in Kazakhstan probably doesn't look the part either, and anyway, if you didn't know what went on at the Cape why would you be going there – to see the manatees?

Before the Kennedy Space Center came into being, all the rockets were fired from the Air Force facilities at Cape Canaveral, a few miles down the coast. Where the big new launch pads now stand there was nothing but scrub grass, she-oaks, flowering cactus and palmettos, inhabited to various depths, altitudes and degrees by wild hogs, bald eagles, storks, ibises, fire ants, blue herons, water moccasins, rattlers and alligators. The aforementioned manatees were dozing in the lagoon. Nowadays the manatees are still dozing in the lagoon and all the other wildlife is there as well, heavily protected under the aegis of the Merritt Island National Wildlife Refuge. Indeed the wildlife, known locally as warld-laugh, has a cushier time than ever, now that it has become reconciled to the occasional outburst of the most godawful noise, as of a billion dollars burning in a silver tube.

Actually not even the noise has been so bad lately. While the rockets were still getting bigger, the row they kicked up got louder every year, culminating in the truly thunderous racket put out by the Apollo-Saturn V moon-shots, which did a slow tower-of-power take-off that could spoil a manatee's entire afternoon. The Space Shuttle, however, translates itself from Launch Complex 39 into Earth orbit in less time than it takes a blue heron to lay a premature egg. This is the true story of the Space Center in recent times: that it has become domesticated. The Space Shuttle goes up with no more delay than the average Sunday afternoon Intercity 125 from Paddington to Bristol, and about the same sense of adventure. No matter how they tokenise the payload – with a woman, a black, a black woman or a multilingual encounter group – every trip is a foregone conclusion. The unknown is in the past.

It will come again one day, when the ships built in near space leave for the planets. Meanwhile there is still some excitement to be had by seeing how things used to be, although it helps to have a child-like nature and a patient ear for your fellow-tourists. Highly PR-conscious, the Space Center caters to visitors as if it were part of the Vacation Kingdom that lies only an hour's drive to the West, where EPCOT, Disney World and Sea World process holiday-makers by the million. A lot of the 'vacationeers' come spilling down the turnpike to the Space Center, where there are buses waiting to take them around. The trip isn't as corny as you might think. Some of the commentary is on quite a high level, when you consider that a high proportion of the people listening are under the impression that Walt Disney built this place, too, and that the big building on the horizon has a rocket ride inside it, operated by Mickey Mouse.

The edifice in question is the VAB, or Vehicle Assembly Building, but it is even further away than its statistics might lead you to believe, and first the bus calls in at the Flight Training Building, which contains the mock-ups and simulators on which the Apollo astronauts used to be instructed, and which are now used to instruct tourists on the mysteries of lunar exploration. Apollo 17, the last mission to the moon, went there and back in 1972, so by now all the Apollo programme participants are old enough to be in the Senate and their voices are present only on tape. They are not very thrilling voices, but occasionally they had some thrilling things to say.

'Roger, Tranquillity, we copy you on the ground.' I was in Italy when I first heard these words, at the Pensione Antica Cervia in the poor quarter of Florence behind the Palazzo Vecchio. I can remember that there were fifteen people in the room watching the televisión. The words still excite me, but now they come across time as well as distance. 'An LEM (lunar excursion module) sits there wrapped in gold foil. Beside me on the bench, a lady who looks like a very large wine cask wearing shorts supplies an additional commentary for the benefit of her husband, who looks like a slightly smaller wine cask wearing a peaked cap. 'You just can't *imagine* all of that!' she informs him. 'That big *thing* going up! Up in *space*!' Her husband makes a lot of semi-abstract noises indicating a sense of wonder.

He made different noises, plus louder versions of the same ones, when the bus approached the VAB. The only way to tell you are near the place is by recognising the little dots walking in and out of the bottom of the front door as people. We were informed that the crawlerway from the VAB to the twin pads of Launch Complex 39 is seven feet thick. 'Seven *feet*,' said the lady. When the crawler, loaded with the complete launch vehicle plus mobile launcher platform, moves along the crawlerway, it makes slow progress. The reflection that it would make yet slower progress if loaded with the lady and her husband struck me as perhaps unworthy even as it crossed my mind, and certainly irrelevant. There are a lot of very fat people in the American South, but none of them works for NASA, whose personnel are flat-stomached jogging types to a man, or in Sally Ride's case to a woman.

American space technology is tin-foil post-Bauhaus, Mies van der Rohe minimalist, with no room for an ounce of fat anywhere. Only the Russians, boiler-plate baroque, have the wherewithal to carry any blubber aloft. The Soviet solid boosters could put the Kremlin into orbit. But very little of what goes up from, or stays on the ground at, Baikonur has the elegance of the hardware at the Cape, and even at the Cape there is not much to compare with your first sight of a Space Shuttle where it sits pointing straight up on one of the Launch Complex 39 pads. The open-air museum for launch vehicles is full of very classy-looking rockets, but the Shuttle is something else. It's a plane that goes straight up instead of along. You can tell just by looking at it that it really goes all the way.

For once having remembered to bring my Press credentials, I used them to get away from the bus and out into the boondocks for a better angle. Launch Complex 39 Pad A was the departure point for the first lunar landing, which makes it a shrine for anyone interested in that sort of thing. Even if you swallow the line that the Space Shuttle is just a more reliable version of a no. 27 London bus, the fact that it takes off from such a lucky spot makes it worth a glance. The Shuttle was boxed in with servicing equipment but its general shape still held the eye. So did a sign beside me in the scrub: DO NOT ENTER ROUGH AREA INFESTED WITH POISONOUS SNAKES.

Back on the bus within seconds, I reflected, not for the first time, that my temperament is all wrong for an astronaut. As John Glenn has recently been demonstrating with his hypnotic speeches, it takes placidity to survive in space, where the whole object is to deprive events of their excitement by reducing them to routine. The Apollo 13 mission was the only time things went so wrong that the men on board actually had to fly the space-ship instead of making sure that it was flying itself. But one day the romance will come back, and there is a case for believing that it never went away. We just got used to the idea of people going up through the air and out of this world. The Space Center is a monument to our adaptability. We can do so much, or think we can, that we can't surprise ourselves. But all that the manatees ever do is just lie there, and occasionally swim around for a while when they hear that dreadful noise.

Observer Magazine
23 September, 1983

How wrong could I be? The subsequent loss of the *Challenger* proved that the humdrum routine of the space programme had never been more than an illusion. There had always been explosive danger close underneath. But if I had been fooled by the air of safety, I was right about the romance: it came back with a bang. No clever journalist will dare to suggest again that the astronauts are office-workers in white suits.

You Little Bobby-Dazzler

WHEN a certain young Australian writer left Sydney for Europe in the early 1960s, the Opera House had barely risen above its foundations. He didn't come back until the building was finished, whereupon, in an article for the *Observer*, he said, among other things, that the Opera House looked like a typewriter full of oyster shells. The Australian newspapers picked the remark up and front-paged it under the headline THE POMS ARE THE WORST KNOCKERS. It was clear and humiliating proof that he was not only unregretted for his absence, he was unremembered for ever having been there in the first place.

The certain young writer was by that time no longer young, and by this time he is not even certain. He was and is, you will have gathered, myself. I don't think that I ever really knocked the Opera House very severely, except by pointing out the obvious fact that a good number of the most important operas couldn't be easily put on in it. To say that it looked like a typewriter full of oyster shells was merely to evoke the appropriate image, that of an old Olivetti Lettera 44 after an office party. But if a carping tone came easily then, it is gush that threatens now. Enthusiasm is the sign of the late convert. I can hold it at bay – the place *still* looks like a broken Pyrex casserole dish in a brown cardboard box – but there are moments when the eye turns dewy, especially on a spring night when one is inside the building gazing out. Seeing the glass wall of the foyer filled with city lights made lustrous by the clean air and the harbour bridge cutting a black lattice out of the starlight, you would need to feel ill not to feel well-being. Somewhere under that wrecked bathroom of a roof, the household gods are having a good time.

The Opera House has its imperfections, but it is perfectly placed. Half the secret of a great building is to be on the right spot. Bennelong Point was begging to have an opera house built on it almost from the time that Bennelong himself was active. An aborigine who took easily to the white settlers' ways, he would probably be pleased with the building they have now put up on his old stamping-ground, although less pleased that they took his name away to make room for it. There is no Bennelong Point left: between the Botanical Gardens and the harbour there is now nothing but the Opera House. But before the Opera House there was a very ugly tram depot, so there was room for improvement, even if New South Wales's long-term Labor premier Joe Cahill scarcely seemed ideal casting to bring great beauty into being. He had already disfigured Circular Quay with a construction called the Cahill Expressway, a combined railway station and four-lane flyover that preserved the original innocence of Sydney Cove by walling it off behind a towering revetment of raw concrete so solid that a hydrogen bomb wouldn't singe it.

But however suspect Joe Cahill's eye for aesthetic values, his heart was in the right place. He wanted eminence for Sydney, and not just for the usual reason, i.e. to get the edge on Melbourne. He cherished a vision of a great cultural monument, an aim made no less worthy by the consideration that it would be in part a monument to himself. So what the combined wishes of such musical giants as Sir Eugene Goossens could never have brought about was brought about by the man of the people, Joe Cahill. Twisting arms and kicking ankles, he pushed the project through. An international competition was set up, with judges exalted enough to recognise genius when they saw it. Joern Utzon of Denmark was the genius. Eero Saarinen was not alone among the judges in pronouncing Utzon's design a prodigy of the imagination. They all did, and they were right.

Utzon's conception had the stamp of authority. The shells of the roof floated above the Mayan-massive podium with no apparent point of contact. In the throat of each shell, a filmy curtain was draped in art nouveau folds as if glass were water. Anybody who could draw such a thing, it was assumed, must be able to build it. Only slowly did the realisation dawn that Utzon wasn't at the frontier of technology, he was beyond it. King's College chapel and the cathedral of Chartres took a long time to build, but the men who built them began with the advantage of knowing how to do it. Utzon didn't: he merely had faith that he would find out.

Joe Cahill's adroit use of the state lottery system ensured an unlimited supply of funds, which was lucky, because the Opera House shared with its curvilinear friend Concorde a sensational capacity to keep on getting so expensive that it couldn't even be abandoned. In Utzon's original sketches the roof shells had a sexily complex curve rather like a Mucha négligé, an old Paris Métro entrance arch or a full set of false teeth without the actual teeth. The consultant engineers, Arup and Partners, discovered that these curves simply could not be built, whether in concrete or in anything else. All the time that the neo-Aztec sacrificial platform was rising from the ashes of the old tram depot, Utzon and Arup wrestled with the problem of how to build the roof that would echo the yachts in the harbour and the strato-cumulus in the sky. The podium was clad in pink slabs of reconstituted granite quarried from the Blue Mountains. It was impressive, but would mean little if it had to be roofed with corrugated iron. The tiling system for the roof shells was all worked out – a pet project of Utzon's, it would combine ceramic tiles of alternating Swedish buff and high-gloss into a surface that would dazzle without blinding, startle without stunning. But without the shells, there would be nowhere for the tiles to go.

Time went by, the costs went up and Joe Cahill grew older. Finally, it was Utzon himself who hit on the solution. Instead of complex curves there would be only one curve. Every surface of every shell would conform to an imaginary sphere of 246-foot radius. All the ribs could thus be poured in only four moulds, on site. It took three years to erect the resulting ribs, but with a system of error-correction devised by Arups the shells clicked together with no daylight showing anywhere. One idea, plus thousands of hours in the computer, had made most of Utzon's dream come true.

Unfortunately there were other parts of the dream for which the elegantly simple idea that might have made them real simply refused to come. Glass, for example, won't drape like that. The completion date receded further into the future, far beyond the fading eyesight of Joe Cahill, who perforce had to depart for the beyond with his Opera House only a spectral shadow compared with the solid magnificence of his beloved expressway. Utzon fell out with the politicians, headed by Mr Davis Hughes, who was cast as the villain, as the realist often is. The Dane might have alienated the politicos and survived. But he also alienated Arups, and that left him without any support inside the project. There was plenty of support outside in the streets, but all it could do was wave placards. Utzon left in a huff for Denmark and a team of locals took over the job, which included the as yet unsolved problem of how to drape the glass.

Cast as betrayers of Utzon's vision but in fact doing their best to keep faith with it, they sweated over the computer until the answer came up. The curtains of glass which now hang in the shells have not quite the Beardsleyesque swirl that Utzon imagined. The metal mullions look heavy individually and when seen obliquely they combine to block the view. But if you stand centrally in the upper foyer and look out through the glass into the harbour at night, you see the splendour of the water-city as Kenneth Slessor first registered it in his poem 'Five Bells'. John Olsen's mural of the same title hangs behind you, but there before you is the miracle itself, an oil-field of light-towers driving down their drills of pastel into the lush dark:

> Deep and dissolving verticals of light
> Ferry the falls of moonshine down.

Slessor was a great talent finally unfulfilled, and the Opera House – his memorial because he found the words for the spectacle into which it glides – is like him. Too much is made of how Utzon's original conception was distorted. Probably it would have been distorted even if he had stayed on the case, since not even genius can sew plate glass like cloth. But what is really unfulfilled about the Opera House is something more fundamental. It is just not a very good place to put on operas. It is a very good place, but not for that.

As the world well knows by now, Utzon, according to the brief given him, designed two main halls, the large one for opera and the smaller one for concerts. Half-way through construction their designated functions were switched, mainly because the Australian Broadcasting Commission, which had most of the clout, wanted a four-second reverberation time that only the larger hall could give. The opera people were left with the smaller hall. Actually they still would have been in trouble even in the larger hall, because Utzon had not designed any wing space in that one either. Squeezed by the site, he had rethought the conventions of theatrical lay-out and dreamed up some special machinery which would enable the fly-tower to do the work of the wings as well. There is good reason to believe that the conventions of stage management – by which what can't be flown from a bar is pushed on from the side – are no more susceptible of being re-thought than the laws of gravity, but in the event the whole question became academic. The halls were swapped, the hugely expensive stage machinery was scrapped like TSR-2, and the opera and ballet people were left with a small hall almost devoid of wing-space. Sir Robert Helpmann, who later became a valued resident producer, pointed out at the time a truth which no amount of subsequent euphoria has ever quite managed to falsify – that La Scala doesn't look too terrific from outside but it's got everything you want inside, whereas the Sydney Opera House looks like a billion dollars but hasn't got what it takes where it counts.

It has been said that the Opera House should never have been called that in the first place, since it was always meant to be an entertainment complex in which opera would be only one function. In Australia the word 'function' applies to any kind of staged event no matter how grand, but as the Sydney Function Centre the project wouldn't have sold a single lottery ticket. The people, with a sure democratic instinct, know that the Opera House belongs to them. Only the intelligentsia is ever foolish enough to believe that opera is élitist. The common people are well aware that melody is a blessing from Heaven which, although by definition not given to everyone, can be given to anyone. When Joan Sutherland won the Sun Aria Competition and sailed for Europe, she had Australia behind her as if she had been challenging for the America's Cup. The main reason why the Opera House now sells out every seat of the year is the general assumption, which no amount of sophisticated argument has yet contrived to dispel, that an opera consists principally of beautiful sound. In this respect, the smaller hall is as much a success as the larger one, if not more so. Voices sound rich and lift easily, so that in the first row of the circle the ensemble singing will push you back in your seat and a soprano's upper register will massage your scalp.

On my first trip back to Sydney I was depressed to see,

from an only moderately angled seat, the *corps de ballet* in *The Sleeping Beauty* queuing up to get off through a doorway in a solid brick wall and the Bluebird trying to achieve, from a standing start, the kind of mid-air entrance that not even Nijinsky could manage without room to run up. You can't, I correctly deduced, swing a cat back there. But by now, several years later, when I have become used to flying home again every so often, the Opera House looks a more and more cheering sight down there on the left-hand side of the sinking 747 as it lines up to land. Visiting the place, one still sees the limitations, but accepts them as quirks. When Wagner is put on, the orchestra can't be the size he specified, there not being enough room in the pit. So in effect you have got a building that does less than Bayreuth at a thousand times the price. But although the cramped working space is a draw-back impossible to gloss over, the gifted resident designer Luciana Arrighi has made a virtue of the restricted stage. The current *Trovatore*, with its brooding stage picture of funereal black and impassioned purple, grown strongly on the spot instead of weakly imported, looks both unique and integrated, a true belonging of the house. And on the first night of spring this year the production made a beautiful noise to go with the pictures. Rita Hunter looked as if she had perhaps made the occasional afternoon trip around to Harry's Café de Wheels at Woolloomooloo, but she sounded glorious; the lady singing Azucena had a gold-rush chest-voice like Zinka Milanov; and Manrico, as well as being built like a block of four home units, sang to strip the brushbox plywood off the roof of the auditorium.

As a baby opera house, the opera auditorium within the function centre known as the Sydney Opera House is a place to be glad about. If a full-scale opera auditorium should become an absolute necessity instead of just something regrettable for its absence – if, that is, the world really does turn upside-down and Sydney becomes one of its great artistic capitals instead of just the very pleasant city that it is today – then perhaps another Utzonesque edifice could be built on a nearby headland. There are plenty of prime sites, all the know-how is still in the computer, and the current building is such a living creature that it is sad to see it so alone.

Meanwhile, in addition to its practical capacities, the Opera House admirably serves whatever symbolic functions are imposed upon it. Earlier on, it symbolised local-yokel cultural pretension, which placed the order for a bobby-dazzler of an opera house without stopping to find out whether the actual operas could be put on inside it. Later on it has come to symbolise a new, confident national ability to see a dream through to reality and love the result even for its faults. On a world scale, it symbolises the belated but total rebellion against the doctrinal architectural precept that form must follow function: the shells have nothing to do with the shape of what happens inside them, they are true only to themselves, and to the joy of the spirit. But finally and lastingly the Opera House symbolises the barbarian's thirst for beauty, towards which he sails open-mouthed, breaking everything he touches but bringing a precious gift of his own – new energy.

Observer Magazine
23 October, 1983

Part Three

AT THE OTHER END
OF THE EARTH

On the Library Coffee-Table

An Illustrated History of Interior Decoration by Mario
Praz, translated by William Weaver
(Thames and Hudson, 1982)

Degas by Keith Roberts
(Phaidon, 1982)

Monet at Argenteuil by Paul Tucker
(Yale University Press, 1982)

IN 1982, the year of his death, Mario Praz's *An Illustrated
History of Interior Decoration* was once again made available,
after being out of print for a decade. William Weaver's
English translation of *La Filosofia dell'Arredamento* was first
published in 1964, which means that there were about ten
years when you could buy it new, and then about ten years
when you couldn't. No doubt it was obtainable second-hand
if you looked hard enough. For myself, only recently did it
begin occurring to me that some of even the most famous
books on art would have to be bought second-hand if they
were to be bought at all, since their chances of being re-
printed in any form weren't bright, and if they did get a
reprint they wouldn't necessarily look their best – no small
consideration when the quality of the design was part of the
original appeal. As it happens, *Interior Decoration* is now
reissued looking almost as good as before, even if some of the
colour plates are a bit lipsticky. But the book might just as
easily have done a quiet disappearing act. Our reassuring
assumption that Thames and Hudson, Phaidon, and a few
other imprints, are looking after the whole business – the
business, that is, of getting our eyes educated and keeping
them that way – is not necessarily well founded. They've

done just that for a long time, but by now the job of transmitting the past seems to have used up some of the energy that was once available for it. The sense of mission is gone. There is no need to beat one's breast at its passing, especially if it was a response to catastrophe in the first place, but perhaps it is time to begin appreciating some of its fruits at their true high value.

If it is now more apparent that *Interior Decoration* is a serious book, this is because other books like it have provided a context. Most of the books like it were written out of the same passion to preserve, which further implies that their authors similarly felt as if civilisation were under a threat. In 1958 Praz published *La Casa della Vita*, which was later, in 1964, brought out in English as *The House of Life*. The book is a kind of spiritual inventory of Praz's house in Rome, which survived the war where so many other houses didn't. The impact of recent destruction started him on the long job of weighing what had been preserved. The contents of the house were not especially valuable in market terms – no millionaire, Praz was restricted to tertiary pieces at best – but they had been chosen for their associations, and now that the devastating wave had moved on, these fine connections to the past were revealed in a new and startling importance. The great works of art were mainly safe in the museums, even if some of them had had to be retrieved, miraculously unharmed, from the tunnels in which Hitler had planned that they be for ever buried. But the artistic households – in which the cultivated life had been led and everything had been chosen according to often unspoken standards of taste and intelligence – were heaps of wreckage all over Europe. *The House of Life* is thus a book written under pressure: the pressure to transmit, or anyway restore, a sense of value in a period when value had been attacked in its fabric. *Interior Decoration*, though written later, carries the same story forward: it is about a hundred different households, but they are all looked at with something of the same intensity inspired by the author's own house when he had absorbed the full implications of the arbitrariness by which it had been left standing. Praz rather liked decadence, as *The Romantic Agony* shows, but only as an artificial occurrence: ruins ought to be by Piranesi.

As the great scholars of the German-speaking Jewish emigration were driven to do their best for the fine arts at the moment when civilisation had been revealed in its full vulnerability, so Praz was driven to do his best for the applied arts. They were, after all, more breakable. He wasn't luxuriating so much as touching things to see if they were still real. The book's ostensible sumptuousness is now revealed as a strength. On page 193 there is a black-and-white reproduction of a little watercolour dating from 1812 showing 'Princess Schwarzenburg Reading in the Austrian Embassy, Paris'. Praz tells you that the original watercolour is one of a pair now kept in the confiscated Schwarzenburg castle of Orlik, near Vltavou in Czechoslovakia. It was typical of Praz to use his grand connections in order to find out what had survived and where it was kept. It was why he *had* his grand connections. There are hundreds of instances in the book which tell you, without his having to say so, that he was putting a world back together bibelot by bibelot, watercolour by watercolour, miniature by miniature. A catalogue of rooms, some preserved but so many lost, the book is an imaginative reconstruction, like Walter Mehring's *Die Verlorene Bibliothek*, in which Mehring, who had to leave his library behind for the Nazi firebrands when he fled, reaches back, after the war, to fondle his books through memory.

So really dilettantism, if it is an accusation, is just about the last thing Praz should have been accused of. He was usually trying to get at a principle, rather than just air his knowledge. Even in such a cluttered essay as 'The Art of the Bourgeoisie' (which forms the introduction of his 1971 book *Conversation Pieces*) there is a real attempt at historical definition under the ponderous massing of comparison and example. But of course he *was* accused of dilettantism – and of connoisseurship, eclecticism and all the other crimes whose names have been made familiar to us by the puritanical side of the modern British critical heritage, which in dealing with the recent history of Continental Europe has suffered from the drawbacks of its advantages. The chief advantage being moated detachment, the chief drawback has been provincialism, which I think threatens to return with new force now that the direct memory of what organised barbarism was like is fading out. Perhaps if Praz had been more obviously a victim, a Jew in Germany, his attempts to retrieve past time would have seemed less like luxury. But he was a non-Jew in Italy, making a fuss about furniture.

In the field of art appreciation, Hitler's unintentional gift to Britain and America was as precious as in the field of the physical sciences. By driving the Jewish publishers, scholars, critics and editors out of Continental Europe he enriched the English-speaking countries just as thoroughly as he impoverished the German-speaking ones. And in no other humanist field was the effect as palpable as in that of the appreciation of the visual arts. The story has several times been told of which universities and institutions, mainly in Britain and the United States, the art scholars went to. At such an exalted level the transference of talent was a relatively smooth story, if not quite painless. But at the more humble, practical level of the commercial publication of art books for the average intelligent reader, Britain acquired the Phaidon Press, for example, as a gift out of the blue. For two generations, not just the instructive content but the engaging appearance of Phaidon books have been of a quality taken for granted. But it was an imported quality, which attained its first high state of development somewhere else.

At present there is a good opportunity to build up one's own private picture of how a whole institution of modern intellectual commerce – thought, writing, printing, design and distribution – moved from one country to another. The now lavish use of full colour in art books, a change partly made possible by Phaidon itself, has led to a lot of people, or more likely their grown-up children, releasing an avalanche of old, largely black-and-white illustrated art books on to the second-hand market, where the bookshop owners tend to price them low for resale, on the assumption, no doubt correct, that the casual collector is unlikely to want a book which has been rendered technically obsolete. If the emphasis is on paintings rather than drawings, then any volume whose plates are mostly in monochrome is sure to look like a back number. So for a few pounds you can take your pick between multiple copies of those crown folio albums which often had the double function of introducing a major artist to the general public while allowing a qualified scholar to get his thoughts down, albeit in compressed form. If the qualified scholar had first expressed those thoughts in some unattainably expensive multi-volume standard work, then to have them expressed in a short version was a clear gain even at the time. Lately I have picked up the crown folio volumes devoted to Botticelli, Vermeer, Raphael, Velázquez and Leonardo. I note them in the chronology of their publication, which was a chronology of war and the time leading up to it. The Leonardo was published in 1944, the Velázquez in 1943, the Raphael and Vermeer both in 1941. The Botticelli first appeared in 1937, and, though printed in English, was not printed in England. The letterpress was done in Innsbruck and the plates in Vienna. The firm was still based in Vienna and the copyright was attributed to Phaidon's owner and prime mover. In print, his first name, Bela, was never mentioned: it was always Dr Horovitz.

In all these large-format volumes – and in many more which I haven't mentioned here – the presiding spirit over the selection and treatment of the plates was Ludwig Goldscheider. He was there in Vienna, and later on, for a long time, he was still there in London. (Dr Horovitz died in 1955 but Goldscheider stayed on with the firm until its first change of ownership in 1964.) A surprisingly high proportion of the plates, incidentally, are in colour: not the major proportion that would nowadays be required as standard, but a solid minor proportion, readily detectable as you browse through. (Indeed, if you don't readily detect a solid minor proportion of colour plates as you browse through, watch out: many incipient ex-owners have found that a tipped-in colour plate can be souvenired with only a fleeting pang of conscience, and second-hand bookshop proprietors rarely check the interior condition of low-priced books.) The colour plates are not as lush as those of today but are often the better for it. Goldscheider, who in all these volumes personally supervised the standards of reproduction and usually did the selection as well – there is often a discreet note saying so – had an infallible eye for the balance of colour. In recent art books the plates often have an over-cleaned look, as if the dazzle of the double-coated art paper had made the inks too luminous. But Goldscheider's plates were the culmination of a great tradition going back to the time when technical limitations imposed a long pause for thought, so that the Medici Society in England, and comparable outlets in France and the German-speaking countries, were producing results before the First World War that have not been surpassed for their delicacy since the Second. Even if the colour plates were not there, however, the volumes would almost invariably be worth having for the introductory essay, in which the scholarship often remains a model of humanism despite some of the details having gone out of date. Wilhelm Suedos's text for the Raphael album is a particularly good example.

In the same crown folio series I recently found the Van Gogh volume in the original German. Copies of it in English abound in the second-hand bookshops because Van Gogh, like most of the Impressionists and Post-Impressionists, is an artist whose paintings the average reader understandably doesn't want to look at any other way except in colour. But the original edition, dated 1936 *In Phaidon Verlag Wien*, takes you back to near the source of the Phaidon enterprise. The introductory essay by Wilhelm Uhde is fairly elementary but once again, although the black-and-white illustrations undoubtedly look out-of-date, there are more colour plates than you might expect, and once again they have been personally supervised by Goldscheider. The text is printed in a sans serif type to suit the Modernist theme. In retrospect, the design looks untypical and agitated – an indication that the serene interior proportions of the various Phaidon formats was attained not by a happy fluke but by calculation against pressure from within and without. With the Van Gogh book they were trying hard to look advanced, as if Van Gogh's special contemporary importance needed defending. (It did, as things turned out: Van Gogh was one of the painters held up for mockery in the exhibition of decadent art staged in Munich the following year.) The press found its style during years of threat, and it was by no means predestined that it should have been such a poised style. Hysteria would have reflected the circumstances more naturally. When you go in search of these books and begin finding them, it becomes harder and harder, instead of easier and easier, to believe that such a classically balanced general appearance could have been attained during the frightened lustrum which remained to Vienna before the Anschluss confirmed that to fear the worst had always been the only sensible attitude.

The style was complete by the time it got transferred to England. During the Viennese years we can see it forming. The short version of Mommsen's *Romische Geschichte* was one of the founding books. A plump volume of some 1,000 pages in demy octavo, it was first published in 1932. My copy dates from 1934 and is from the print run extending from the 60th to the 74th thousand. If you think of the chances of such a book selling so many hardbacks so quickly in the English-speaking countries today, you start getting some idea of how widespread general culture was in the German-speaking countries at the time Hitler came to power – a disturbing idea, because it leads to the further idea that widespread culture is not much protection against vandalism.

But the immediate consideration about this compact Mommsen is the visual authority with which it demands to be picked up, leafed through and read. The many black-and-white photographs were chosen by Goldscheider, who also was responsible for the abridgment and lay-out of the text, which he selected from the first four volumes of Mommsen's original work. Mommsen's original fifth volume, conceived as a separate entity anyway, formed the basis of a further Phaidon book in the same format, called *Das Weltreich der Caesaren*. Ludwig Friedländer's *Sittengeschichte Roms* made up the trio, and there were other books the same shape, including Woldemar von Seidlitz's *Leonardo da Vinci* and Joseph Gregor's *Weltgeschichte des Theaters*. This last book I had to leave behind in a Munich bookshop recently, having expended all my cash on its companions. They make a brave show lined up together, stout but graceful tubs of distilled erudition. The photo-illustrated book on cultural history was already a tradition going back to Burckhardt, but with these chunky volumes Phaidon was restating the theme with a new conviction, as if learning needed a bulwark – which it did, at the very least.

The appearance of the thinner but taller and wider volume, the *grosse illustrierte Phaidon-Ausgabe*, was thus already half established. But the larger format, naturally enough, gave more latitude for the interplay of massed text and white space, tipped-in colour plate against matt black page, gold classical capital letters on ivory buckram binding, and all the other characteristic devices which Goldscheider brought to perfection while time ran out. Meanwhile Dr Horovitz, the pioneer of co-production, arranged for the translation of the books into English. At least one of them was translated *from* English, and never translated back again in such a sumptuous form: J. H. Breasted's *History of Egypt*, which was brought out as *Geschichte Aegyptens* in 1936, with a rich selection of illustrations from Phaidon's own archive. That same year Phaidon brought the picture section of the book over into English, complete with its superb colour plates, but for the full effect you need to see the unabridged work, thick as a brick yet full of light and air, the tipped-in plates of falcons and pharaohs seeming to hover just above their black mountings with the pearl-grey sans serif captions, and the hundreds of pages of opaque *holzfreies Werkdruckpapier* providing the ideal palimpsest for the faultlessly arrayed legions of Baskerville antique.

Even by the high printing standards which had for a long time obtained in the German-speaking countries, no books for ordinary consumption had ever looked like these. Books about art, they were works of art in themselves. Collecting them now, I feel like a buyer for the Pierpont Morgan Library commissioned to make a hoard of all the best illuminated books of hours, except that the cost is negligible and they belong to me instead of Morgan. One could be

accused of gluttony. But there is a difference between invest-
ment and enjoyment. The print runs were too big for the
books ever to attain high cash value. Their intrinsic value,
however, is incalculable. Leafing through them, you can tell
that a single creative impulse was controlling every detail.
Goldscheider's name is on most of the Phaidon books some-
where, and looms large on his personal *tour de force*, *Fünfhun-
dert Selbstporträts* of 1936. There was an English version but I
have seldom seen it outside a library. In a London bookshop
I recently found the German original complete with dust-
wrappers and the loose tissues protecting the colour plates,
as if the book had never been opened. Once opened, it is not
an easy book to close. Understandably a large number of the
self-portraits were taken from the Uffizi collection, but in all
other respects the work is a testament to Goldscheider's
archival passion, which represented the fulfilment of
Burckhardt's original intention, conceived in the previous
century, to enlist photographic reproductions as an aid to the
study of history. Part of Burckhardt's intention might have
been to give the study of history a lighter side. If so,
Goldscheider fulfilled that too: all his books invite rather
than forbid.

The Phaidon directors were obviously aware of Burck-
hardt's pioneering importance and took great trouble to
publish his works in a way which would have gratified him.
Their quarto edition of *Die Zeit Constantin des Grosses* is plump
with illustrations which the reader so soon discovers to be
indispensable that he might need reminding what an innova-
tion it was to have a whole photographic archive appended
to the text. Both the book on Constantine and the fun-
damental *Kultur der Renaissance in Italien* were taken over into
English, where the latter, when magically shrunk to the
crown octavo format, was the style-setter for the range of
heavily illustrated thin-paper Phaidon pocketbooks of which
almost any general reader over the age of forty possesses at
least one example. Usually it is *The Civilisation of the Renais-
sance in Italy*, but there are several other likely possibilities,
especially Gregorovius's *Lucrezia Borgia*. By now I have
managed to bag most of the others on the list, including the

Brothers Goncourt on *French 18th-Century Painters*, Cellini's *Life*, Baudelaire's *The Mirror of Art*, Fromentin's *The Masters of Past Time*, and the essential *The Journal of Delacroix*, which ideally should be owned in no other way.

By the time Huizinga's *Erasmus of Rotterdam* was added to the list in 1952, thin paper was obviously no longer an economic proposition: the book looks pudgy. But its predecessors, taken together, represent the peak of small-format publishing in Britain. Lately Phaidon has taken to reprinting some of these books in the series of retreads called 'Landmarks in Art History', but the way to own them is in the original format, which for 1944 was a cleverly appropriate thing for anyone to devise, since it reeked of luxury but on an acceptable scale. *The Civilisation of the Renaissance in Italy* must have been responsible for a lot of heart's ease at that stage of the war. In a battledress jacket pocket it might not have stopped a bullet, but it would have staved off the feeling that all was lost, especially at a time when most of the works of art illustrated had only recently ceased having bombs dropped on them. Until lately in the second-hand bookshops it was possible to snap up these Phaidon pocketbooks cheaply, but now it is becoming necessary to pay through the nose, which is only proper, because their real worth was always high above the asking price. Looking at my set – some of them badly shaken but most of them still as firmly compact as an unopened tin of State Express 555 – I still can't quite see how they were allowed to come into existence. Even as limited editions they would have been remarkable, but as popular printing they amounted to a small miracle.

It was, however, a European miracle, not just a British one. The German *dünndruck*, or thin paper, printing tradition had merely expressed itself in English. We became accustomed to it as part of the look of our post-war publishing, but when you trace it back you find that not even Phaidon invented the whole thing on their own. The high-quality pocketbook was commonplace in the German-speaking countries between the wars. The Viennese publishers in London, like the refugees who stained the glass for King's College Chapel, reached the apex of their craft in a foreign country, but they learned its fundamentals before they left home. Gregorovius's *Geschichte der Stadt Rom im Mittelalter* was published, with 240 full-page photographs, in two crown octavo volumes by Wolfgang Jess Verlag in Dresden in 1926. Squarely bound in vellum, printed on more than 1,500 pages of thin paper each, they are books that would make a humanist out of a Viking. When you look at the uncluttered lay-out of the title page, you can see everything that was to come later from Phaidon and Penguin. If nothing else were left over from Dresden, here, in a few cubic inches, would be sufficient evidence that a high civilisation once flourished in that city. The history of fine printing by specialist printers is interesting to the antiquarian market: the history of fine printing by ordinary publishers would tell us a lot about modern Europe.

Nowadays there is still an astonishing number of German and Austrian small-format books done to the same high standard, or near it. But they tend not to be in the field of art history, from which the Jews, when they were driven out or worse, subtracted the necessary capacity to see what needed doing. By the time the Nazis in Vienna had got through rendering the city *judenrein*, there was not much left on Phaidon's list fit even to steal. Dürer was still all right. Not only did he date from a suitable epoch, but the book on him was written by an Aryan, Wilhelm Waetzoldt. Before the Anschluss, Waetzoldt's *Dürer* had already gone through four editions. The English version is easy to find second-hand. Like all the Phaidon quarto monographs it is well worth having, but in its original language it had a sinister career. Under the Third Reich the book achieved a fifth edition in 1942, printed from the same plates but published by Kanter-Verlag in Königsberg. There is a dedication, sad in every sense, to the author's son-in-law, killed at Kalinin in October 1941. But the tragic element is in the author's note thanking his new publishers because they have reconquered the book for Germany.

There is no point in getting on a high horse now. *Zurück-erobern*, 'to reconquer', is a terrible word for what really amounted to robbery with violence. But perhaps the author was just playing along. If the Thousand Year Reich had lasted longer than twelve years it would probably, like the Soviet Union, have demanded positive allegiance in every department of life, but as things were it was possible for an art historian to make a few token gestures and continue working, provided he stuck to a safely traditional subject. Though the annihilation of the Jews cauterised the brain of German art-scholarship, the corpse kept walking. Picking up copies of Third Reich art books second-hand can be a weird experience, not because they are different from what went before but because they are so like it. As Wolf Jobst Sedler pointed out in his excellent book of social commentary *Behauptungen* (Berlin, 1965), the really unsettling aspect of Nazi culture was the large areas of life that were left untouched, yet were made sinister by a new silence. Nazi radicalism was essentially retrogressive, even when viewed from the right-wing angle. The official party thinkers, such as they were, regarded even Fascism as international, avant-garde, and thus inherently Bolshevistic and un-German. Nazism left bourgeois life pretty much as it was, while depriving it of the self-generating critical element which had made it civilised. The result was a false normality worse than chaos. The awful fact of the train full of deportees leaving the station was made more awful by the train full of holiday-makers that left an hour afterwards.

The same frightening reassurance is breathed by the German art books published during the Third Reich. There is usually nothing repellent present in the book, nor are there very many signs of awkward facts being suppressed. A scholar such as Ulrich Christoffel goes on as before. It's just that he has no competition. Pantheon Verlag, Christoffel's publishing house, had previously been a second-rate Phaidon but now ruled the roost. His popular coffee-table book *Meisterwerke der Französische Kunst* (Leipzig, 1939) even has a picture by the Jew Pissarro. Christoffel could have given himself points for being brave, while reflecting that the Nazis were probably too ignorant to know much about Pissarro's ancestry. Anyway, Impressionism was ideologically all right: it was only after Van Gogh that the official line got tough. Everything up to then was considered suitable house-furnishing in an approach to the arts which was, under the hysterical idealism, numbly materialistic. Nevertheless it was safer to stick to the established old masters of unquestionably Aryan origin, particularly Dürer and Cranach. Heinrich Lilienfein's *Lukas Cranach und seiner Zeit* (Bielefeld and Leipzig, 1944) has a text printed on butcher's paper but the colour plates are arrestingly good for a country being bombed around the clock. Here is palpable evidence for the thesis that the Nazis had ony a rhetorical, and never a realistic, notion of total war: with no efficient central planning there was little hope of the country's full resources ever being committed, so these strange pockets of peaceful enterprise continued, as if nothing was going on. Christoffel himself spent a large part of the war preparing a new edition of his standard work on Holbein, which he finally managed to get published by Verlag des Druckhauses Tempelhof in 1950. The colour plates are unimprovably good and the reproduction of the drawings is the equal of the Phaidon *Holbein Drawings at Windsor Castle* done in England after the war. Yet you can't open the book without seeing ghosts. 'The book should have appeared in its new form in 1943 to commemorate the 400th anniversary of Hans Holbein's death,' begins the author's foreword. 'The circumstances at that time prevented the printing.'

The circumstances at that time included, for nearly all of Christoffel's most eminent contemporaries, forced exile at the very least. But at this distance we should be slow to judge. The Viennese critic Alfred Polgar, one of the most glittering figures of the emigration, had a right to be scathing about the opportunism of Wilhelm Furtwängler, but pitied him instead. All we have leave to say about a tiddler like Christoffel is that he seems to have flourished in the circumstances at that time, when the giants of the field were dead, foully imprisoned or on the run.

The emigration ended up in England or in America, but it had several preliminary stages. People could go from Berlin to Vienna in 1933, and then from Vienna to Prague in 1938, and then to Paris or Amsterdam. Only the very eminent found the path at all smooth. Even for so great a scholar as Max J. Friedländer, an old man at the height of his learning and reputation, there were some chancy steps on the way to safety, which until the war was over he never quite reached: he had to hide out in Amsterdam. A fundamental collection of his essays, *On Art and Connoisseurship*, was published by Bruno Cassirer in Oxford in 1942: the publishing imprint of Cassirer was itself at the end of a long trail into exile which had started in Berlin. The translation from the German was by Tancred Borenius, othewise prominent as a contributor to Faber's list of books on art, the Faber Gallery.

On Art and Connoisseurship is simply one of the best books of criticism in any field that I have ever read: learned yet actual, compressed yet clear. The same applies to its companion volume *Essays über die Landschaftsmalerei* which Cassirer brought out in German in 1947 (The Hague and Oxford) and then in R. F. C. Hull's English translation (distributed by Faber) in 1949. So the octogenarian's later essays, the distillation of his wisdom, had been made safe. As for his earlier, central work on the Netherlandish painters, in the 1950s it was published in English as *From Van Eyck to Bruegel* and became one of the books which proved that scholarship could sit well on the coffee-table. Gombrich's *The Story of Art* was to be, as it still is, the all-time best-seller, but Friedländer was only the most prominent of a whole range of important scholars whose work was drawn upon by the firm to show that the general reader would buy a hard text if it were well presented: library shelf and coffee-table, it was assumed, were in the same room.

Perhaps Vienna, where bright ideas were hatched in coffee-houses, was a natural place for such a notion to get started. But really it was a tradition going all the way back to the aforementioned, spiritually omnipresent Burckhardt. Anyone who haunts the second-hand bookshops in even a few European cities will gradually find himself tracing the succession back through the generations. Friedländer's incumbency at the Berlin Picture Gallery and Print Room (terminated abruptly in 1933) he inherited from the mighty Wilhelm von Bode, the subject of an especially valuable chapter in Friedländer's last book, *Reminiscences and Reflections* (London, 1969), a misprint-laden slim volume which was out to remainder for what seemed like years, but is now not so easy to find. Bode, as well as being tough enough to give a Jew like Friedländer a leg up, had other moral qualities. Above all, though a tremendous connoisseur who built up the Berlin collections to world importance, he was unsnobbish enough to be a confident populariser. The German multi-volume art-history encyclopaedia, the *Propyläen Kunst-Geschichte*, has an impressive contribution by Bode. Called *Die Kunst der Frührenaissance in Italien* (Berlin, 1923), it is a thumping volume on the Quattrocento which starts with a 150-page essay – Friedländer said that Bode was no great shakes as a writer, but perhaps the gifted pupil was being tough on his master – and goes on to provide more than 400 plates of which the tipped-in colour reproductions are beyond reproach. I found it in a London bookshop for a few pounds and can only imagine it got there because an émigré had died and his descendants didn't see the point of keeping such an out-of-date-looking whopper. The self-consciously Neo-Classical spine does rather seem like a ponderous gesture by Ludwig I of Bavaria towards the ancient world, but when you look inside the book, it is like looking into the future which is now our present. The whole appearance of the Pelican History of Art is already there. The way that Phaidon was to mount its plates on coloured paper is also there. Even the texture of the art paper, which we tend to think of as a post-war luxury, is there. And all this finely judged solidity was produced in the Weimar Republic only a year after the inflation was at its height.

Going further back still, there is a clear stylistic connection between Bode's *Propyläen* volume and Karl Koetschau's pre-First World War gallery guide *Das Kaiser Friedrich-Museum zu Berlin* (Leipzig, probably 1911). Whatever other aspects of civilisation had been shaken by the First World War, art history survived it as a direct continuity. The main difference between Bode's time and Koetschau's was that the Berlin collections had grown richer. It took the Nazis to break the connection. Otherwise you can go from 1933 all the

way back to Burckhardt, who was himself as much a culmi-
nator as an instigator, since in writing general cultural
history he was fulfilling a requirement which had already
been proposed by Schiller. But Burckhardt's genius lay
exactly in that – he fulfilled it. He had the Olympian
sovereignty and the disinterested judgment. (The words,
which I wish were mine, are from Egon Friedell's 1918 essay
on Burckhardt collected in *Abschaffung des Genies*, Munich,
1982.) Also Burckhardt had the necessary lack of snobbery.
He knew too much about art to be put off something just
because the public liked it. His collections of letters are
unputdownable. The year before last in London I found
Briefe an einen Architekten 1870–1889 (Munich, 1913). It is
amusing and instructive to see how Burckhardt gives Verdi
and Wagner an equally thorough hearing but won't be
budged from the conviction that Verdi is the superior artist.
After his second hearing of *Aida* in Munich he had to calm
himself down with beer. Touring the European museums
and galleries, he collected photographic reproductions with
the same enthusiasm. There are peeved letters about how
much the photographs cost in London. It was the basis of the
whole pictorial tradition by which German and Austrian
books on cultural history, and on history generally, were to
set world standards. But as Friedell suggested, probably
none of it would have happened if Burckhardt hadn't been
Swiss. It needed a politically stable base to allow such scope.

Nevertheless there was no intention to be soothing in
Burckhardt's belief – expounded in *Weltgeschichtliche Betrach-
tungen* – that pessimism leads to a false view of history.
Pessimism he merely distrusted. Optimism he loathed.
Though it was true that we could not define good fortune if ill
fortune did not happen, still there were some evil events
which produced nothing but devastation and could not be
looked upon as edifying even at long range. Not every act of
destruction, he said, is succeeded by a new creativity. Some-
times the loss is total. One of his examples was Tamburlaine,
with his pyramids of skulls and his walls of stone, lime and
living men. Burckhardt, for all his curiosity, was a realist by
conviction. But not even with Burckhardt's historical

imagination could anyone have guessed that so blindly damaging a force as Nazism would appear in the age to come.

It didn't last, but it did lasting damage. Not, perhaps, such lasting damage as was done by the Russian revolution of 1917, which sent learning into an exile that for many of its best exponents was tantamount to oblivion. So accomplished a cultural historian as Paul Muratov, for example, never attained the place in the worldwide intellectual community that should have been his. Some of his lesser works were translated into French and a very few into English. But his major works were published only in Russian, by émigré Russian publishing firms in the various European cities – firms which were dispersed all over again with the advent of the Nazis. *Obrazi Italii*, Muratov's three-volume work on Italy, published in Leipzig in 1924, belongs with Symonds, Gregorovius, Burckhardt and every other book of its kind back to Goethe's *Italienische Reise*, except that it is better than almost any of them: a survey of the Italian cities and towns which brings in all the literary background while assessing the works of art with an untiringly fresh eye. The thought that such a book can have become lost in the turmoil of emigration is daunting. Even more daunting is the thought that in the case of the Soviet Union such books are still being lost now. Less blatantly than with the Nazis but more enduringly, the Soviet Union has imposed a thoroughgoing cretinisation on its own culture, and especially on the ability of that culture to examine itself. The Russians turn out some beautiful-looking art books – the colour plates are as good as you can get – but the text invariably shows that when history is rewritten, cultural history must be rewritten along with it. No stronger proof that the two things are allied could be forthcoming, and no sadder one either.

Not that the Nazi disaster has been redeemed. We çan be grateful that it was brought to an end so quickly, but when the pyramid of skulls was dismantled, the air wasn't clear so much as empty. The standard of German and Austrian book production is as high as ever, which means it is higher than ours. But too many of the people went away. Phaidon, like the Warburg Institute or the theory of relativity, was a child of German-speaking parents but it grew up speaking English. The refugees had a mission to preserve civilisation. They were the democratic equivalent of a monarchy in exile, except that afterwards they mostly did not go home. The very intensity of their effort is probably the real reason why, except for the tirelessly productive Gombrich, it could not be maintained, since the succeeding generation lacked the same desperate incentive. The indigenous British art writers added some important titles to the list during the first twenty-five years since the war, but even to the casual eye, Phaidon rather lost its way in more recent times, although under yet another set of new owners it says that things will pick up. With Gombrich's *Story of Art* as a cash cow, Phaidon in Britain was in the same position as Capitol Records in America, which with the Beatles on its list could theoretically make any mistake and still be in profit. But Capitol went broke anyway. Phaidon did not go broke but it did seem to go haywire. All kinds of catch-penny titles came into the catalogue and editorial control showed signs of desperation. In the 1982 enlarged edition of Keith Roberts's *Degas* – one of the books in the old Colour Plate Series which has been bumped up to the new Colour Library format – the flap refers to Edouard Degas, which makes you wonder whether there will be a book on Edgar Manet. Meanwhile the remainder shops fill up with stacks of the Phaidon Colour Plate Series. These I buy at a cut rate as I would not have bought them at full price, having been spoilt by second-hand bookshops and also wanting more for that money than just pictures.

But probably not enough people had felt the same way, so that the competition from all the picture-book firms from Skira on down had made too chancy the business of publishing serious works for the general market, especially when, as in Skira's case, some of the writers doing the short text were well enough qualified to persuade you that the book was half-way to being a scholarly monograph anyway, and not just an album. By now Skira itself has been outflanked: some of its titles seem to be going straight to remainder, where they are hard to resist at the price – the Pissarro is the pick of the current bunch.

The art book boom is either over and done with or else is splitting up again, with albums of captioned colour plates for the general reader and serious works of original research for the student. The two functions are all too easily separated. In China I bought art books I couldn't read just for the pictures, and in the West I have bought books about Chinese art mainly for the text: the book that satisfies both requirements is perhaps hard to bring about, now that the old European scholar-popularisers have died off. The generation they trained is now mainly employed in the universities, and that mainly means the American universities. Paul Hayes Tucker's *Monet at Argenteuil* is the kind of rock-solid scholarly contribution which Phaidon might once have published but could today only republish. Professor Tucker thanks the University of Massachusetts for a Faculty Development Grant and the Samuel H. Kress Foundation for its support from 1975 to 1977. A lot of travel and research went into the book, which shows the benefits: a simple thesis, that Monet edited the landscape to make it seem more rural, has been backed up with a wealth of on-the-spot investigation. It looks like a Phaidon book now, but reads the way a Phaidon book used to. Phaidon continues to bring over some of the important Continental works into English, such as Pierre-Louis Mathieu's *Gustave Moreau*, which it published in 1977. And there are even a few such efforts still being initiated within this country. But the old coherent picture has broken up, as it probably had to do, having been held together by external pressure, which has since relaxed. MacNeice's refugees are no longer prominent in the vicinity of the British Museum. The popularisers are now publicists, the scholars are specialists. Any British art historian based on a university will probably take his next book to whichever firm is likely to do the best job. If he is part of a community of scholars, it is not based on a publishing firm. The old Phaidon *was* a community, but perhaps it was the same kind of community you get in a lifeboat.

In which case the price was too high. You can't wish all

hell to break loose just so that civilisation might once again become fully aware of itself. Max Friedländer learned his famous quality of selectivity from Schopenhauer, who always warned against the danger of reading about something instead of looking at it. There was humility under Friedländer's pride, as there was under Burckhardt's, who knew that to show his students a photograph of a work of art was at least as important as anything he could say about it. Eventually it is the pictures that count. Connoisseurship and scholarship put the pictures in the right place, so that we can see them. We see pictures, and we see pictures of the pictures, forming in our minds what Malraux called the museum without walls. But Malraux's idea was already there in Elie Faure's *L'Esprit des Formes*, and anyway it was implicit in the behaviour of Burckhardt, part of whose collector's impulse was the urge to have all the world's visual wealth at arm's reach. The photograph of the work of art is not the work of art, but then neither is the work of art. The material object is a registration of the human spirit, that alleged abstraction which becomes so tangibly precious during a catastrophe, like the one brought about by the failed artist Hitler, in the circumstances at that time.

London Review of Books
17–31 March, 1983

Montale's Capital Book

L'opera in versi by Eugenio Montale, edited by
Rosanna Bettarini and Gianfranco Contini
(Einaudi (Turin), 1981)

Xenia and Motets by Eugenio Montale, translated by
Kate Hughes
(Agenda Editions, 1980)

**The Man I Pretend to Be: The Colloquies and Selected
Poems of Guido Gozzano**, translated and edited by
Michael Palma
(Princeton University Press, 1981)

POETRY, Eugenio Montale said in his Nobel Prize address,
is not merchandise. On that basis he excused himself for
having turned out comparatively few poems. Put together,
however, they make a volume of impressive dimensions,
especially if you count in the fourth dimension, time. Anno-
tated with unimpeachable scholarly patience and critical
judgment by Gianfranco Contini and his pupil Rosanna
Bettarini, *L'opera in versi* is the book with a capital 'b', or *libro*
with a capital 'l', which this great poet, as personally modest
as he was vocationally proud, always looked forward to in
trepidation and worked towards with confidence. Unless,
which seems unlikely, Montale wrote a hill of material in the
very year of his death, there is not much that escapes its
purview. It contains all the poems, all the variants which led
up to the established texts, and a closely relevant selection
from the poet's prose, ranging from pertinent sentences
drawn from already well-known articles and interviews to
excerpts from letters never before seen in public. If this book
is not the first and best way for the average reader to become
acquainted with Montale, for the average reader who *has*

become so acquainted it is likely to be appreciated as the ideal assemblage and distillation of everything he has come to know and respect about a great national poet. A national poet and a world poet, since his cultural significance extends to providing a living definition of civilisation applicable beyond any kind of national barrier, including that of language – and now that he is dead the living definition becomes more alive than ever.

When the book with a capital 'b' finally materialises, those readers who absorbed its component volumes as they came out are apt to be loud in their admonitions to the younger student that there is something soulless about approaching a poet by way of a tombstone-sized tome, especially when, as in this case, the binding appears to have been carried out in Carrara marble. Such warnings have in them an element of age envying youth, but there is no gainsaying that Montale, the least bombastic of creative mentalities, is an unsuitable subject for monumental treatment. Once through its clinically white portals, however, even the novice will soon realise that here is no sepulchre, although he should equally realise that this is no way to begin. He should begin as Montale would have wished him to, with the individual volumes in Mondadori's *Lo specchio* series, starting with *Ossi di seppia* and being shamelessly ready to employ every teaching aid that comes to hand – including, if possible, one or two live Italians. Montale stripped Italian poetry of its rhetoric, but that doesn't mean that he simplified its vocabulary. Quite the reverse. The cuttlefish bones, the *ossi* of his strategically chosen first title, are emblematic not just for their being picked clean but for their particularity.

What Pasternak said of Pushkin's poetry – that it was full of things – is conjecturally true of all poetry and certainly true of Montale's, which even at its simplest is lexically so analytic that the Italians themselves must underline words to be looked up later. Students do it with a ballpoint and often with impatience, thereby manifesting in little that temporal frenzy to which Montale opposed himself and all his work, cultivating, and to a heartening extent attaining, a divine detachment. There is consolation in this for the

English-speaking reader whose Italian is not fluent. When he buys a copy of *Ossi di seppia* or *Le occasioni* or *La bufera* which has been heavily scored by a student and sold after the examination has been passed or failed, he may possibly make up in spiritual resource for the previous owner's geographical advantage. While emphatically disclaiming the title of linguist, Montale was a devoted reader in the other European languages, and something of what he undoubtedly got out of them we can legitimately hope to get out of him. He writes the universal language of considered experience. Youth, even when it speaks fluently in the same tongue, finds that language hard to hear, while those who have grown older can sometimes recognise it in a foreign face.

If one is reluctant to let the point go, it is because of a proprietary eagerness to assure younger readers now coming to Montale that the permanent currency which he will in future seem to possess was once actual. He was there. You could buy *Corriera della Sera* off the news-stand and read an article by him. *L'Espresso*, while occupying itself as usual with the imminent downfall of capitalism, would devote its colour magazine to some of the *Xenia* poems and decorate them with the poet's own drawings. Without benefit of clergy, he made a subtle but immediate impact on everyday Italian life. There were always critical articles about him by other hands, but the critic who mattered most was the man himself and everything he wrote in prose was devoted to keeping the space uncluttered between his poems and anyone who might want to read them. He could be an elusive poet and sometimes an outright difficult one, but never wilfully and always in the belief that at least to some extent art had to be possessed in common if it was to be individual at all. Mayakovsky is reputed to have admired Montale's first poems. Montale conceded that this was just possible, but couldn't imagine a greater difference than the one between his own voice and that of a man-megaphone. Another difference, which he was too modest to claim, is that it was he, rather than Mayakovsky, who found the natural measure with which to represent a people. He found it not through loudness but through quietness; not by the striking of public attitudes but by the searching of the private soul; not in wooing the future but in cherishing the past. As the decades of variously inflated eloquence succeeded each other, his unique tone gradually revealed itself for what it was – the sound of natural speech.

Natural but compressed. Montale enjoyed insisting that when he wrote at all he wrote easily, without much revision. He said the secret of his way of working was all in waiting for the miracle (*un'attesa del miracolo*) and that miracles, in these times without religion, are rarely seen. But all this can mean is that he did a lot of composing in his head. The proof is in the variants, which show that the work was not always complete before being set down in manuscript and some-times went on after the first printing. In 'I Limoni', the first full-sized poem in *Ossi di seppia* and consequently the first poem of Montale's that most of us ever read seriously, the very first word in the famous first line (*Ascoltami, i poeti laureati*) was just *Ascolta* at one stage of the manuscript. In other words, he was merely saying 'Listen' in the im-perative instead of inviting the reader's complicity with the intimate 'Listen to me' which now seems so prophetically characteristic of his tone.

In *Le occasioni* one of the poems which most admirers would recommend to a beginner is 'Carnevale di Gerti', even though certain aspects of it are notoriously something of a puzzle. The mysteries could remain unclarified without damaging the poem's status. Perhaps its incantatory po-tency to some extent depends on them staying ravelled. Nevertheless it is useful to be able to look up the notes and discover, from relevant citations out of essays and inter-views, just who Gerti was and exactly what form her sortilege took. Gerti lived in Graz and told the future by dripping hot lead into cold water. But the poem is also set in Trieste and Florence. Montale himself is quoted as finding the poem diffuse and obscure, but he was looking back on it through his own life. For those of us who must try to remember 1928 through writings by him and others, the diffuseness and the obscurity seem more like a clarity so concentrated that its depths dazzle. There are many times when Montale will make us think of Mandelstam and here is one of them. They had a similar way of remembering their toys. The forms and colours in 'Carnevale di Gerti' were all once played with in the nursery. And those very forms and colours, we find out, were sounds and colours in an earlier version. If you move the hand of your little wrist-watch, says the narrator, everything will fall back inside a disintegrating babelic prism *di forme e di colori*. Only it used to be *di suoni e di colori*. Strange that so perfect an image was once so different.

Gerti, it turns out, is also the woman in the second part of that other famous poem in *Le occasioni*, 'Dora Markus'. In the first part, Dora Markus is the woman addressed because the story being told is of a life not yet lived. Thirteen years later, he added the second part, making the subject Gerti, whom he had known. Dora Markus, it transpires, he never knew. He heard about her in a letter from his friend Roberto Bazlen, here adduced. Bazlen told Montale that Gerti had a friend called Dora Markus who had marvellous legs (*gambe meravigliose*): a poem should be written. Montale wrote the first half out of pure imagination. When he came to write the second half he needed to write from experience, so he addressed Gerti as Dora (*La tua leggenda, Dora!*) and thus, according to his own later judgment, gave the poem a conclusion, if not a centre. But any amount of such ancillary information, fascinating though it is, will scarcely deflect the reader from his conclusion that 'Dora Markus' is all about the one woman, her lost country, and the ivory amulet that enables her to exist. The marvellous legs, incidentally, were left unmentioned.

After *Le occasioni* comes *La bufera*, and so on to *Satura* (including the *Xenia* poems), the *Diario del '71 e del '72*, the *Quaderno di quattro anni*, all the otherwise uncollected verse and finally the complete translations, minus, no doubt for reasons of space, the original texts which appear on, the facing pages in *Quaderno di traduzioni*. Montale's later work poses the same sort of aesthetic problem to the Italians that Auden's later work poses to us. From *Satura* onwards, he becomes steadily more sparing with the lyrical incantation that abounded in his early work even at its most dedicatedly austere. Perhaps his lyrical impulse worked like a mathematical gift and was exhausted comparatively early. More likely, as with Auden, he simply wanted, as he grew older, to find more direct ways of telling the kind of truth experience brings without its having to be searched for. At least one reader has found Montale's 'diary' poems more and more interesting as time goes on. But for all their plainness – you can read them almost as easily as his prose – they attract at least as much documentation as the early work, so that after an hour or so of ferreting among the notes you could be excused for wondering if poetry should need so much help to sustain itself.

The first answer is that in Montale's case it definitely doesn't. If the back of this book were torn out and thrown away, the front of it would still be something to take with you. The second answer is given in a tiny poem from *Satura* which says that although poetry rejects with horror the glosses of the scholiasts, it can never be quite sure of being sufficient to itself. Contini's archival, scholarly and critical accompaniment to Montale's poetry goes back to well before the Second World War and has obviously always had Montale's co-operation, however diffidently given. The extracts from Montale's half of their correspondence would by themselves be sufficient to make this volume a treasure-house. It is impossible to tell how the two editors divided up the work. Whatever Rosanna Bettarini's share of the painstaking labour, she has done it with the pellucid logic and thoroughgoing economy befitting a *continiana*. But the presiding curatorial spirit is Contini's. His critical articles on Montale are collected in a little book of which the title, *Una lunga fedeltà*, is exactly right – a long faithfulness. For all the long time they knew each other, he paid Montale the compliment of giving him the same quality of attention he gave to the great poets of the past. In his central book, *Varianti e altra linguistica*, the essays on Dante and Petrarch – essays which for their combination of learning and penetration excel even those of his master, Ernst Robert Curtius – there is nothing said which he was not equally ready to say, *mutatis mutandis*, about Montale. He studied the poetry of the past on the assumption that in the present there could be great poets too.

For Contini history is now and now is history. His memorabilia give off light and gather no dust. His apartment in Pian de' Giullari outside Florence boasts no negotiable wealth apart from a single small Morandi. The bullion is on the bookshelves and in the desk drawers. It is a comfort to realise that there are usually one or two people like him whatever the circumstances: in the Soviet Union, for example, where recent conditions could not have been more inimical to the documentation and iconography of the creative life, the few genuine scholars among the party functionaries of *Literaturnoe Nasledstvo* have achieved prodigies. Facing, during the Fascist era, pressures not entirely dissimilar, Contini dedicated himself to serving the continuity of humane studies. Even in the *tour de force* of stylistic analysis by which he claims the anonymous *Fiore* as the work of Dante, he is manifestly dealing with his chosen writer as a living human being: he once jokingly called himself a structuralist before structuralism, but it was a joke he could afford to make, since it never would have occurred to him that there could be any such thing as a text separable even momentarily from the individual expressive personality. But, like Curtius, who greeted Proust in the same terms with which he had appraised Dante, Contini never lapsed into the common scholarly vice of allowing familiarity with the past to breed contempt for the present. On the contrary, he further developed his innate capacity for treating now as if it were as rare and cherishable as then. Montale himself, when a young man, formed a friendship with Svevo which was instrumental in preserving the senior writer's achievement and making it known to the Italian public. Such friendships are basic to modern Italian cultural history, which has gone through times when a lot has depended on trust. Just such a friendship later obtained between the mature Montale and the brilliant young philologist Contini. The scholar recognised the poet's importance and set about making sure that the paperwork was properly attended to. In less tactful hands, the job might have looked like hagiography, but Contini's critical sense is too human for that: a love of literature that can make Arnaut Daniel seem contemporary was never likely to make a contemporary seem mummified.

Contini's critical sense participates in this book only by implication, as the intellectual foundation underlying the scholarly edifice. The critical sense which becomes more and more pervasive as one consults the notes belongs to Montale himself. But once again this is not the first and best way to start. In this book he is necessarily talking only about his own work: he can be interesting about that, but he is positively illuminating when talking about other poets and he is one of the touchstone modern critics when writing about art in general. Just as the beginner should go to the individual volumes in order to become intimate with Montale's poetry, so he should go to *Auto da fé* and (especially) *Sulla Poesia* in order to take the full measure of Montale's criticism, which apart from anything else is such a model of apparently relaxed style that it provides an unbeatable means of attaining fluency in reading modern Italian prose. A trained singer in his early days and a practising painter all his life, Montale possessed a genuine background, not just pretensions, across the whole range of the arts. He was as variously curious as Auden and less frivolous. He was as aphoristic as Valéry but less exquisite. He was as deeply read as Eliot but less keen to prove it. Beyond all that he was reasonable. He was fond of quoting Tommaso Ceva to the effect that a poem is a dream in the presence of reason. His criticism is reason made tangible over the whole field of artistic creativity in recent times, with particular emphasis on making sense of Italian cultural history in the nineteenth and twentieth centuries. Readers who have not previously moved outside the field of modern criticism written in English are likely to encounter Montale's prose with surprise, relief and delight at hearing a voice which is intelligent, serious, rigorous and generous all at the same time.

Montale, like Contini and every other modern Italian who thinks seriously about literary matters, has the immense advantage of inheriting the philosophical and critical achievement of Croce. Broadly it can be said that these later writers, disciplined by the tumult of events, have nullified

Croce's compulsive system-building while extending the consistency which helped make the vast edifice of his idealism so imposing. Students of philology will know the importance of Contini's arguments against Croce's dismissal of the study of variants. But at the practical level of everyday critical opinion, Montale himself has always shown a similar ability to refine the theoretical heritage and combine it with what he has learned as a working artist. If you can imagine a Randall Jarrell less worried about the place of the superior mind in a democracy, you will gather something of Montale's capacity to talk about art in general without being carried away by general ideas. He had an unerring ear for the dogmatic no matter who was pronouncing it. It might have suited the first part of his book with a capital 'b' to agree with Gide that what mattered about poetry was the element of incantation. Montale (in *Sulla poesia*) said Gide seemed to have forgotten that the accord, or let it be the compromise, between the sound and what it signifies does not allow partial solutions in favour of either term. Montale believed that the emphasis which Gide was favouring had in fact helped to sterilise French poetry after Baudelaire. Montale's insistence on maintaining an inclusive view of what poetry might be would have been persuasive in itself, even if his later poetry had not gone on so thoroughly to shift the emphasis away from any vestige of word music as it had commonly been conceived.

Perfectly conversational yet unfaltering in its dignity, Montale's critical prose is difficult to translate well and all too easy, some of the evidence suggests, to translate badly. Perhaps the Italianist academic community in Britain might have formed a committee to ensure that the job of translation would be, if not inspired, at least learned and consistent. However that may be, the matter of translating Montale's prose into English is in a very unsatisfactory state. He is in almost as big a mess as Croce, who was entombed by the slapdash enthusiasm of his principal translators and lives on only to the extent that he was incorporated – some might say plagiarised – by Collingwood.

Lacking a centralised, responsible strategy for translating Montale's critical writing into English, the English-speaking

Italianists resort to isolated individual efforts. Not surprisingly, the Americans do the job most lavishly, having the larger grants. Edited by Michael Palma, *The Man I Pretend to Be* presents *I colloqui* and selected poems by Guido Gozzano in parallel text, the English translations being by Mr Palma, who also translated the introductory essay by Montale. Gozzano was a predecessor whom Montale valued highly, so that by reading this essay you can get some idea of what his critical prose is like when he is being affirmative – not that he was ever really anything else. In another essay, collected in *Sulla poesia*, Montale compared Gozzano with his beloved Puccini and said that their fruitfulness was no less valuable just because it had to be eaten with a spoon. Mr Palma certainly has the linguistic resources in Italian to provide a useful crib for anyone who wants to read Gozzano's poetry. But when it comes to Montale's prose, you quickly find that what he lacks is the necessary control of English. He makes Montale sound stiff – harsh treatment for a style which in the original flows with such ease. In a footnote to Montale's introductory essay we find Mr Palma wondering about a reference to Francesco De Sanctis. Is Montale, Mr Palma asks himself, talking about the distinction De Sanctis drew between 'the idea of a work of art and its manifestation'? He is talking about something much more elementary – namely, the distinction De Sanctis drew between poetry and art. That distinction, one of the fundamental ideas in De Sanctis's aesthetic theory, is mentioned everywhere not only in his criticism but in Montale's too, and thus constitutes a fairly large topic for Mr Palma to be puzzled about.

If unsatisfactory translation from Montale's prose is to be regretted, unsatisfactory translation from his poetry is pretty well inevitable. There is no need to rehearse here the various attempts, beyond saying that poets with strong personalities of their own tend to make Montale sound like themselves, while poets with no special individuality tend to make him sound like nothing. Montale himself was an assiduous translator from other languages, employing someone else's literal translation of Cavafy's Greek but working without intermediaries when dealing with English, which was his passion.

The *Quaderno di traduzioni* proves that he was a patient translator, fully aware that even to begin registering the idiomatic and syntactical subtleties of another language was no light matter. He called English '*una lingua che non si impara mai*' – a language that one never finishes learning. Nevertheless he thought translating some of his favourite English poems worth trying even if what he came up with was no better than a crib. Probably the same holds true in reverse for his own poetry, of which any translation, especially of the early work, is unlikely to exceed the status of a crib, but for which cribs can come in handy even with the later poems at their most prosaic. By this measure, Kate Hughes's *testo parallelo* of *Xenia* and the *Mottetti* is welcome. It would be an even better crib if it were more strict. Possibly in deference to poetic imperatives of her own, Miss Hughes does quite a lot of leaving out, putting in and switching things around. In the fourteenth poem of *Xenia* I, the lines '*Dicono che la poesia al suo culmine/magnifica il Tutto in fuga*' come out as 'They say poetry/celebrates the All in flight', which means that *al suo culmine* has gone missing, perhaps because it means 'at its height' and Miss Hughes didn't want a rhyme with 'flight'. But she could have said 'at its peak' or 'in its fullness' or something similar. And in the beautiful thirteenth motet, the gondola that slides by in a dazzle of tar and poppies might, I suppose, almost as well slide by in a glare of tar and poppies, but what it can't possibly do is slide by in a *diamond* glare of tar and poppies: by imposing the idea of a diamond Miss Hughes makes you momentarily wonder if she knows whom she is dealing with. Montale's self-imposed task was to divest Italian poetry of cheaply poeticised effects, not to increase their number.

Examples, alas, could be multiplied. Nevertheless Miss Hughes is right to see that *Xenia* is a good way for the English-speaking reader to begin acquiring Montale in Italian. Not only has the bewilderingly specific vocabulary of the early poetry been left behind, there is a story to follow. The heroine of the *Xenia* poems, Mosca, was Montale's last and most transfigurative *ispiratrice*. Her emergence into straightforward narrative sums up and transcends

Montale's various preliminary dedications to a mysterious female interlocutor, constantly changing definition and probably identity. With his earlier muses Montale established a spiritual communion as subtle as Rilke's, but without the plaintive longing for the unattainable. With all his muses through to and including Wera Ouckama Knoop, Rilke apparently depended, for the ability to generate his febrile metaphysical excitement, on never attaining his object. Montale has the same certainty that the mental connection is what lastingly matters, but the certainty is made doubly certain by emanating so obviously from ordinary love as most of us know it. In Rilke, the *Sehnsucht*, the longing, begins before love and happens instead of it. With Montale the sense of loss happens after the event – in the case of Mosca, after her death. In all of modern poetry it is hard to think of a similar example of the loved one evoked as a fully alive, fully individual human being rather than as the poet's imaginative figment. Montale translated 'La Figlia che Piange' and was as susceptible as anyone to the revelation of divinity through the female form, but while never growing out of it he grew on from it, so that although at the end all the original intensity of vision is still there, it has been joined by the facts of ordinary human personality, which have become radiant too. Mosca is an old woman who can't see and who can hardly walk, but like Dante's Beatrice and Petrarch's Laura she is the light-source of the poet's vision and, unlike Leopardi's Silvia and Nerina, she has been talked to, touched, lived with for a long time and *then* lost. There is no one quite like her in Italian poetry or any other poetry I can think of, but the reader, even through the imperfect medium of a parallel text, will immediately recognise her as poetic, and all the more so for being real.

The sense of place that Montale brought with him from Liguria he gave to the world. Like all the historically sensitive poets in the 1920s – Yeats, Eliot, Rilke, Valéry and Mandelstam are only some of them – he found his creative impulse dominated by a hypertrophied urge to preserve the texture of civilised life. They all reacted in different ways and it is easy to play favourites. Miss Hughes unreservedly recommends Leavis's *Listener* article on Montale, but those of us who read it when it came out are apt to remember that Leavis characteristically employed Montale as a means of finding Valéry inadequate and was thus able to belittle Eliot because Eliot had admired Valéry. I am only one of many people who would have liked to be a fly on the wall when Montale and Leavis were reciting 'Le Cimetière Marin' at each other. But no greater opposition of two critical minds can be imagined: Leavis's heresy-hunting was exactly the kind of thing Montale was against. Montale believed in separate individual talents adding up to a collaborative society of the intelligence. But then he had been obliged to believe that, with no room for self-indulgence: in Italy, where orthodoxies had been imposed at administrative level, the kind of argument Leavis was employing could be recognised for what it was.

Nevertheless we can't help feeling a greater affinity with some writers than with others, or thinking that some took a more fruitful course. Montale speaks for the century as unmistakably as Mandelstam, with the additional consideration that by chance he was able to live on, and so reach his full, slow flower. ('*On respire*,' wrote Contini when introducing Montale to a French audience, '*d'avoir affaire pour une fois à un poète qui n'a pas été un enfant prodige.*') The fragments Eliot shores against his ruins belong to a civilisation which he says we would have lost whatever happened. Yeats, too, is farewelling something that was never ours. Even Valéry's lost kingdom is somewhere in fairyland and Rilke has to be in a castle before he can give you his sense of the past: he needs all those armigerous trappings, and if his patroness is not in the *Almanach de Gotha* he feels uprooted. But Montale and Mandelstam both avoided social nostalgia. Mandelstam's nostalgia was, famously, for a world culture. Apart from that, as history crumbled around him, he sought salvation, not by harking back to the lost society, but by focusing with ever-increasing sharpness on the furniture of his own memory and so giving his individual life more and more meaning the more it was officially denied that such a thing could matter. Threatened with death, he hoped to be born again in the form of children's games. It was an angelic wish, an annunciation. The new reader will find Montale's poetry bathed in the same light.

Montale was a long time bringing the full facts of his everyday life into his poetry, but the feeling of the thingness of things is there from the start. Rhetoric was already official state policy when Montale, through the *Ossi di seppia*, insisted that it was stone walls, stagnant ponds, blades of grass and the instantaneously apprehended cloud of sea spray that really lasted. Leaving to others the attempt to preserve the memory of a vanished social order, he set about preserving the memory of everyday landscapes too ordinary ever to have been enrolled in anybody's scheme of the spectacular. At the beginning his propensity for regarding the unregarded sounded like despair: people thought that Montale's waste land was like Eliot's. But Montale's pessimism was more robust. If I cry, he later wrote, it is a counter-melody to enrich the great cloud-cuckoo-land which is the future.

Always realistic in his expectations, Montale dreamed in the presence of reason: no matter how jaundiced the view he took of life in Italy, he never gave the impression that it was the whole of modern life he was rejecting. Democracy, if it could be re-established, might not be paradise but as this world went it was a lot better than nothing. For this reason, and unlike most of the other major contemporary poets I have mentioned in connection with his name, Montale seems to give the present time the credit it has got coming. His poetry and prose taken together offer a complete literary personality which it is possible for the reader to embrace in its entirety, with no need to make allowances for neurasthenia or a self-consciously reactionary political stance. Montale had the robustness to face the world as it was and is. As the Italianists will know from the *Carteggio Svevo/ Montale*, what the young writer and his master recognised in each other was the determination to learn from life and not from books. In Montale's case, this principle made his wide reading all the more telling as he pursued it further. It isn't the man who wants to, he said, who continues the tradition, it's the man who can – and he's sometimes the man who knows least about it. He was the man who can. But he was also, gratifyingly, the man who knows everything about it.

Always thrilled by the emotional abundance of grand opera, Montale said he didn't trust anyone who preferred *Falstaff* to *Trovatore*. He didn't mean that he disliked refinement. He just meant that refinement means nothing without energy. Without posing as the man inspired – he called himself an artist among bourgeois and a bourgeois among artists – he was the embodiment of literature as a way of being true to life. Believing that the particular truth comes first and the general truth grows out of that, he began as the tutelary spirit of his own bleached region and ended by handing a whole country back to itself. When his compatriots read him they look back into their own lives and find the meaning of what they have been through. Our own experience is not so different from theirs that we can't share something of the same revelation. He cultivated his solitude until it belonged to us all.

London Review of Books
15 October–4 November, 1981

How Montale Earned His Living

The Second Life of Art: Selected Essays of Eugenio Montale edited and translated by Jonathan Galassi
(Ecco Press (New York), 1983)

Prime alla Scala by Eugenio Montale
(Mondadori (Milan), 1981)

IF EUGENIO MONTALE had never written a line of verse he would still have deserved his high honours merely on the basis of his critical prose. The product of a long life spent clearing the way for his poetry, it is critical prose of the best type: highly intelligent without making mysteries, wide-ranging without lapses into eclecticism or displays of pointless erudition, hard-bitten yet receptive, colloquial yet compressed. The only drawback is that it constitutes a difficult body of work to epitomise without falsifying.

For a long time Montale's English translators added to the difficulty by not being able to read much Italian or, sometimes and, not being able to write much English. Then a few competent, if restricted, selections emerged. But the problem remained of transmitting Montale's critical achievement in its full, rich and all too easily misrepresented subtlety. Now Jonathan Galassi has arrived to save the day. His style does not always catch Montale's easy rhythm, but much of the time he comes close, and the explanatory notes on their own would be enough to tell you that he has mastered all the necessary background information. One of the most active of Montale's previous translators was under the impression that Dante employed the word *libello* to mean 'libel' instead of 'little book'. A dedicated and knowledgeable student of the tradition from which he emerged, Montale was a stickler for detail, so Mr Galassi's wide competence comes as a particular refreshment. In all his phases as a poet, from the early, almost Imagist toughness to the later anecdotal relaxation, Montale started with the specific detail and let the general significance emerge. His prose kept to the same order of priority, so it is important that the details be got right. Galassi had several volumes of prose to consider, all published late in the poet's life. *Sulla Poesia* of 1976 is the principal collection of literary criticism as such, and indeed one of the most interesting single collections of literary essays in modern times, but the earlier *Auto da Fé* of 1966 (Montale must have been unaware that Elias Canetti had given the English version of *Die Blendung* that same title) is its necessary complement, being concerned with the question of mass culture – a question made more vexing for Montale by the fact that, although he didn't like mass culture, he did like popular culture and thought that élite culture would kill itself by losing touch with it.

There are also some important discursive writings on

literature in *Fuori di Casa* (1969), the book about being away from home, and the *Carteggio Svevo/Montale* (1976), which chronicles Montale's early involvement with the novelist whose merits he was among the first to recognise, and whose concern with the artistic registration of the inner life helped encourage Montale in the belief – crucial to his subsequent development – that what mattered about modern art was not its Modernism but the way it allowed private communication between individuals, the sharing of deep secrets in a time of shallow rhetoric. In addition, there is the abundant music criticism, but most of that, at the time this book was being prepared, was not yet available in book form, so Mr Galassi largely confined himself to the general articles on music scattered through the volumes mentioned above.

Even with so considerable a restriction, however, there was a lot to choose from. The *richesse* must have been made doubly embarrassing by Montale's habit of returning to the same point in essay after essay in order to elaborate it further, so that there is a real danger, if you settle on a single essay in order to demonstrate how he has aired a given topic, of getting the idea that he glosses over difficulties in passing, whereas in fact one of his salient virtues was to stay on the case, sometimes for decades on end, until he had it cracked. To sample him is thus almost always to belittle him: it is misleading, for example, to have him speaking as an anti-academic unless you also have him speaking as an appreciator of solid scholarship, and no representation of Montale as the hermeticist young poet can be anything but a travesty unless he is also allowed to speak as the reasonable man who didn't just end up as the advocate of appreciability, but who actually started out that way. One of the big compliments Mr Galassi should be paid is that, given this very real problem, he has selected well. All the books are fairly represented, most of the main different emphases in Montale's stable but manifold critical position are touched upon if not covered, and the quiet giant comes alive before us, as a personality and a mind.

To an extraordinary extent the two things were co-extensive. Like one of those periods in Chinese history when Confucian self-discipline and Taoist impulsiveness nourished each other, Montale's inner life was both naively fruitful and sophisticatedly self-aware. It makes him great fun to read, as if the smartest man in the world were a friend of the family, one of those good uncles who aren't avuncular. In Italian the title essay of the book was called 'Tornare nella Strada' ('Back into the Street'), but the term 'second life' recurs throughout the piece and comes right from the centre of Montale's essentially generous artistic nature. No poet could be more learned about the cultural heritage of his own country and his learning about the cultural heritage of other countries is impressive too, but he says, and obviously believes, that it is not the appeal of art to adepts that interests him most. It is not the first life that matters, but the second life, when a theme from an opera gets whistled in the street, or a phrase from a poet is quoted in conversation. This view might sound crudely populist or even philistine when excerpted, but as argued in a long essay, and fully considered during a long career, it proves to be a highly developed exposition of the elementary precept that art must be appreciable, even if only by the happy few. It doesn't have to be immediately appreciable, and indeed in modern times any attempt to make it so is likely to be just a coldly intellectualised programme of a different kind, but if it rejects the possibility of being appreciated then it disqualifies itself as art. 'The piece goes on and on,' he says regretfully of Schoenberg's *Ode to Napoleon*, 'but it does not live during the performance, nor can it hope to do so afterward, for it does not affect anything that is truly alive in us.'

Montale realised quite early that to propose such a line would involve a perpetual obligation to dissociate himself from unwanted allies who would mock any kind of difficulty, even when it was legitimate. That there could be such a thing as legitimate difficulty Montale did not doubt, since he himself embodied it as a poet. But he also didn't doubt that Modernist enthusiasms would open the way for illegitimate difficulty in large quantities, and that the enemies of art would therefore have a lot at which to point the finger while they made their strident calls for a responsible culture.

Mussolini liked quotable quotes, and Palmiro Togliatti's idea of art was of something which people could sing or recite while they were lining up to join the Communist Party. If you don't much like Expressionism, the way you say so is bound to be modified by the fact that Hitler didn't like it either. Montale's lifelong apoliticism was very political in this sense – that he spoke for the autonomy of culture at a time when political forces were trying to co-opt it. Art should be responsible only to itself. But responsible it should be. 'Mastery,' he said in twenty different ways, 'consists of knowing how to limit yourself.' It was the necessary corollary of his other famous proposition, the one about how it isn't the man who wants to who continues the tradition, but the man who can.

The man who can is the man with inspiration. But the inspiration has to come from life. This was where Montale parted company from the Modern movement as a whole. For Montale, art which had nothing except its own technique for subject matter could only be a monster. 'An art which destroys form while claiming to refine it denies itself its second and longer life: the life of memory and everyday circulation.' It would be a conventional enough conclusion for any artist to reach in old age but all the evidence suggests that Montale started out with it. Even back in the 1920s, when he was the unfathomable, linguistically revolutionary young poet of *Ossi di Seppia*, he had that social humility to go with his fierce artistic pride. Maturity was part of his gift.

'Style,' he wrote in 1925, the year of the first publication of *Ossi di Seppia*, 'perhaps will come to us from the sensible and shrewd disenchanted, who are conscious of the limits of their art and prefer loving it in humility to reforming humanity.' The idea had been made very relevant by the events of the 1920s. The international avant-garde had already projected, and was bringing into being, an art without limits. Fascism was bringing into being a reformed humanity, or supposed it was. To this latter end, the mobilisation of art was alleged to be essential. In the event, Italian artists and intellectuals were slow to provide Mussolini with the accreditation he would have liked. He gave them medals but, as Montale points out, even when they accepted the medals they did not give much in return.

Montale accepted no medals and gave nothing – not to the state, anyway. What he gave, he gave to his country. As a poet he continued and deepened his original course of writing a new, compressed poetry which, from the puffy and sugared *cappuccino* that the Italian lyric had become, was a direct and vertiginous return to the Dantesque *espresso basso*. Later on, when his early manner relaxed into the luminous transparency of the love poetry and the slippered reminiscence of the verse diaries, that initial rigour was still there underneath, keeping everything in terse proportion. In the most rhetorical age of Italian history, his poetry was always as unrhetorical as could be. His prose kept the same rule, to the end of his long life – a *serietà scherzevole*, a joking seriousness, a humane ease whose steady claim on your attention reminds you that he is the opposite of dispassionate. He is a passionate man in control of himself, having seen, or guessed in advance, what self-indulgence leads to.

Montale's defence of art against utilitarian pretensions, whether from the state or on behalf of the mass audience, has general relevance for the modern world, but the specific conditions of recent Italian history brought it into being. Faced with the stentorian claims of bogus novelty, it was inevitable that he would appeal to tradition. Yet it was a tradition from which he personally was trying to fight free. Certainly his unusual capacity to speak generally about the arts without declining into abstraction springs partly from a detailed engagement with his European literary predecessors. But that much he had been born to. Eliot, with whose name Montale's was often linked, got into the European tradition from outside. Montale, born inside, had to get out from under its crushing weight. He talked his way out. Mr Galassi's selection from Montale's many essays on Italian writers shows the poet humanising the past, pointing out what is permanently current. The great figures rise from their tombs of scholarship and speak as contemporaries, even the grandiose and torrentially eloquent D'Annunzio, the poet who was everything Montale strove not to be. In fact, the essay on D'Annunzio leaves you thirsty for more. If it were as long as the one on Svevo, you would feel that D'Annunzio was at arm's reach, instead of still soaring around above you with goggles preposterously flashing, pursuing those 'flights of omnivorous fancy which does not always turn what it touches into gold, but which will never cease to amaze us'.

Montale's admiration for D'Annunzio was real, but a long way within bounds. For Svevo it was a profound sympathy. D'Annunzio wanted to conquer the world – an uninteresting prospect. Svevo's universe was in his own soul, and that interested Montale very much. Montale's young enthusiasm helped the diffident Triestine businessman to the recognition he deserved as Italy's most important modern novelist. But here again it is necessary to emphasise that Montale was much less concerned with Svevo's technical advance into Modernism than with his thematic return to a solid, communicable, everyday subject – which just happened to be the one subject everybody could recognise: namely, the failed adventures in the soul. At a time of heated bombast, Svevo offered concreteness and the slow maturity of considered awareness. 'Removed from contact with the world of letters, Svevo developed in solitude.' Montale was also talking about himself. He was not removed from the world of letters, which was never likely to leave him alone, but he always cultivated his solitude in a way which Svevo had helped show him was the key to being a modern artist. The life had to be private before it could be public. The other way round was just publicity.

The essay on Svevo would be enough by itself to demonstrate that Montale, if he was ever anti-academic, was not so for lack of scholarly instinct. He had respect for scholarship but was early aware that it would tend to put the past beyond reach, if only by providing 'too much light'. He had a knack for making then seem as close as now – the obverse of another knack, equally valuable, for sensing what was eternal about the present. The section on foreign artists has essays about Valéry, Auden and Stravinsky which bring out their full dignity. A keen student of English, he enjoyed Auden's verbal playfulness in a way which would have horrified F. R. Leavis, who admired Montale and therefore assumed that he took a stern line against frivolity. But Montale was always willing to forgive intellectual sleight-of-hand if something unexpectedly lyrical should come out of it. His admiration for Stravinsky was withdrawn only when Neo-Classicism, which at least allowed the possibility of spontaneous feeling, gave way to serialism, which didn't. Apart from a few sour words about Brancusi, who was a bad host, Montale never belittles a real artist, no matter how variable his work or questionable his personal odyssey, believing that 'true poetry is in the nature of a gift, and therefore presupposes the dignity of the recipient'. But he isn't dewy-eyed either: the false positions that creative people can get themselves into, especially politically, fascinate and appal him.

Foreign students who own the monumental, fully annotated Contini/Bettarini *L'Opera in Versi* of 1980 are likely to remain deprived for a long time yet of an equivalent edition of the prose. They will find Galassi's book a useful tool even if they don't need the translation. Experts might sniff at being told who Svevo was, but it doesn't hurt to be told that Federico Frezzi was a poet of Foligno who wrote a long poem in imitation of Dante, thus, apparently, earning himself immediate and lasting oblivion. Montale would have approved of a footnote that gave Federico Frezzi of Foligno the dignity he had coming. Even a very minor artist was a good thing to be.

I can't see that Mr Galassi has fudged much in the way of information. Where Montale speaks of genius as a long patience, I think he expects us to know that Flaubert said it to Maupassant, although lately I have seen the remark attributed to Balzac. Here it is attributed to no one but Montale, who was good enough at aphorisms of his own not to need other people's wished on him. Also when the humiliated and offended are mentioned at one point, and the humiliated and afflicted at another, these are indeed accurate translations from two different essays, but Montale is almost certainly referring to the title of the same novel by Dostoevsky in both cases.

But this is nit-picking. Montale's range of literary reference is so wide that even the most alert editor is bound to let a few allusions get through unannotated. More serious is Mr Galassi's seeming determination, despite his evident familiarity with Benedetto Croce's basic works, to remain unaware that you must be very careful not to translate the word *fantasia* as 'fantasy', when it should be 'imagination'. In English, thanks to Coleridge, 'imagination' is the categorically superior term. In Italian, after Croce, *fantasia* is categorically superior to *immaginazione*. Imprecision on this point is made galling by the fact that for Montale, as for every other Italian writing in the twentieth century, it was Croce who made precise discussion of the subject possible.

More serious still, the translation is often glutinous. Montale's enviably colloquial flow can't be reproduced unless you are sometimes content to write several sentences where he wrote one. The arbitrary genders of Italian enable a *prosatore* of Montale's gifts to construct long sentences in which you don't lose track. It's impossible to transpose them intact, as Mr Galassi proves on several occasions by producing a construction so labyrinthine that Ariadne's thread would run out half-way.

This prevalent fault of lumpishness – so unfaithful to Montale's conversational urbanity – is exacerbated by a light peppering of strange English usages, or misusages. On page fifty-seven, to take one example, 'the game is up' should be 'the game's afoot' or possibly 'the game is on', but as it stands it means the exact opposite of what Montale wrote. 'Poetry is the art that is technically available to everyone: all it takes is a piece of paper and a pencil and the game is up.' On page 134, 'gild the pill' literally translates the Italian expression (*indorare la pillola*) but in English sounds like an unhappy conflation of 'gild the lily' and 'sugar the pill', which mean something separately but not a lot together.

The Second Life of Art, of the books in English by or concerned with Montale, is easily the most important to date. Of the books in Italian, *Prime alla Scala* has been long awaited. From 1954 to 1967 Montale wrote regular opera notices for the *Corriere d'Informazione*. It was always clear that when the pieces were collected the resulting volume would be one of the strongest on his short shelf. But the complete work, which he did not live to see published, is beyond expectation. It shows him at his best: in love with the subject and full of things to say.

Montale attended most of the La Scala first nights in the great period when much of the conducting was being done by his ideal maestro, Gianandrea Gavazzeni. The *bel canto* operas were being rediscovered, mainly because of Callas. Early and middle Verdi was being honoured for the first time as the full equivalent of the later operas and not just as the preparation for them. Meanwhile it was becoming ever clearer that the tradition could be added to only by re-assessing the past. The new composers, with the qualified exceptions of Stravinsky and Britten, lacked the secret.

Montale's criticism, underpinned by his early training as a singer, was part of all this. The book abounds with solid detail. ('Her diction was clear and precisely articulated,' he says of Callas, 'even if her almost Venetian Italian rendered difficult the doubling of consonants.') Beyond that, in his usual way, he draws conclusions about art in general. The crisis in music is traced as it happens, by someone who was there, in 1916, at the first performance of one of Leon-cavallo's last operas and lived to hear the endlessly repeated notes of a new work by Nono bore the audience starry-eyed in the name of social awareness. Yet Montale's own repeated note is one of endurance, a refusal to be crushed under the weight of justifiable pessimism: the new composers might have lost touch with any possible public except themselves, but Bellini lives again, Verdi is reborn in full glory, the past enthralls the present and reminds it of what art is. In the modern era there is no way for music *not* to be self-conscious. Being that, it has small chance of being spontaneous. But Montale, remembering how he himself found a way of being both, always talks as if other people might somehow manage it too.

These are necessary books about the arts, in a troubled period when one of the threats facing the arts is that there are too many books about them. Montale said he thought of journalism as his *secondo mestiere*, the day-job whose demands relegated his real calling, poetry, to evenings and spare time. But the fact that he was obliged to spend so much time thus earning a living is a good reason for liking the age we live in – a liking that he shared, despite everything. He was the kind of pessimist who makes you feel optimistic, even when he can't do the same for himself.

London Review of Books
11 February – 2 March, 1983

Elastic White Thighs

Bawdy Verse: A Pleasant Collection edited by
E. J. Burford
(Penguin (New York), 1983)

E VERYTHING has been done to make this little anthology of off-colour verse as repellent as possible. It is subtitled 'A Pleasant Collection', for coyness. On the title page there is a jocular penguin reading a book equipped with a flagrant pair of fake boobs, for vulgarity. Finally there is the editor's introduction, for embarrassment. Ephraim John Burford, 'born and educated in the City of London', is 'currently preparing a book on the rise of organised bawdry in London'. On top of this, he 'has also lectured on London and particularly old London Bridge for the City of London Society'. At least one resident of London has never bumped into Mr Burford, but no doubt he is indoors a great deal, preparing his books and lectures.

To aid him in this activity he has a killing prose style with several main attributes. There is his alliterativeness, by which we hear of 'bawdy ballads, lubricious lyrics and salacious songs'; there is his word-play, by which such

vocables as 'lions' and 'loins' become hilariously inter-
changed. ('We can be sure that Blondel sang bawdy songs to
his lecherous master, Richard the Lionheart, extolling the
theme of his loins rather than the lions.') And there is his flair
for innuendo, evoking for us 'the ostensibly mysterious
female pubic triangle'.

The book itself, however, does not quite live down to
expectations. Comprising versified filth by variously com-
petent authors from the fourteenth century through to the
late eighteenth, it is indeed disgusting – even more disgust-
ing than Mr Burford's introductory remarks might lead you
to imagine. But by the end of it I had to admit that Mr
Burford, though I liked him no better, had done a useful job,
and probably out of a sort of innocence. If the catchment
area had been extended to the nineteenth century, things
would probably have become much nastier, because of
Victorian hypocrisy. As it is, what we are given is honest
even when frightful. Mr Burford is right to be fascinated.
There is truth to life in what he studies, and it has probably
done good to his soul, if not to his prose.

Dating from the middle of the fifteenth century, 'A Talk of
Ten Wives on Their Husbands' Ware' ringingly sets one of
the themes which are fated to recur throughout the next
several hundred years.

> The fourth wyffe of the flocke
> Seyd 'owre syre's fidecocke
> Ffayne wolde I skyfte.

Mr Burford gets in at the bottom of the page to explain
that this last line means 'My husband's penis I'd like to
change' but the meaning would have emerged from its
context, as the second half of the stanza reveals.

> He is longe and he is smalle
> And yett he hath the fydefalle;
> God gyve hym sorry thryfte!

Once again Mr Burford is there (somebody like him was
probably there at the time) to explain that if the wyffe's

hosbonde hath the fydefalle it means 'he can't get it up'. Nor was getting it up the supreme challenge. Yet more important was keeping it up. Even at this early stage in the written history of modern Britain, the measure of manhood seems to have been the ability to satisfy the woman's burning desire. Feminists might object that there were few songs written about unwilling women, but even the most rabid among them could hardly claim, on this evidence, that men have always thought only of their own fell needs.

> Then off he came and blusht for shame
> So soone that he had end it;
> Yett still she lies and to him cryies,
>   'Once More, and None can mend it!'

So goes the song 'Walkinge in a Meadow Greene', written before 1600. Recently there was an idea vaguely in circulation that the female orgasm had been first discovered in the 1960s and that in pre-modern times a man took his satisfaction with no thought for the woman's. Here is an indication, if such were needed, that this notion is baseless. More interesting, however, is the further indication that men not only set out to secure the woman's pleasure, they drew the essence of their own pleasure from doing so. Even the most subtle feminist finds it hard to believe that for a man who loves women, love-making is not a refined version of rape but its absolute opposite. Yet the truth of the matter is older than the hills, and omnipresent even in Burford's mainly awful collection, of which Nashe's 'The Merrie Ballad of Nashe His Dildo' is merely a more adroit example than usual.

> 'By Holy Dame' (quoth she) 'and Will't not stand?
> Now let me roll and rub it in my Hand!
> Perhaps the silly *Worm* hath laboured sore
> And worked so that it can do no more:
>
> Which, if it be, as I do greatly dread,
> I wish ten thousand times that I were dead.
> What ere it be, no means shall lack in me
> That may avail for his recovery!'

No means lacking, she effects the recovery in the following few stanzas, which we will omit here only for reasons of space. More interesting, from the viewpoint of the mature student, is the reciprocity of the subsequent rapture.

> On her his Eyes continually were fixed
> With his eye-brows her melting Eyes were mixed,
> Which like the Sun, betwixt two Glasses plays
> From the one to the other casting rebounding Rays.

There is a proto-Metaphysical stamp to this which harks forward to the knottier conceits of Donne, although a close reading shows the lady to be in serious ophthalmic trouble. Getting so much hair in her lachrymal ducts could easily lead to galloping conjunctivitis on top of the strabismus which she apparently has naturally, unless Nashe means that the rebounding rays are going from both her eyes to his, and not from one of her eyes to the other. This is to quibble, however: Nashe raised the standard of what Mr Burford would call 'ribald rhymes', just as Rochester was later to raise it again, and Walpole later still. Raising was something it would always need. Except in times of censorship, the major writers got the scabrous element into their writings along with all the other elements. That left the minor writers to plug away at their one topic, not always with an abundance of invention.

> Faine would I go both up and downe,
>   up and downe, up and downe
> No child is fonder of the gig
> Than I to dance a merry Jig
> Faine woulde I try how I could frig
> Up and downe, up and downe, up and downe,
> Faine would I try how I could caper

This probably sounded better sung than it reads now, and even if it didn't, to echo such sentiments in what Mr Burford would call 'convivial company' must have been at least as enjoyable as watching an old Matt Helm movie alone in your hotel room after midnight. Or try 'The Sea Crabb', conceived circa 1620.

The good man went home and ere he wist
Put the crabb in the Chamberpot where his wife pisst.
With a ging, Boys, ging, ging, boys, ging.
Tarradiddle, farradiddle, ging, boys, ging!

As any nightclub comedian knows, once the atmosphere of salacity is charged up high enough any word will acquire a double meaning, even if the word makes no sense at all. The song 'A Maid and a Younge Man' capitalises on this fact.

A Man and a younge Mayd that loved a long time
Were taken in a frenzy in the Midsummer prime;
The Maid she lay drooping, Hye;
The Man he lay whopping, Hey;
the Man he lay whopping Ho!

But even in Arcadia there was no whopping without a price. The usual price was the pox. If human tenderness is shown to have been always possible, divine retribution is shown to have been always present, and just as ready to strike the innocent as the guilty. Not that the guilty cringed. As 'The Westminster Whore' loudly pronounces, it goes hard with the professional when there are so many eager amateurs.

'Now, the Curse of a Cunt without Hair
And ten thousand Poxes upon her:
We pore Whores may go hang in dispaire;
Wee're undone by the Maydes of Honour.'

So went a harlot's song in 1610. Blake later said that the harlot's song from street to street would weave old England's winding sheet, but perhaps the main reason he cast his warning as a prophecy was that the song was very old and had not yet done so. From the accession of the Stuarts to the Glorious Revolution of 1688, the commerce between the court and the stews was a constant theme, only enriched during the Civil War and the Commonwealth, when each side accused the other of buggery, it seems with some cause.

Certainly Rochester, the great syncretic spirit of Restoration rakery – it will be seen that Mr Burford's style is getting into mine – included sodomy among his repertoire of talents. But Rochester most clearly adumbrated our own time by making stars out of whores, as in 'An Account of Cuffley'. In 1670 Molière wrote *Le bourgeois gentilhomme*, Racine wrote *Bérénice*, Dryden wrote *The Conquest of Granada*, and Rochester wrote this:

> Then the next morning we all hunt
> To find whose fingers smell of Cunt.

With the advent of Rochester you really feel that it might start raining brimstone at any moment. Here is a first-rate talent whose chief concern is to grab the back of the reader's neck and shove his face right in it. Three stanzas of 'A Ramble in St James's Park' should be enough for one gulp.

> Did ever I refuse to bear
> The meanest part your lust could spare!
> When your lewd Cunt came spewing home
> Drenched with the seed of half the Town.
>
> My dram of sperm, was supped up after
> For the digestive surfeit water.
> Full gorged at another time
> With a vast meal of nasty slime
>
> Which your devouring Cunt had drawn
> From Porters' backs and Footmen's brawn,
> I was content to serve you up
> My Ballock-full for your grace cup.

This is jealousy talking the way it usually only thinks. Two hundred years before the French poets, Rochester made the descent into hell on behalf of English literature, and did it without posturing. What is inspiring about him – along with his energy, imagination, and driving rhythm – is that he found humanity down there. Later in the same poem, jealousy gives way again to the adoration that fired it.

When, leaning on your faithless breast
Wrapped in security and rest,
Soft kindness all my powres did move,
And Reason lay dissolved in Love!

But Rochester's poem, for all his seeming determination to seek out the worst diseases and make sure he catches them, is poetry, not bawdry. A more typical creation of his time is the anonymous 'Last Night's Ramble'. The scene is Lady Jane Southcott's up-market cat-house. The matron speaks:

'The Lady within's tis, whose husband's old.
She comes to swive for Pleasure, not for Gold:
While quondam Judge is taking fees at home,
She, for that same, sometimes abroad does roam.

'Such a Belle tall, such a Bon Mein and Air
So witty, so well-shap'd and such a Hair!
A snowy skin, such sparkling eyes, and then
Rough as you'd wish, strait as a girl of ten!'

The lady of quality who wanted to play the hooker might not have been entirely a dream, inasmuch as there has no doubt always been some young woman ready to cast herself as Belle de Jour. Yet clearly she was a dream to whoever bought the broadside. Lewdness gives way to pornography when instead of being an inducement or accompaniment to lubricious conduct it becomes a substitute. But probably it would be a mistake to suppose that there was ever a sexual version of Eliot's dissociation of sensibility. A more likely assumption is that there were always men who sat around loudly singing rude songs while their more astute fellows were off somewhere quietly getting lucky. Imagine the sheer noise-level that must have gone into the collective composing of that dependable show-stopper, 'The Brown Cunts of Old England'.

When mighty brown cunts were the Englishman's taste,
With strong curled hair that could tie round the waist.

Our offspring were stout and our wives were all chaste
    Oh! the brown cunts of old England
    And Oh! the old English brown cunt.

There is ingenuity in this but a forlorn longing too. It is
written to be sung by men without women, whereas the
saving grace of earlier verse, however scurrilous, lay in the
assumed complicity of the sexes, to the extent that it is now
often hard to tell which sex wrote it. But the pills to purge
melancholy went on being produced in the eighteenth cen-
tury, and although many of the examples cited by Mr
Burford induce more melancholy than they purge, neverthe-
less the urge to be merry is still patent. Even in low forms,
however, there is no substitute for talent. No appeal to
tradition could mitigate the perfect tedium of 'The Travel-
ling Tinker, and the Country Ale-wife'.

A Comely Dame of Islington,
    Had got a leaky Copper;
The Hole that let the Liquor run,
    Was wanting of a Stopper:
A Jolly Tinker undertook,
    And promised her most fairly;
With a thump thump thump, and knick knack knock,
    To do her Business rarely.

Whether you call it ribaldry or protest, the rotten folk song
is perennial. But some genuine enthusiasm went into 'White
Thighs', dating from about 1735.

Poets praise Chloe's shape, her complexion, her air,
    Coral lips, pearly teeth, and fine eyes;
A fig for them all, they can never compare
    To my charmer's elastic white thighs.

The eighteenth century's representation suffers from the
absence of Swift, but Horace Walpole's 'Little Peggy' proves
that the politically levelling sexual impulse could still be felt
as more of a blessing than a threat. The Earl of Lincoln
fathered a daughter on his great love, a famous whore called

Peggy Lee. Walpole, a full-blooded man himself, predicted great things for the child.

> Arise, O maid, to promised joys arise!
> *Lincoln's* sweet seed and daughter of the Skies!
> See joyous Brothels shake their conscious Beds,
> See glowing *Pricks* exalt their crimson Heads!
> See Sportive *Buttocks* wanton in the Air
> And Bawds, *cantharides* and *punch*, prepare!
> The youths unbuttoned to thy arms advance
> And feather-tickled Elders lead the Lech'rous Dance!

The best thing from later in the century is 'The Bumper Toast', in which once again the democracy of lust finds happy expression. It would be nice to think the desire was father to the ability. Alas, the evidence suggests that an exclusive concern with these matters almost guarantees a leaden muse. The anonymous author of the toast was one of those rare singers who through monomania attained the universal.

> Fill a Bumper, my host, and I'll give you a Toast
> We all have conversed with and everyone knows;
> Fill it up to the top and drink every drop
> Here's Cunt in a bumper wherever she goes.
> Your high-sounding titles that Kings can create
> Derive all their lustre and weight from the Donor;
> But Cunt can deride all the mockery of State
> For she's, in herself, the true fountain of honour.

Sincerity and generosity are here unmistakable. In the nineteenth century they were harder to find. The genteel arrived and locked pornography in the cellar, where it flourished until released to overwhelm us. Perhaps Mr Burford was right to leave all that out. Some notable artists have written scurrilously in our time, but nearly always with a purpose. Auden's 'The Platonic Blow' would fit into this anthology because of its lack of didacticism, its pure sense of enjoyment. It would also fit because of its consuming – the word seems not inappropriate – dullness.

With the salient exceptions I have mentioned, Mr Burford's 'pleasant collection' makes pretty unpleasant reading. Not even Rochester could make a symphony out of one note. But among the catch-penny titles with which Penguin nowadays tricks out its poetry list, this one has a more solid reason for being than its presentation might suggest. As I sit typing this article after midnight in the City of London, I see, outside the window, white concrete, plate glass, and a smooth asphalt street being cleaned by a machine. The whole neighbourhood was destroyed by the fire raids of 1940. But once it was Moorfields, the bubbling stew from which many of the verses in this book emerged. Here was Grub Street, and before that there were Mother Cresswell's brothels. Around here, people rotted from the pox or were maddened by its cure. *And* were maddened by its cure. When you imagine the suffering, it is a wonder that anyone ever felt pleasure at all, let alone sang for the joy of it. There is never any harm in being reminded that the way we live now is not normal.

New York Review of Books
13 October, 1983

Necessary Inhibitions

T. S. Eliot: A Study in Character and Style by Ronald Bush
(Oxford University Press, 1984)

HERE IS a learned, literate, thoughtful book about T. S. Eliot that ought to bring his poetry closer. Then why does it make you feel, long before you have finished reading it, that Eliot's poetry is drifting further away? Eugenio

Montale once said that there is a danger that scholarship and criticism will act together to shed 'too much light' on a work of art. Only the captious would accuse Ronald Bush of having shed too much light here, but it will be a forbearing reader who does not sometimes conclude, while puzzling his way through this densely argued monograph, that any poetry which induces such a complexity of exegesis might just possibly have something wrong with it.

Mr Bush himself voices doubts about the consistency of Eliot's achievement after *The Waste Land*, but modestly refrains from adducing, as supplementary evidence, the fact that he felt compelled to write a book-length commentary which might have been a mere article if Eliot had gone on succeeding – or, at any rate, had not failed in a way that requires so much help from explicators in order to be made intelligible. Mr Bush does not blame Eliot for needing him. Professor Denis Donoghue, we remember, betrayed no such hesitation in the case of Yeats, saying that what was wrong with Yeats was that he needed so much learned attention from the likes of Professor Donoghue. It is possible, however, that Professor Donoghue picked up this notion from the late Dr F. R. Leavis, who thought that the total number of 'fully achieved' poems written by Yeats was two, and that everything else was vitiated by its crying need for illumination from an outside source. Leaving aside its infernal arrogance, the palpable falseness of this idea did not stop it from becoming a talking point in its turn, a contribution to the exponentially expanding literature *on* Yeats, as opposed to the relatively contracting literature *of* Yeats.

Mr Bush has composed a distinguished increment to the literature *on* Eliot. Before deciding whether the literature *of* Eliot has been further shrivelled as a consequence, we can count ourselves lucky that a scholar with a critical mind – or a critic with scholarly equipment, if the converse priority is preferred – is on the case. Admittedly, Professor Hugh Kenner covered the same subject more than twenty years go, but *The Invisible Poet* was a volume of his modern marvels encyclopaedia only marginally less frenzied than the one devoted to Ezra Pound. Besides, Eliot's private life was hard to discuss at that time. Relevant data having piled up in the interim, the way is clear for another very clever, but this time less hagiographic, book connecting the man who suffered with the mind that created. Mr Bush takes the opportunity with enthusiasm, especially in the matter of Eliot's human frailty, which gets a lot of emphasis – to the point where we might be inclined, perhaps unwisely, to regard the man who wrote *The Waste Land* as an ordinary human being like the rest of us, who didn't write it.

But if Mr Bush can't fully approve of what came after *The Waste Land*, at least his disapproval helps him to approve of *The Waste Land*, so to some extent he stays attached to the reality of the matter, which is that Eliot, when he did succeed in writing poetry, wrote something no amount of explanation can fully explain. Having remembered in this one case that he is dealing with an entity rather greater than the sum of its elements, Mr Bush is able to talk informatively about the elements. That *The Waste Land*, whether or not it is a lament for a wrecked civilisation, is certainly a lament for a wrecked marriage has been argued before, most notably by Ian Hamilton in *A Poetry Chronicle*, whose chapter on *The Waste Land* seems to have escaped Mr Bush's otherwise panscopic attention. A pity, because its example might have kept him down to earth. But he stays down to earth long enough to get some pertinent things said concerning the various ways Eliot avoided speaking outright about his personal suffering, and so wrote a poem whose impersonality became, and still becomes, the private property of any reader.

Eliot's two main stratagems, one of which Mr Bush likes a lot and the other of which he likes less, were the 'accidental image' and the applied myth. The accidental image had its heritage in French Symbolism, and there can be no doubt that Eliot, as well as being intellectually drawn to the technique through the opportunities it offered for compression and resonance, really did find his own psyche more accessible when he took it by surprise, rather than through a frontal assault.

Mr Bush gives the poet good marks for achieving in *The Waste Land* even more of what he had achieved in the earlier poems by way of outsmarting his inhibitions. He gives bad marks, though, for how the same poet, looking upon what he had wrought, foisted a myth-schema on to it so that it would look more portentous or, at any rate, less vulnerable. The poetic moments, the critic concludes, are the real McCoy, but the overall pattern is a put-up job.

Though Mr Bush makes too much of this when dealing with *Four Quartets* later on, its relevance to *The Waste Land* is hard to question, and for a while we are given some real criticism to ponder. But the attendant speculation might have been of higher quality, instead of just high-flown. The biographical details that are not supposed to be available (if the poet's widow had allowed an official biography straight away, it might have dished out neatly the beans that the unofficial biographies have so clumsily spilled) are brought in by Mr Bush with welcome tact, but not even so fastidious a scholar can resist constructing a straw man with them. Mr Bush's straw man was always inhibited. He always had difficulty expressing himself. Mr Bush might have asked himself again, if he asked himself at all, whether the real man was that simple. Suppose, for example, that Eliot knew all about his own mental condition and cherished it as the motor of his gift. Would a poem that *directly* complained about the agony of his marriage have been a desirable, or even imaginable, artistic object? When Eliot, towards the end of his life, finally achieved the bliss of married love, it produced exactly one lyric.

Mr Bush finds the poems between *The Waste Land* and *Four Quartets* too incantatory, too dependent on wilful echolalia – in short, too patterned. Before, myth was doing the patterning at a late stage of composition, but now the patterning was being done from the jump by Eliot's weakness for assonance: that is, by his strength for assonance left unguarded. Again, this is well argued, but the essential point is left out, which is that 'The Hollow Men' and 'Ash-Wednesday' are full of lines hard to forget even at their most obviously contrived.

It is no doubt true that Eliot, in shifting his admiration from the poetry of Donne to the prose of Lancelot Andrewes, renounced the self-indulgence of the metaphysical quiddity and embraced the chastening ideal of a reasoned verse. To add that 'Eliot fastened upon philosophical precision not as a mode of public speech but as a way of avoiding it' is a justifiable turn of the screw. But even when you take into account – as Mr Bush perhaps too generously does not – the sheer tedium of the choruses from *The Rock*, there is nevertheless enough in Eliot's period of plain and fancy chant to remind you that although incantation may be a bad word in Mr Bush's vocabulary, André Gide thought that poetry should consist of nothing else.

But Mr Bush has a line to push. Eliot's proneness to pattern-making, he says, reaches its culmination in *Four Quartets*, which is, or are, damaged as a consequence. Once again, there is enough in this notion to save it from being self-evidently silly. There *is* something wilful, even mechanical, about the sequence of 'movements', a pretension to musical form that makes Eliot sound unmusical for the first time in his life. But Mr Bush might have asked himself whether Dante – to take an example closely relevant to Eliot – was not being equally mechanical when he decided to write three canticles of thirty-three cantos each with each canticle ending on the same word. The *Divine Comedy* proves that a work of art can be mechanically organised and still be organically alive. So does *Four Quartets*, which is not only as marvellous in its poetic parts as Mr Bush says it is but also much more poetic in its prosaic parts than he seems to realise. Throughout the book he underestimates the value that Eliot placed on – and that we should place on – the verse that was just prose but more than just prose. When Eliot wrote the 'No! I am not Prince Hamlet' sequence in *Prufrock*, he hit pay-dirt.

Not all of his image-free verse is his best, but much of his best verse is image-free. Mr Bush, stuck with his theory of the accidental image, finds this fact harder to appreciate than he ought, and he is thus too ready to believe Professor Donald Davie's confident pronouncement that the passage in 'The Dry Salvages' containing the line about the 'very good dinner' is disastrously dull. But Professor Davie's 'devastating critique' of this supposed lapse would be disproportionate even if it were correct. Eliot is either pretending to be an old buffer, or he is an old buffer, but it fits either way. If those lines are blemishes, so are liver spots.

Deafness to tone is not among Mr Bush's drawbacks, but he parades enough academic affectations to make it seem to be. The occupational hazard of strained argument automatically produces the deadly catch-phrases that try to say the argument isn't strained at all. 'It's no accident, then . . .', 'It is not surprising, then . . .', '. . . it is neither accidental nor surprising . . .', 'It is not for nothing that . . .' This is not too gruesome a tally as publish-or-perish texts go, but it is lucky that the body of the book contains nothing to match a lulu in the notes at the back: 'My gesture towards *Finnegans Wake* is deliberate.' My own gesture, upon reading this, was equally deliberate: a hand pointing towards the door. Get out, sir, and come back when your tongue is clean.

Mr Bush's tongue will be a healthy pink again after the fever of book writing passes. Too appreciative of his subject to be completely fooled by his own theories about it, he retains at the end some of the excitement with which he began. As Brecht said in his little poem, when the fork with the lovely bone handle breaks, the trick is to discount your new knowledge that it must always have been flawed, and remember how you thought it flawless. Mr Bush tells the story of a fork revealing its flaw, but at the end he remembers. Indeed, he remembers too well, calling 'Little Gidding' not just the high point of Eliot's poetry but the high point of modernist verse, beyond which the post-modernist variety has not gone and apparently may not go. Any literary criticism that sounds like science is bad, but this sounds like bad science.

The book contains enough good criticism to redress the balance. It is a solid contribution to the literature on Eliot. Bright students may be directed towards it in the certainty that they will pick up something, if only a decent respect for the author's wide reading. But surely the chance is getting slimmer that they will have the time, the energy and the necessary innocence to make the literature *of* Eliot their own.

Atlantic Monthly
January, 1984

Lively Copy

London Reviews edited by Nicholas Spice
(Chatto & Windus, 1985)

The New Review Anthology edited by Ian Hamilton
(Heinemann, 1985)

Night and Day edited by Christopher Hawtree
(Chatto & Windus, 1985)

Lilliput goes to war edited by Kaye Webb
(Hutchinson, 1985)

Penguin New Writing: 1940–1950 edited by John
Lehmann and Roy Fuller
(Penguin, 1985)

WITH MORE than 800 high-grade items to choose from, *London Reviews* gets the number down to just twenty-eight. But already it is the third such selection from the *London Review of Books*. Is three neat volumes sitting on a shelf better than hundreds of copies of the magazine mouldering in a corner? Yes, but not emphatically. When a literary magazine is as good as this one it hurts to throw old copies away. Visiting I. F. Stone once in Washington, I was impressed by his complete bound files of the *New York Review of Books*, and more impressed still that he had extracted these from the editor as part-payment.

Perhaps contributors to the *LRB* could work the same trick on Karl Miller, who for this anthology hands over to Nicholas Spice, who in turn sensibly makes sure that Karl Miller's long essay about the *LRB* heads the list of contents. This essay is to be relished, not least when it is most uncertain. If the style is less tortuous than usual, the stylist is even more tortured. His highly developed sense of scruple has not let him rest easy since he chose Ursula Creagh as the reviewer of a book by A. Alvarez about divorce. Ursula Creagh, in addition to her sharp critical faculty, had the qualification of being divorced from A. Alvarez. Or should it have been the disqualification? The estimable Alvarez, brave as well as bright, will not mind my saying on behalf of several thousand subscribers that the piece was read keenly.

If the editor didn't print it just as keenly, certainly he managed to overcome his reluctance. But it can't be denied that the adversarial casting of reviewer and reviewed is more commonly practised down at the tattier end of Grub Street, to produce what is known as 'lively copy'. Let me give an example, based on close personal experience. Suppose, say, the *Literary Review* has printed an attack on one of your books a year after it was published. This might be an insult but so far there is no injury. The editor of the magazine then writes you a letter saying that the attacker is about to bring out a book of his own and asking whether you would like to review his book 'in reply'. You deal with the letter in the only way appropriate, by pretending you haven't seen it. The assistant editor of the magazine then rings you up to repeat the offer. You reply to the effect that revenge is a bad reason to write book reviews. A more graphic reply is ruled out by the fact that both the editor and the assistant editor are young women, new to the job but learning fast.

In the editorial half-world of the property-market give-away glossies and Naim Attallah's *corps de ballet*, lively copy is pursued in all innocence by fashionable female honourables whose idea of a rigorous literary magazine is *Vanity Fair*. In the arts-update departments of the fashion mags – and, increasingly, the back ends of the weeklies – lively copy is generated with a greater awareness of how seriousness is being sacrificed to trivialisation, and consequently with a more strident self-righteousness. But Manichean explanations are otiose. The Grub Street jobbing editor not only doesn't see anything awful about being slipshod, he doesn't see anything slipshod about being slipshod. He isn't transgressing his standards. Those *are* his standards. Hence the guileless charm of Karl Miller's self-searching. Worried about a momentary lapse from a principle the other chaps don't even know exists, he is so far above the battle that his anxious feet shuffle empty air. Imagine Wittgenstein high up in the grandstand, painfully arriving at his celebrated formulation that a game consists of the rules by which it is played. Imagine, down on the pitch, some clapped-out Third Division football side wanly attempting to avoid relegation by hacking at its opponents' raw ankles. The discrepancy is of that order.

The ethical point is not just relevant but crucial, because it is to the principled editor, the worrier, that the talented contributors come in search of prestige. As editor of a literary magazine he will have almost nothing else to pay them with, so all depends on his moral clout. He must conjure up a sense of mission. It is no coincidence, as the academics say, that what joins Karl Miller, now of the *LRB*, to Ian Hamilton, some time of the *New Review*, is a dominant, not to say overbearing, personality. Either man is able, by force of self-belief, to make good contributors expend, on an article, energy that they might otherwise have saved up to write books. Getting less good contributors to do this is no problem, but good contributors are more retentive, and eventually reach the stage when they yield up copy like a stone giving blood. It then becomes a matter of the editor's will. Without a Napoleonic inner certainty, he won't get the stuff. He must convince the best minds in the country that his magazine is a key factor in its survival as a civilisation, and he can do this only if he first convinces himself. My *Observer* colleague Neal Ascherson – present in this anthology with an exemplary piece on Ken Livingstone – once observed that the task of the literary editor is to ruin the next generation of writers. In diverting them from what they think they should be doing to what he thinks they should be doing, he had better believe that it is a far, far better thing they do for him than they might have done if left alone. Voice any doubt except that.

Below Karl Miller's troubled conscience is an assurance worthy of John Knox, if rather more tolerant. His magazine reflects this – is, indeed, its embodiment. The *LRB* is the house magazine of the British intellectual élite. In the *TLS* they talk to the world. In the *LRB* they talk to each other. The dons let their hair down. Professor Ricks tears his out. Everyone is in character. Ellipsis, allusiveness and casual snidery propagate a coffee-house atmosphere which is no doubt part of the appeal. More important, however, is that good minds are at their best when writing like this, on their mettle rather than up on stilts. Here again, the editor's personality is decisive. He gives the licence to be quirky. The contributor is encouraged to speak for the paper only in his cogency of argument. Otherwise he speaks for himself. The assumption is that a communal effort can be brought about only by individuals. The individual style is consequently cherished. Within the bounds of grammar, you may speak as you please. Contributors to any American publication at an equivalent level will know that the same privilege, however freely offered by the editor, will effectively be withdrawn by his minions. Edmund Wilson's famous letter to the editor of the *New Yorker*, complaining of how the very characteristics of style which had presumably led to his being hired in the first place were comprehensively expunged during the process of editing copy, has been much reprinted but paid little heed. The thrill of earning a dollar a word soon wears off when it turns out that the fact-checkers and guardians of house style will never be off the transatlantic phone.

Writing a single piece for an American magazine which I won't specify beyond saying that it is not published weekly in the Pacific, I had encounters at length with the disembodied voices of three separate editorial assistants, the last of whom wanted to convince me that the phrase 'redress the balance' made no sense, because only an imbalance could be redressed. I gave in for the same reason that rock splits under the impact of dripping water. So small a point ought not to matter, except that having the way you write absorbed into house style is only a step away from having the way you think absorbed into editorial policy. American critical papers, aware of their constitutionally guaranteed role as part of the government of the nation and therefore of the world, must be seen to have weight. Even if a writer has been hired for his light touch, he will find the editor collaborating with him lest due gravity be compromised. The heavy contributor will be encouraged to grow heavier still, by putting down footnotes as a baobab tree puts down roots. At its most extreme the effect is of a learned journal plus woodcuts.

The *LRB*'s contributors are encouraged to wear their learning lightly and will find their prose interfered with only in aid of clarity. Here again, the editor's reputation is decisive. As literary editor of the *New Statesman* and editor of the *Listener* he proved to a whole generation of writers that his blue pencil hurt only to heal. The *LRB*'s taste for poetry is a sure sign of its ear for prose. Craig Raine is represented in this selection by a poem of his own and another by David Lodge, who parodies the Martian approach so successfully that you wonder if it has quite enough to it. Blake Morrison's 'Xerox' is a poem to be memorised now if you did not cut it out of the paper and keep it, but he already had a reputation so anyone might have printed it. Fiona Pitt-Kethley, however, was little known until the *LRB* started printing her poems. For anyone with a teenage daughter their scabrous subject matter is hard to take. They would scare Martin Amis. It needed a true appreciation of literary talent to spot their quality.

The same true appreciation ensures that the prose in the *LRB* rarely falls below a certain standard and that the level of argument is kept up. Not all of the best *LRB* writers are here. Such is the paper's plurality of casual labour that the most diligent contributor can hope to be anthologised only every second time. I can think of several writers for whom this rule should be relaxed. Barbara Everett, for example, is proof that the traditional academic study of English literature, armed against theory and sensitive to real life, is the only sort of attention adequate to the subject. Her presence in the anthology would be a powerful reminder of just why the pseudo-scientists are absent from the magazine. The *LRB* knows what it wants to keep out. Therefore it is the paper to be in.

A don can make it into the *TLS* if he is one of the only two authorities on Punic zinc-smelting and the other has just written a book. He will thus be increased as a don. But in the *LRB* he becomes more than a don: he becomes someone whose intelligence counts generally. The magazine's invitation brings him half-way out of the cloisters and half-way into Grub Street, where the obligation to make himself plain must incidentally ensure, to our benefit, that he gives us the *haute vulgarisation* of his subject. Attracted by the same laurels while moving in the opposite direction, freelance literary journalists are also constrained to do their best. They are a dying breed, partly because the moonlighting of the dons has kept remuneration artificially low throughout the field. Time spent on writing a review for the *LRB* is time taken away from fabricating lucrative stuff for the glossies, an activity which doesn't hurt the conscience all that much because nobody reads it anyway. But one surprises within oneself the church-going urge to be more serious. Alan Bennett's piece on W. H. Auden, which seemed so good when it appeared in the paper, seems better still reprinted. For this, the justly famous Bennett can have got no royalties, no curtain calls, no green-rooms cries of 'Darling!' His reward was the special, monkish sense of release that you get from embracing a discipline, from doing your bit to transcribe the codex. The paper's monastic air of frugality would be called its bottom line if there were a PR person on the staff.

But this attribute needs no promotion, since the paper's format embodies it. The *LRB* started life as the cisatlantic *Doppelgänger* of the *New York Review of Books* (for a while they travelled together, like the pre-war Short-Mayo composite flying-boat) and was thus ordained to be a broadsheet on butcher's paper. But on its own it grew even more austere, without even a resident cartoonist. Nothing except a few photographs and the occasional drawing relieves the letter-press, which if it is to sparkle must do so by itself. The seemingly paradoxical, but in fact logical, result of this harsh physical regime is more latitude for exuberance, as' in a playground with high walls. The paper is bright because the editor's idea of lively copy is the truth told in a short space. This can be a tricky criterion when it comes to the hard sciences, and even in the humanities there is such a thing as fluent falsehood, the enchantingly specious. The editor must follow his strict nose while allowing for the possibility of legitimate controversy. In this respect it is a pity the anthology has no more room than it has for extracts from the letters column, a water-hole at which proud beasts appear fortnightly and charge at one another head down, sometimes for months on end. At the time of writing, Craig Raine and Tom Paulin are still colliding in a dispute which began over a small failure to recognise a quotation and an even smaller disagreement over whether a spondee can be made to rhyme oxytonically with an iamb. The clash would be from Laputa, not to say Lilliput, if the quality of intelligence brought to it were not so generally illuminating. For such a brouhaha not to degenerate into the kind of raree show which elsewhere in Grub Street might be cried up as a 'feud', the editor must know when to impose his authority. To do that, he must have it. A literary magazine is a personal creation.

Another case in point is, or was, Ian Hamilton's *The New Review*, now excerpted from and introduced by the editor himself. This modest-looking anthology is crammed with good things. Unfortunately the magazine never looked modest, and even when the good things squeezed out the makeweights the effect was seldom one of value for money. The format was too lush. This single error of judgment dogged *TNR* from the start. The *LRB* would still look like money well spent if it were to be discovered that the editor was scattering half of his Arts Council grant on the blackjack tables of Las Vegas. *TNR* would have looked profligate if it had been as well managed as Marks and Spencer. A single copy cost less to produce than you might have thought, but what made this information so startling was the air of extravagance. As Jeffrey Archer might say, it was a problem of presentation. In theatrical parlance, the show was over-billed. The format promoted more expectations than the content could fulfil. Printed on double-coated paper perfect-bound between card covers, excellent material looked merely normal and anything average counted as a minus. More had to be average than the editor would have liked. The magazine's forerunner, *The Review*, could go on rejecting material and delaying publication until every issue was a little keepsake. *TNR* was so much bigger that even had it come out with the same blessed irregularity it could not have been better. But it came out every month and was a Moloch for material.

Speaking as one who supplied *TNR* with some of its makeweight copy under an assumed name, I can confidently assert that Ian Hamilton's infectious dedication to an altruistic, non-commercial ideal of cultural duty never ceased to inspire the troops when they gathered in the Pillars of Hercules to be given their assignments. Bohemian virtue, however, was a vice when it came to bourgeois practicalities. '*The New Review*'s grant,' says Hamilton in his preface to this anthology, 'was the largest ever given to a magazine – a lot of people took offence at this – but was never large enough, alas, to safeguard the enterprise from penury.' The sincerely meant candour of this statement would have been more luminous if it could have found space to concede that a budget is something it is wiser to start out with, not be forced by circumstances to adopt piecemeal as you go along. The enterprise being in the hole from the start, lack of money, to adapt Dylan Thomas's epigram, continued to pour in. A dearth of the ability to calculate meant that blows inflicted by reality were rarely interpreted as lessons: an ad for subscribers placed expensively in the *Listener* resulted in the enrolment of exactly one subscriber, but this harsh fact did little to dampen some confident talk among the staff of opening a wine bar to defray costs. The prospect of the ailing brewery organising its own piss-up as a fund-raiser did not reassure those of us who were already working a double shift.

Its atmosphere of fiscal unreality made the venture hard to defend with a whole heart when it was attacked. A sitting duck dolled up like a flamingo, it was attacked often, most tellingly on grounds of waste. It should be emphasised that *TNR* was a Stroheim movie only in the sense that the artists had taken over the accounts department. The total amount of money involved was peanuts – when Ian Hamilton so grippingly interviewed Calvino in a recent edition of BBC2's *Bookmark*, the perhaps not entirely necessary scene-setting sequence on an Italian railway station must have cost more than *TNR*'s annual grant. But they were Arts Council peanuts. Grub Street journeymen who could point to no artistic achievement beyond a nose full of burst veins were able plausibly to complain about a waste of the taxpayer's money. They were less plausible when they complained about weak material, but honest rebuttal had to encompass the realisation that the good things in the magazine might have been packed closer together if the demand for copy had been matched with more foresight to the possible supply. There is only so much good critical writing to be had – a fact of which Hamilton, with a long history of extracting articles deeply lodged in feverishly elusive contributors, was well aware going in.

Coming out, his innate sense of cogency reasserts itself. As the pall of dust dissipates around the crashed bandwagon, it becomes clear that *TNR* largely fulfilled its editorial aim of printing the extended critical pieces that the other literary papers would not commission even as disguised book reviews. The verse is of a high standard. We see poems that helped establish the reputations of James Fenton and Craig Raine; poems by Heaney and Lowell; and Peter Porter's 'An Australian Garden', which counts among his best things. Of the short stories, 'Solid Geometry' is a reminder that *TNR* played host to Ian McEwan when he was still regarded as a fairly nerve-wracking guest. But the essays are the chief boast. Lowell's piece on John Crowe Ransom was a much weightier contribution than some of his later poems, which Hamilton politely greeted without obvious signs of diminishing excitement when they arrived in Greek Street by the cartload. John Carey's 'Down with Dons' is a *locus classicus* of the *odium theologicum*, boiling with the deep-down unreason which so often underlies, and possibly fuels, the ratiocinative dazzle of the star dons, but wonderfully entertaining in the texture of its prose. What makes Carey the most rewarding of the nutty professors is that he writes so well. He has wit, for example, where Professor Ricks can only pun.

Yet not even Professor Carey can do without a good editor. Ian Hamilton might not have actively interfered in the composition of 'Down with Dons' but his own example helped set the mark, as it did for every other contributor to *TNR*, the old *Review* and the *TLS*, when he was one of the assistant editors. Hamilton wields a meticulous blue pencil. When he goes through your typescript he gives you a free writing lesson. But he also gives you that when he writes. Of all the critics in his generation (there were droves of them to start out with) none commands a prose so supple, pointed, acidly laconic. When *TNR* packed up he was free again to fulfil his best gift, and mellow for the experience. The excellent biography of Lowell duly followed. His 'Diary' contributions' have been among the highlights of the *LRB*, which perhaps also benefited from the general lesson provided by *TNR*'s short career. In the music business the same general lesson is sweated down to one piece of advice: don't give up your day job. A British critical review should be edited as a sideline and look austere. The culture demands it. But the culture also readily forgives a business failure. Artistic integrity is rightly valued above financial acumen, although it can't hurt to point out that the first is not automatically acquired by despising the second.

Justly legendary and now usefully anthologised, the pre-war high-life weekly *Night and Day* adumbrated *TNR*'s touching good faith by making the same miscalculation four decades earlier. Its editors assumed that a certain number of well-off, well-informed, artistically inclined people must want a magazine reflecting their interests. It was painfully discovered that the number is uncertain and there is no must about it. Knowledgeably editing this selection, Christopher Hawtree dismisses the cosy idea that the magazine's early demise was due solely to the libel suit brought by Shirley Temple after Graham Greene, the magazine's cinema reviewer, suggested that she knowingly flaunted her precocious sexuality. It would be nice to think that the asinine law put the magazine out of business. But it put itself out of business. Under-capitalised from the start, it was a luxury magazine short of money – a contradiction in terms. Properly funded, it might have survived. Though it smacked of Maytime in Mayfair, it was a lot more than just a homegrown *New Yorker* and there was no real competition from *Punch*, which it far outstripped in its writing. As with the *New Yorker* before it got fat, *Night and Day*'s strength was in its departments. The personnel sounds like a dream roster, an all-time heavenly cricket team. Greene on cinema, Osbert Lancaster on art, Elizabeth Bowen on theatre, William Empson on travel . . . and Evelyn Waugh on books. Waugh's lambasting of the milquetoast Left sounds like mere common sense now, but by making truthfulness of prose his first criterion he achieved a permanently refreshing generosity of taste. With poetry he gave way to rant, calling the poems in *Letters from Iceland* 'rough Byronic verses'. Auden's 'Letter to Lord Byron' is less rough than anything by Byron himself. But Waugh must be allowed his prejudices. What startles is how few of them he allowed to show. The magazine made him well-mannered. It brought out the best in all its contributors, some of whom – Hugh Kingsmill and Malcolm Muggeridge are two examples – came fully alive only in such a context, where they were, in Cyril Connolly's phrase, praised on the nail. Cheaply bound but breathing value for money, this compendium should do good business as a Christmas present and bring in for its publisher the kind of revenue which might have saved the magazine at the time. Fifteen years ago, I bought the complete run of *Night and Day*, in two volumes buckram bound, for twenty pounds. Since then it has appreciated alarmingly. The unwitting possessor of a rare book, I have been afraid to handle it lest the uric acid in my sweaty palms diminish its value.

Where *Night and Day* failed, *Lilliput* lasted. On a smaller scale it had something of the same urbane look, but it was more down-market. Down-market is bigger. This probably explains why there was backing available at the crucial moment. *Lilliput goes to war* is only one of the many possible anthologies which could be made out of the complete run, much of which as a pre-teen in Australia I read until the covers frayed. I was particularly attracted by the retouched nudes but it was clear even to me that *Lilliput* represented a whole view of existence. From this distance, it is easier to see what that view was: it was the refugee's view, cherishing the free variety of British life while the Nazis rampaged in the old homeland. *Lilliput* was not strictly a literary magazine, but Stefan Lorant, the Hungarian who was its driving spirit, had a cultural gusto of a type well-known on the Continent and which Hitler did the rest of the world a tragic favour by scattering to the winds. Younger readers now will be surprised to find how accurately the magazine's editors and contributors saw what Hitler was up to.

Penguin New Writing, although it ran pictures later on, was the literary magazine pure, simple and austere. The war made it a popular hit, in the same way that water gets popular in a drought. John Lehmann does not emerge from his three-volume autobiography as the most charismatic of editors, but obviously he was the right man at the right time. Apart from Cyril Connolly's *Horizon*, Lehmann's *Penguin New Writing* was the only game in town. It was almost the only game in Europe. Thus it had everything to choose from, so there is no reason to be astonished by the roll-call of contributors in this anthology, although the fame of some of the poems might give even the prepared reader a prickly neck if he can imagine them hitting the editor's desk. 'Lay your sleeping head, my love . . .' Yes Wystan, we'll be glad to print that one. Got anything else? Orwell's 'Shooting an Elephant' and Isherwood's 'A Berlin Diary' are among the prose. It's an era *in nuce*. But it isn't just a British era. The European names bulk large. At a time of national crisis, the magazine had the international outlook, the world view.

Now that the country faces a different crisis, or a later phase of the same one, a critical paper is more than ever enjoined to take the world for scope. The *LRB* does gratifyingly well in this respect. Without belittling its politics, one can say that its cultural politics are the politics that matter most. Social democrats *avant la lettre* were glad to be rescued from limbo by the formation of the SDP. Now, in the columns of the *LRB*, they can talk to one another as Brian Magee and Bernard Williams no doubt talk in the Garrick. It is comforting to hear the bright minds of the political centre being so clubbable. Further to the left, space is made for Tam Dalyell to pursue his *Belgrano* studies. Things are a bit thin on the right, but perhaps the editor believes the Right to be a bit thick. More important is the supervening realism, the devotion to the world as it is, to what is the case. This is the tone for which Goethe and Eckermann took the *Edinburgh Review*. It is not just a matter of keeping the paper free from the lively copy which Coleridge, in his 'Remarks on the Present Mode of Conducting Critical Journals', called intrusive personalities. Grub Street has always had an open sewer running down the middle of it. The stench is probably less toxic now than in the last century, and certainly than in the century before that. Hacks have always been vindictive, but unless *habeas corpus* is suspended they can hurt only your feelings. Oxbridge baby dons cutting a dash in the glossies would do more damage if denied the limelight. The fashionable literary glitter-girls would rather meet Boy George than George Eliot, but they brighten life and Pope would have written a poem about them. Come to think of it, he did: 'The Rape of the Lock'. New, however, or at any rate returning in a more insidious form, is a certain cocksure, know-nothing Little Englandism. Marginally talented writers find cachet, and credibility along with it, by flaunting their parochialism. Ignorance has become aggressive. Grub Street is infested by unfunny Beachcombers, Chestertons without magnanimity, and – a truly sinister development – Bellocs bedewed with the same cold, xenophobic sweat. Migrants customarily spot signs of decay in their adopted country; perhaps I have been here too long, or am just growing old. But deluded or not, I can't imagine a bigger danger for Britain now than to shrink under its shell. There is no shell. The only safeguard lies in the country's peculiar intelligence – empirical, proof against big ideas, uniquely sensitive to its own language. The critical papers help keep it unclouded. This kind of wealth is still well worth coming here to seek, even if the more usual kind has become harder to get hold of. The best reason for being in London is to get a paper like the *LRB* on the day it comes out, or in my case – the dubious privilege of a subscriber – a couple of days later.

London Review of Books
7 November, 1985

An Affair of Sanity

Required Writing by Philip Larkin
(Faber, 1983)

EVERY reviewer will say that *Required Writing* is required reading. To save the statement from blinding obviousness, it might be pointed out that whereas 'required writing' is a bit of a pun – Larkin pretends that he wouldn't have written a word of critical prose if he hadn't been asked – there is nothing ambiguous about 'required reading'. No outside agency requires you to read this book. The book requires that all by itself. It's just too good to miss.

Required Writing tacitly makes the claim that it collects all of Larkin's fugitive prose, right down to the speeches he has delivered while wearing his Library Association tie. There is none of this that an admirer of his poems and novels would want to be without, and indeed at least one admirer could have stood a bit more of it. The short critical notices Larkin once wrote for the magazine *Listen* are, except for a single fragment, not here. As I remember them, they were characteristically jam-packed with judgments, observations and laconic wit.

If Larkin meant to avoid repetitiveness, he was being too modest: incapable of a stock response, he never quite repeats himself no matter how often he makes the same point. On the other hand there is at least one worrying presence. The inclusion, well warranted, of the prefaces to *Jill* and *The North Ship* can hardly mean that those books will be dropped from his list of achievements, but the inclusion of the long and marvellous introductory essay to *All What Jazz*, an essay that amounts to his most sustained attack on the modernist aesthetic, carries the depressing implication that the book itself, which never did much business, might be allowed to

163

stay out of print. That would be a shame, because jazz is Larkin's first love and in the short notices collected in *All What Jazz* he gives his most unguarded and exultant endorsement of the kind of art he likes, along with his funniest and most irascible excoriation of the kind he doesn't.

Jazz is Larkin's first love and literature is his first duty. But even at the full stretch of his dignity he is still more likely to talk shop than to talk down, and anyway his conception of duty includes affection while going beyond it, so as well as an ample demonstration of his capacity to speak generally about writing, we are given, on every page of this collection, constant and heartening reminders that for this writer his fellow-writers, alive or dead, are human beings, not abstractions.

Human beings with all their quirks. Larkin proceeds as if he had heard of the biographical fallacy but decided to ignore it. 'Poetry is an affair of sanity, of seeing things as they are.' But he doesn't rule out the possibility that sanity can be hard won, from inner conflict. He has a way of bringing out the foibles of his fellow-artists while leaving their dignity at least intact and usually enhanced. To take his beloved Hardy as an example – and many other examples, from Francis Thompson to Wilfred Owen, would do as well – he convincingly traces the link between moral lassitude and poetic strength. This sympathetic knack must come from deep within Larkin's own nature, where diffidence and self-confidence reinforce each other: the personal diffidence of the stammerer whose childhood was agony, and the artistic self-confidence of the born poet who has always been able to feel his vocation as a living force.

The first principle of his critical attitude, which he applies to his own poetry even more rigorously than to anyone else's, is to trust nothing which does not spring from feeling. Auden, according to Larkin, killed his own poetry by going to America, where, having sacrificed the capacity to make art out of life, he tried to make art out of art instead.

It might be argued that if the Americanised Auden had written nothing else except 'The Fall of Rome' then it would be enough to make this contention sound a trifle sweeping. It

is still, however, an interesting contention, and all of a piece
with Larkin's general beliefs about sticking close to home,
which are only partly grounded in the old anguish of having
to ask for a railway ticket by passing a note. He is not really as
nervous about Abroad as all that: while forever warning us of
the impossibility of mastering foreign languages, he has the
right Latin and French tags ready when he needs them, and
on his one and only trip to Germany, when he was picking
up a prize, he favoured the locals with a suavely chosen
quotation in their own tongue.

Lurking in double focus behind those thick specs is a star
student who could have been scholarly over any range he
chose. But what he chose was to narrow the field of vision:
narrow it to deepen it. He isn't exactly telling us to Buy
British, but there can be no doubt that he attaches little
meaning to the idea of internationalism in the arts. All too
vague, too unpindownable, too disrupting of the connections
between literature and the life of the nation.

Betjeman was the young Larkin's idea of a modern poet
because Betjeman, while thinking nothing of modern art,
actually got in all the facts of modern life. Like all good critics
Larkin quotes from a writer almost as creatively as the writer
writes, and the way he quotes from *Summoned by Bells* traces
Betjeman's power of evocation to its source, in memory. The
Betjeman/Piper guide-books, in which past and present
were made contemporaneous through being observed by the
same selectively loving eye, looked the way Larkin's poetry
was later to sound – packed with clear images of a crumbling
reality, a coherent framework in which England fell apart.
An impulse to preserve which thrived on loss.

In *Required Writing* the Impulse to Preserve is mentioned
often. Larkin the critic, like Larkin the librarian, is a keeper
of English literature. Perhaps the librarian is obliged to
accession more than a few modern books which the critic
would be inclined to turf out, but here again duty has
triumphed. As for loss, Larkin the loser is here too ('depriva-
tion is for me what daffodils were for Wordsworth') but it
becomes clearer all the time that he had the whole event won
from the start.

Whether he spotted the daffodil-like properties of depriva-
tion, and so arranged matters that he got more of it, is a
complicated question, of the kind which his critical prose,
however often it parades a strict simplicity, is equipped to
tackle. Subtle, supple, craftily at ease, it is on a par with his
poetry – which is just about as high as praise can go. *Required
Writing* would be a treasure-house even if every second page
were printed upside-down. Lacking the technology to
accomplish this, the publishers have issued the book in
paperback only, with no index, as if to prove that no matter
how self-effacing its author might be, they can be even more
so on his behalf.

Observer
25 November, 1983

Part Four

WE SHALL HAVE
STARS

'Tis Vidocq!

AN EX-CONVICT who founded the Sûreté in 1811 and whose fame rivalled Napoleon's even while Napoleon was still alive, the master sleuth Eugène François Vidocq, at the height of his renown, published his *Memoirs* in 1828, thus arousing more adulation than ever. The first star cop had written a classic book. Vidocq's assertive personality declares itself on the first page.

> I was born at Arras. My continual disguises, the flexibility of my features, and a singular power of grimacing having cast some doubt concerning my age, it will not be deemed superfluous to declare here that I was brought into the world on the 23rd of July, 1775, in a house adjoining that in which Robespierre was born sixteen years before. I had a most robust constitution, and there was plenty of me, so that as soon as I was born they took me for a child of two years of age, and I soon gave tokens of that athletic figure, that colossal form, which have since struck terror into the most hardened and powerful ruffians.

Vidocq's superabundance of energy quickly proves to be more than Arras can contain. His flexible features and singular powers of grimacing, combined with a weakness for young ladies and a remarkable capacity to steal from his mother's purse, soon land him in trouble. The revolutionary guillotine is still busy but Vidocq manages to get himself sent to prison instead. Supplied with a disguise by his girlfriend Françoise, Vidocq makes the first of many escapes. 'I passed, one day, muffled up, by the sentry: who, taking me for a municipal officer, presented arms.' It is to be a continuing theme in Vidocq's career, that even the people who know him most intimately completely fail to recognise him when he puts on a disguise. Misled by the flexibility of his features and his singular power of grimacing, they address him as a stranger and engage him in a conversation which, to his secret amusement and without his prompting, invariably turns to the subject of Vidocq and his awesome capabilities.

But most of that happens later. First Vidocq has to be recaptured many times, amounting to a grand total always exceeding by one the number of his escapes. Inevitably he is sentenced to the galleys. Loaded down with fetters and manacles, Vidocq's colossal form is temporarily immobilised, but his power of grimacing luckily remains unimpaired. Having somehow procured sailor's garb, he puts it on under his galley-frock and trousers. But how to pass inspection? 'They examined, as usual, our manacles and clothing; knowing this practice, I had pasted over my sailor's garb a bladder painted flesh-colour.' The guards having been fooled by the bladder – which must have made his colossal form even more colossal, but presumably he distracted their attention with some singularly powerful grimacing – Vidocq ducks behind a stack of planks.

'I soon threw off my galley-frock and trousers, and put on a wig.' He doesn't mention that he removed the bladder, but no doubt he did so, otherwise it would have looked pretty weird in combination with the wig. Nor should the question delay us of how one puts on a sailor suit under a prison outfit without having first removed one's manacles. Others abide our question: Vidocq is free. 'I disappeared, cautiously gliding behind the piles of timber.' Gliding is something Vidocq is destined to do a lot of. For a big man, he moves noiselessly.

But not noiselessly enough to avoid being nabbed yet again. Busted back to the galleys, he rapidly escapes, finding sanctuary among robbers. 'They all exclaimed: "'Tis Vidocq!" They surrounded and congratulated me.' Still at an early stage of his brilliant career, before he had even begun the fateful transformation from poacher to gamekeeper, Vidocq already exemplified the essential conundrum posed by all his famous successors up to and including

Charlie's Angels – though extremely recognisable, he was also invisible. ''Tis Vidocq!' they cried, but when he wanted to he could pass unnoticed, eking out with a few tufts of hair his power of grimacing. Somehow his opponents never latched on to the possibility that the colossally formed individual who had joined their company unbidden was at least reasonably likely to be Vidocq in disguise, just as no gang of heavies in recent American history has ever been disturbed by the sudden appearance in their immediate environment of three glamorous young women dressed up as firemen, road-menders, etc.

On the run, Vidocq hears voices whispering at the door. '"He is a powerful man," said one; "we must be wary!"' Who else can they mean but Vidocq? A note having been concealed in a pie ('Be careful of yourself, and trust no one'), the agents are fooled. But not even Vidocq can run for ever. Collared again, he is offered remission if he turns around. 'I was no less famed for courage than for skill, and it was the general opinion that I was capable of any deed of renown in case of need.' In simpler words, Vidocq had decided to turn stoolie.

As the resident fink of the galleys, Vidocq has merely to sit there while the criminals, awed by his fame, rush to unburden themselves of their secrets.

> Not a robber arrived at LaForce, who did not hasten to seek my company, even if he had never seen me, to give himself consequence in the eyes of his comrades; it fed his self-love to appear to be on terms of intimacy with me. I encouraged this singular vanity, and thus insensibly made many discoveries; information came to me in abundance.

Information is a big word with Vidocq. He was the first man to realise that in the modern age inside knowledge would constitute the only reliable meal-ticket. Vidocq the thief-taker was a data-bank dressed up. In the *Memoirs* he understandably stressed the flexibility of his features, but what really gave him the bulge over his rivals was the retentiveness of his brain, which later on he buttressed with a card-index.

As a cop, Vidocq was a roaring success from the start. Soon he was ready for the big time: Paris, where his name struck terror in the vicinity of the rue des Mauvais-Garçons. Not only was Vidocq infinitely malleable as to his facial structure, he had the physical endurance to conceal himself under beds or in small cupboards for days on end. At the right moment, he would suddenly employ his most devastating technique, the vigorous dart forwards. 'I made a vigorous dart forwards, and seized him by the hair of his head.' Thus many a hardened desperado was sent back where he belonged.

> I was fortunate enough to send back to the galleys a considerable number of those individuals whom justice, for want of the necessary proofs for their conviction, might have let loose upon society.

Vidocq, the Dirty Harry of his day, was the first rogue cop in history, and as such was duly loathed by the regulars. They had a lot to be envious of. In addition to his physical prowess, Vidocq had the divinatory capacity of a seer. How did he suss the criminal propensities of the notorious knife-wielder Boudin? 'He was bow-legged: a deformity I have observed amongst several systematic assassins, as well as amongst many other individuals distinguished by their crimes.' Much later in his career, Vidocq might have been ready to deepen this insight by pointing out – as he was among the first to do – that most criminals sprang from the undernourished orders, and that cruel punishments tended to create a permanent criminal class. But at this stage he was still on the make, and ambition likes to keep things simple.

Onward went Vidocq, ever deeper into the low-life purlieus later flattened by the city planning of Haussmann, but still darkly pullulating in our hero's heyday. Having infiltrated himself into the nefarious presence of the hoodlum Guevive ('I accordingly provided myself with a suitable disguise'), Vidocq does the mandatory sitting around while

the unsuspecting Guevive expatriates on the familiar subject
of a certain secret agent's genius for camouflage.

'God bless you!' cried he, 'it is easy to perceive you are a
stranger to this vagabond Vidocq. Just imagine, now,
that he is never to be seen twice in the same dress; that
he is in the morning perhaps just such another looking
person as you; well, the next hour so altered that his
own brother could not recognise him, and by the
evening, I defy any man to remember ever having seen
him before. Only yesterday I met him disguised in a
manner that would have deceived any eye but mine.'

Vidocq relishes Guevive's misdirected encomiums for
several pages before flinging off his disguise and making the
vigorous dart forwards.

Rising steadily in the estimation of his police chief, M.
Henry, Vidocq is given what amounts to a free hand. 'Soon
M. Henry took no steps without consulting me.' M. Henry's
trust proved well founded, because Vidocq's next feat was to
bust the notorious Madame Noel, the Music Mistress of the
Marais, a piano-playing putative ex-aristocrat equipped
with 'that indescribable air of superiority which the reverses
of fortune can never entirely destroy'. Barely able to conceal
his affection even in retrospect, Vidocq evokes Madame
Noel as:

a little brunette, whose sparkling eye and roguish look
were softened down by that gentle demeanour which
seemed to increase the sweetness of her smile and the
tone of her voice, which was in the highest degree
musical. There was a mixture of the angel and demon in
her face, but the latter perhaps preponderated; for time
had developed those traits which characterise evil
thoughts.

It was Bulldog Drummond versus Irma Peterson, but in
the long run there could be only one winner. The victory
went to the possessor of the more adaptable physiognomy.

My hair . . . was dyed black, as well as my beard, after it had attained a growth of eight days; to embrown my countenance I washed it with walnut liquor; and to perfect the imitation, I garnished my upper lip thickly with a kind of coffee-grounds, which I plastered on by means of gum arabic.

Thus transmogrified, Vidocq glides into Madame Noel's fragrant vicinity.

In my quality of a newcomer, I excited all Madame Noel's compassion and solicitude, and she attended to nothing but me. 'Are you known to Vidocq and his two bull-dogs, Levesque and Compère?' she enquired. 'Alas! yes,' was my reply; 'they have caught me twice.' 'In that case, then, be on your guard. Vidocq is often disguised; he assumes characters, costumes, and shapes to get hold of unfortunates like yourself.'

Vidocq would have had to restrain himself from smiling at this, for fear of dislodging the coffee-grounds.

But if Madame Noel excited Vidocq's compassion, the vile Fossard merited no mercy. A crook of rare alertness, Fossard required to be snuck up on. Never was Vidocq's gliding ability put to a more severe test, especially when you consider that he was now accompanied by a growing entourage of helpers – one of the more obvious penalties of success. 'The denouement was near at hand. I made all my party take off their shoes, doing the same myself, that we might not be heard whilst going up stairs.' Fossard was caught with his *culottes* down.

At the same instant, with more rapidity than the lion's when darting on his prey, I threw myself upon Fossard; who, stupefied by what was going on, was fast bound and confined in his bed before he could make a single movement, or utter a single word. When a light was brought and he saw my black face, and garb of a coalman, he experienced such an increase of terror that

I really believe he imagined himself in the devil's clutches.

Vidocq's triumph being by now complete, M. Henry had no alternative but to give him his own department, soon to be famous as the Sûreté. Vidcoq does not mention in the *Memoirs* that the Sûreté's funding was handed to him as a lump sum, with the choice of assistants, and their emolument, left to his discretion. This may well have been the basis of the large fortune with which Vidocq later retired from the service. Nor is it beyond possibility that people paid him to look the other way. But there is no telling – certainly not by Vidocq. Expansive on all other topics, he was hazy about the source of his wealth.

Wealth, however, was a side issue. The central issue was fame. 'The name of Vidocq had become popular, and many persons identified me as the person thus known.' Vidocq was among the first to experience the now familiar fact that publicity is limiting. A Rommel rather than a von Rundstedt, Vidocq was always out there in the forward areas, thirsty for battle. It was his drawback – you must grow with your fame or be diminished by it – but it was also his destiny. The celebrated affair of the thief Sablin ('a man of almost gigantic stature') is a case in point. Sablin knew Vidocq from the old days in the galleys and was thus hard to approach, however flexibly one's features were arranged. But Vidocq did one of his renowned long waits. 'I resolved, in spite of the rain, to pass the night before his house. At break of day, the door being opened, I glided quickly into the house.' Gliding in saturated boots is not easy: Vidocq's feet must have been under the same tight control as his face. Sablin's pregnant wife, however, is on the *qui vive*. '"Here is Vidocq!"' But Vidocq presses on inexorably. 'A man was in bed. He raised his head, 'twas Sablin! I flung myself upon him, and before he could recognise me I had handcuffed him.'

Pausing only to deliver the thug's wife of her baby ('I immediately took off my coat, and in less than twenty-five minutes Madame Sablin was delivered'), Vidocq melts into the night, but is later gratified to hear that Sablin, touched by his adversary's moral example, has had a change of heart. 'In spite of the vexation which Sablin necessarily experienced, he was so deeply penetrated by my proceedings that he could not forbear testifying his gratitude.'

Vidocq's success had aroused so much envy that his days at the Sûreté were numbered: while he was out there gliding about and making vigorous darts forwards, the place-men were plotting his downfall. But he had one more triumph to come, and in the *Memoirs* he makes sure it gets pride of place, right at the end: the story of how Vidocq entrapped the scoundrels who stabbed the harmless tradesman Fontaine twenty-eight times with a short dagger. Actually the dagger was so short that Fontaine survived, but Vidocq was implacable on the trail.

Having snared some of the minor figures in the tragedy, Vidocq sweats them to find the ringleader. He employs subterfuge. '"You are not naturally bad fellows," said I to them; "I'll engage that you have been led into all this by some scoundrel or other; why not own it?"' Unmanned by Vidocq's overmastering sympathy, the heavies finger their leader, the homicidal Pons Gérard. '"I must warn you,"' says one of the now contrite goons, '"that he is not to be caught napping. If you surprise him he will make a desperate resistance."' Has even Vidocq got what it takes to go up against Pons Gérard?

All the inhabitants to whom I spoke of Pons Gérard described him to me as a robber, who subsisted only by fraud and rapine; his very name was sufficient to excite universal terror, and the authorities of the place, although daily furnished with proofs of his enormities, durst take no steps to repress them.

The authorities might not durst, but Vidocq dursts. Unpredictably abandoning all recourse to flexible features, powerful grimacing, the rain-soaked glide and the vigorous dart forwards, Vidocq essays the frontal approach.

I walked directly up to the individual whom I supposed to be Gérard, and embracing him with every demonstration of regard, exclaimed, 'Pons, my good fellow, how are you? How is your wife, and all your family? Quite well, I trust?'

Apparently Pons was paralysed.

Astonished at this unexpected salutation, Pons remained in silent examination of my face for some minutes; 'Devil take me,' said he at last, 'if I know who or what you are; where the deuce did you spring from?'

Pons, like all France, is fully aware of Vidocq's existence, but somehow has no clue what Vidocq looks like. Perhaps Pons has never seen the engravings, but more probably he has been bamboozled by the fact that Vidocq has fronted straight up to him, instead of gliding in out of the downpour or vigorously darting forwards after two weeks in the broom cupboard. '"But who is this Vidocq, of whom we hear so much?"' asks Pons conversationally. '"I have never been able to meet him face to face."'
This, for Vidocq, must have been the supreme moment. '"Bless you, it is easy enough to meet with him," replied I; "you may have that pleasure now, for I am Vidocq, and I arrest you!"' It is the climax of Vidocq's career and almost the end of Pons's life. 'The astonishment of Pons defied description.' But it doesn't defy Vidocq's prose.

Every feature appeared distorted, his eyes starting from their sockets, his cheeks quivering, his teeth chattered, and his hair stood on end. After his arms were fastened, he remained for nearly half an hour motionless, as though petrified.

The book ends there. Vidocq had two ghosts to help him write it but there is no reason to doubt that the tone is all his. By the time it was published, Vidocq was a more popular figure than ever, but he was out of a job. Under the Bourbon restoration the regular cops were thought of as more seemly. He got 24,000 francs for the *Memoirs*. In addition he started up his own information agency, having correctly guessed that the age he had helped bring to an end – when a criminal could stay free if he kept moving – would be succeeded by a new era in which, wherever you fled, your dossier would get there ahead of you.

Vidocq was a social lion, but on borrowed time. Balzac put him in *La Comédie humaine* under the name of Vautrin and wrote a play in which Vautrin was played by the great Frédérick Lemaître. The play was a flop. So, eventually, was Vidocq, who like many talented men failed to realise how business requires a talent of its own. He lived out his days as a novelist and a loan-shark. The Second Empire was the kind of police state he had helped make possible, but he did not flourish under it. He made himself ridiculous by pestering the police agencies with help they did not want. It is one of the rules of fame: the innovator must get out early. He can take credit for the world his innovations help to bring about, but he should not compete in it. Yet Vidocq was already immortal when he died in 1857. Eleven women came to the funeral, each clutching a different version of his will. All the super-sleuths since have glided in his footsteps, changed their appearance according to parameters established by his power of grimacing, made the pinch in a pale echo of his vigorous dart forwards. The first man through takes the long glory.

Observer Magazine
12 December, 1982

Kung-Fu Wit

WHEN Oscar Wilde was in his full, brief flower, any witty remark, whoever made it, was immediately attributed to him. Later on the same thing happened to Dorothy Parker. Like the practitioner of no other literary genre, the great wit is assumed to incarnate his gift, leaving room for no one else. While he lives, he is not one among many: he is alone. When he dies, there is a tense wait for the birth of such another.

But what if a great wit were to be born, live out his short life, and pass away unappreciated? By the nature of his talent, it couldn't happen. The news about Bruce Lee was bound to come out sooner or later. Perhaps it was his very fame as a Kung-Fu film star that overshadowed his genius for comedy.

Bruce, before his death at thirty-two, was worshipped worldwide as the young man who brought the Chinese martial arts into the twentieth century and the international arena. With his handsome face distorted by the blood-curdling cry of *kiai*, Bruce would kick the pistol from the hand of any assailant not smart enough to realise that the chief advantage conferred by fire-arms is their ability to kill from a distance.

Now Bruce sleeps, but his fame is greater than ever. In Britain there is vast interest in the details of his life, methods and philosophy: yet further evidence for the theory that mass culture is not imposed from above, like defoliant, but grows spontaneously from below, like jungle. On the surface, the British reading public is interested in Salman Rushdie's living-room and the forthcoming novels of Lisa St Aubin de Terán. Deeper down, however, where the sales are in the millions instead of mere thousands, the people who buy books for love are interested in Bruce Lee.

The Power of Bruce Lee, The Secret Art of Bruce Lee, Bruce Lee's Last Interview – these are the volumes that sell straight off the van. It is a market in which there is no division between pundit and common reader. All readers are pundits, and collectively they have decided that Bruce Lee was not only the foremost modern philosopher of Kung-Fu, but the most penetrating wit ever to come out of the East.

The forty-third issue of *Kung-Fu Monthly* carries a cover-story entitled THE WIT OF BRUCE LEE, OUTRAGEOUS HUMOUR-IST! You won't need to be told about this if you are subscribing to *Kung-Fu Monthly* already. It is statistically likely that you are: no precise figures are available, but estimates indicate that Lambeth Palace is almost the only prominent address in Britain not receiving *KFM* twelve times a year.

If by some slim chance, however, you are not already a subscriber, now is the time to place your order and thus make yourself eligible for a discount on the Bruce Lee one-piece track-suit offer.

> You've waited long enough . . . Yes, *KFM* has finally located some excellent reproductions of Bruce Lee's amazing YELLOW AND BLACK, ONE-PIECE TRACK SUIT. Snug-fitting and comfortable, we are anticipating an enormous response to our offer for this rare and unique garment.

It will be seen that *KFM*'s command of grammar is not always exact. But the master himself was perfect in this respect as in all others. For Bruce, language was just another form of expression, like kicking people in the head. He gazed with narrowed eyes into the deep secrets of human laughter, mastered them, and turned them to explosive use, like his feet which kicked not just 'at' an opponent, but 'through' him, as in *taneshiwari*, or Breaking Techniques. His tongue was like a third foot.

Which is not to say that his foot was in his mouth. Nevertheless, perhaps because the language of the body was even more international than Chinese or English, he seems to have favoured mime as the vehicle for his outrageous humour. 'Once, whilst being chased by a gang of thugs through the back streets of Hong Kong,' *KFM* recounts, 'he managed to get a little way ahead – and then pulled off a neat little stunt.

'He leapt on to a nearby roof, stripped down to his underpants and sat meditating in the cross-legged position. When the heavies arrived he screwed up his face and squinted to such a degree that they failed to recognise him. When asked if he'd seen anybody come by in the last few minutes he nodded – and pointed in another direction. They disappeared in hot pursuit!'

The Bruce Lee one-piece track suit was a functional item of equipment, since if you kick people all day for a living the strain on the crotch of the trousers is immense. (Though not as immense as the strain on the crotch of your opponent's trousers, if, emulating Bruce, you 'execute the roundhouse kick to the exposed groin'.)

This question of split trousers became the occasion of outrageous humour for the high-spirited Bruce, known to his disciples as the Little Dragon. 'One day while on the set of *Big Boss*,' says *KFM*, 'the Little Dragon was talking to support actress, Nora Miao. In a serious voice he asked her, "What do Kung-Fu fighters have more than anyone else?" Nora, and one or two other people around, decided that it was obviously an important question, so they thought long and hard. Eventually they gave up and asked him what it was. He replied, "More torn trousers" – and promptly produced a pair with an enormous gaping rip in them. It was a good joke, and everyone laughed.'

Like all true wits, Bruce seldom repeated himself. He used an idea a second time only if he could make it more humorous. (In *KFM* the word is sometimes spelt 'humerous', probably in homage to Bruce's strongly developed upper arm.) His famous Japanese telephone-engineer disguise is a case in point. 'In *Fist of Fury*, who could ever forget Bruce's Japanese telephone-engineer disguise? Once more, many Western audiences may have missed the absurdity of a Chinese actor disguising himself as a Jap. Out East, it had them rolling in the isles!'

Readers should not jump to the conclusion that 'isles' is a misprint for 'aisles'. Around Hong Kong there are many small islands whose inhabitants, after a long day manufacturing toys for export, ask for nothing more than to watch Bruce Lee bewilder the enemy with a mixture of roundhouse kicks, blows with the extended knuckle and humerous impersonations. But the important point is that the Japanese telephone-engineer disguise is not allowed to rest there. Dining out with friends in Hong Kong, Bruce brings the routine to perfection.

'Eating out,' laughs *KFM*, 'frequently gave the Little Dragon the opportunity to turn on the hilarity. One day he accidentally knocked out one of his contact lenses. The other people at the table were worried he might flare up at this embarrassing incident. The Master, however, saw the funny side of it and, quickly, he donned a pair of heavy, shell-rimmed glasses. At once he seemed transformed into the famed Japanese telephone-engineer disguise – the table rocked with the joke.'

Most of the great wits have had to rehearse their ad libs. Even Byron wrote better than he spoke. Sheridan was the only one who had it to burn. But perhaps Bruce Lee was his equal as a wit, and his superior as a free spirit. To purchase Drury Lane, Sheridan reputedly sold his wife's favours to the Prince of Wales, and ever afterwards was careful not to offend his grand connections. Bruce, secure in the love of an audience larger than Charlie Chaplin's, could be as shocking as he wished.

'One of the best remembered scenes,' says *KFM*, 'has to be in *Way of the Dragon*, where a customer visits the toilet, only to discover the Little Dragon standing on the seat. His knees are bent and he's poised over the basin ready to take his trousers down! Though the impact of the joke was a little lost in the West, for Eastern audiences it was hilarious. Well they could appreciate the difficulties encountered by a Chinese-man brought up with very different toilet facilities to those normally used in our part of the world.'

This shaft of wit might have been lost if someone had not seen it as his duty to interpret Bruce Lee's outrageous humour for an Occidental audience. But someone did. Culture is more robust than we tend to imagine. Creativity arises spontaneously and scholarship along with it. There is something encouraging about the way Bruce Lee's permanent significance as a wit has emerged from his temporary fame as the man who revolutionised the martial arts. The martial arts will be revolutionised again, but the wit of Bruce Lee endures – an important contribution to the world culture which has become a reality in our time.

Observer
20 February, 1983

Boys Will Be Girls

Footlights! A Hundred Years of Cambridge Comedy
by Robert Hewison
(Methuen, 1983)

THE ENGLISH are not at their best, although they may well be at their most characteristic, when they go on a lot about the dear old days at school or the 'varsity. Not even the inspired Cyril Connolly could get his tongue far enough into his cheek to be anything more tolerable than stomach-turning about Eton. George Orwell, who had been there too but thought it was possible to have a life afterwards, was surely right to tell him to come off it. Even if there were room for doubt in this matter, however, there can be no question that an ex-Colonial transplantee who happens to have done some of his growing up in an English school or university should be slow to bring forth his cosy reminiscences, and very slow to hand them over to anyone else. So when the author of this book about the Cambridge Footlights

approached me, in my capacity as one of the club's numer-
ous surviving ex-Presidents, I imitated the action of the
clam. Judging from the relative sparseness of the ac-
knowledgments list, a lot of other alumni did the same thing,
for whatever reasons. Probably they were just being
cautious. For a professional performer after a certain time,
every interview he doesn't give counts as a victory, on the
principle that the label you help them lick is the one that
will stick to you longest.

Nevertheless, or perhaps therefore, Mr Hewison has pro-
duced a respectable book: sensible, well-researched and
solid enough to be unexciting. If the publishers thought they
were going to get the kind of sputtering firework that one of
David Frost's script associates might help him deliver into a
tape-recorder, they haven't. This is a book meant to be read
and even kept. Indeed, it might have more keepers than
readers, since a probable majority of buyers will be the
people mentioned in the appendixed lists of club committee-
members, tabulated on an annual basis. An ex-Junior
Treasurer or Falconer from the late 1960s now sweating it
out in front of a computer terminal in the City will be able to
look up his own name and remember when he suffered from a
different, sweeter form of nerves – trembling on the bench
beside the little stage in Falcon Yard as his time grew close to
go on and do a sketch. He never really got the laughs, but he
learned how to stay alive under the lights. Most important,
he discovered for certain that his path lay elsewhere. By
finding out what he wasn't, he started to find out what he
was.

But if Mr Hewison had confined himself to such a typical
non-story his book would have been for subscribers only.
Understandably he puts his emphasis on those who made
names later on. It is a seductive emphasis because whereas
later on their various relationships and interlockings tend to
be evanescent, circumstantial, conjectural or non-existent,
early on, as he tells it, they seem to have hung out together in
groups of a dozen at the minimum – generation after genera-
tion of tight little cliques busily revolutionising the comic
heritage, usually as a reaction to what was supposedly

achieved by the clique on whose heels they were treading. Since Mr Hewison went to Oxford and was thus never a Footlight himself, his success in making himself familiar with this snug little world is doubly remarkable. Only a man of scholarly temperament could have squeezed along these burrows, although it might be remembered that the same could be said about the author of *Watership Down*. There are commendably few factual errors, and the sole really glaring one is an editorial slip on page 151, where the photograph captioned 'Germaine Greer, 1965' is of a happily unfamous girl called Sheilah Buhr. I was ASM for the touring company of that year's May Week revue (its title, *My Girl Herbert*, was, alas, my suggestion) and can remember Sheilah well. A Canadian graduate student of high intelligence and angelic temperament, she was a typical Footlight in that she was just passing through an amateur dramatics phase on the way to the real world.

But as Mr Hewison well realises, in this club it is the untypical club-members who make the news. Nobody outside Cambridge would give the Footlights Dramatic Society a second thought if it were just an end in itself. It is as a means to an end, a launching-pad for showbiz careers, that it provides copy. Yet here again, the average showbiz career launched from this well-illuminated facility is less likely to achieve orbit than to make a small splash not very far down range. The truly productive Footlights years start comparatively recently, in the early 1950s, but even when considering this undoubtedly busy period Mr Hewison is obliged tacitly to admit that there are only a few real inventors to conjure with. The media dominance exercised by ex-Footlights over the last two decades – it is now coming to an end – had as much to do with run-of-the-mill administrative careerism as with inspired performance, especially in radio. So Mr Hewison finds himself talking about trends and movements, and indeed with reference to the earlier years there is nothing else to talk about, since the real inventors can scarcely be said to have existed.

From the 1880s right through until the post-Second World War National Service years widened the intake, raised the age and lowered the voice of undergraduates, the Footlights was concerned almost exclusively with make-up and drag. Faced with this fact, which the photographs and song-sheets would not have allowed him to shirk even if he had wanted to, Mr Hewison forgivably drifts into relativism, a version of the developmental fallacy by which it is held that what we now regard as the undergraduate sense of humour had to evolve from small, questionable and perhaps not very funny beginnings. In the cold eye of history this assumption has not much substance to it. Hollywood silent-film comedies which are as funny now as they were at the time were being created while the stars of the Footlights were putting on their lipstick, climbing into their frocks, and singing arch little numbers that all too often, by no paradox, poked dismal fun at the idea of providing equal opportunities for women. The Viennese cabaret world produced such great minds as Karl Kraus, Egon Friedell and Alfred Polgar while the stars of the Footlights were putting on their lipstick, climbing into their frocks and singing arch little numbers aimed at European intellectuals. While Carole Lombard was making *Twentieth Century*, the Footlights stars were still putting on their lipstick, climbing into their frocks and swatting each other with their handbags. While Rosalind Russell was making *His Girl Friday*, they were *still* at it.

There is no reason to think that the Footlights would ever have grown up by itself. It was a 100 per cent reactionary institution until forced to change by a changing world, and even then it changed as reluctantly as it could. Nor is there any reason to believe that an intelligent onlooker would have found the goings-on particularly funny, although he might well have found them stylish. Norman Hartnell designed some very pretty dresses for *The Bedder's Opera* in 1922. There are illustrations to show what he looked like wearing them. He was particularly seductive in an off-the-shoulder number with roses appliquéd at the bustline and scattered randomly over the flounced skirt. Cecil Beaton's personal outfit for the 1925 revue *All the Vogue*, on the other hand, is a severely simple basic black high-neck jersey cocktail frock worn with a single choker of huge pearls, a lustrous lip job and a marcelled wig even more convincing than Hartnell's. Fashion papers such as the *Sketch* regularly ran spreads of the Footlights transvestites in those years. IN A WEDDING GOWN OF LACE: MR D. F. CARY AS THE BRIDE. The body copy explained that:

> the 'ladies' of the cast, who include a most attractive beauty chorus, are a really elegant 'bunch' . . . at first sight, no reader will observe that these charming 'ladies' are really members of the sterner sex, for at Cambridge men undergraduates always play the women's parts.

In this atmosphere, which prevailed until sanity at last got a look-in after the Second World War, the occasional member of genuine literary gifts – Malcolm Lowry is perhaps the most distinguished example – would scarcely have been able to make much of an impact even if he had felt driven to. Mr Hewison drums up what excitement he can out of the high professional standards set by Jack Hulbert in 1913, when the immense success of *Cheer-Oh Cambridge* at least ensured that the frocks of the future would be deployed with a quasi-professional swish. But Hulbert's professionalism had little to do with content. He just had a glossier way of being mindless, and the club was soon back under the influence of its long-lived master spirit H. Rottenburg, whose giftless song-sheets, when I read through the club's much-depleted library forty years later, still had their power to induce despair. (Mr Hewison gallantly eschews all reference, incidentally, to the time-honoured rumour that the Footlights' archives were left in the back of a taxi by David Frost during the expensive year when he functioned as the club's secretary.)

Robert Helpmann choreographed all the Footlights revues in the late 1930s. Things picked up under his regime to the extent that the chorus line, instead of being Dadie Rylands protégés dolled up in point shoes and tutus, were rugby-players dolled up in point shoes and tutus. The sketches were innocent of all mention of Hitler but that wasn't entirely the fault of an epicene, style-mad, arrogantly snobbish and incorrigibly anti-intellectual tradition. There was also the Lord Chamberlain, who exercised what amounted to a political censorship of the theatre right through until the late 1960s – one of the chief reasons why television was eventually able to suck theatrical revue dry and spit out the pips. One feels, however, that even if the undergraduate writers had been free to say what they liked, they would not have said much. The dons held sway, and the theatrical dons – less powerful in my time, thank God, than they had been – were intent on keeping undergraduate humour up on its high heels, where they supposed it belonged. There is always the possibility that all the swooping and posing was shriekingly funny to watch, but Richard Murdoch, who was up in 1936 and much later made a solid contribution to the British humorous tradition with *Much Binding in the Marsh*, looked back on his Footlights days with a nostalgia well tempered by a sense of proportion. He said that they weren't as good as they thought they were.

It was different after the war, although not immediately, because for some years the drag artistes were still in control. If a real woman got through the doors it was only as a guest – a fact which remained shamefully true until the precociously capable Eric Idle, President in 1965, finally managed to repeal the exclusion laws. Germaine Greer duly became the first woman elected, playing Gertrude Lawrence in a Noel-Gertie colloquy featuring the present writer as Noel. (As you might imagine, she stood out from the cast.) Before that, such an inventive woman as Eleanor Bron had to be content with guest status. The lads weren't going to give up their boas and beads if they could help it.

The revues of the early 1950s which featured Jonathan Miller still had their quota of rouged youths. But at long last the IQ level of the Footlights rose into triple figures. Successively on to the scene came such butch illuminati as Miller, Michael Frayn and Peter Cook, with results that Mr Hewison obviously finds it much less uncomfortable to write about, even if it simultaneously becomes more difficult to trace the thread. These were and are real individuals, less easily subsumed into a trend, either at the time or in retrospect.

Trend-conscious our author nevertheless remains, but no doubt it was inevitable. In this context you can't *not* talk about *Beyond the Fringe*, *TW3* and *Monty Python*, even when the relevance of the Footlights is marginal. In *Beyond the Fringe* only two of the four writer-performers were ex-Footlights; *TW3* was largely cast from unknown faces in *Spotlight*; and *Monty Python* was an ex-Cambridge cum ex-Oxbridge combination put together at the BBC after its respective contributors had graduated through several other television shows each. But such facts, as Mr Hewison sighingly concedes, are too complicated for the average showbiz journalist to grasp, so the story is always written as if the trends came out of the universities instead of, as happens in reality, going back into them.

Usually it takes years on the outside before an ex-Footlight, or an ex-anything else, is in a position to influence anybody. Jonathan Miller, who arrived on the university stage as a fully formed intellectual, was so much the exception that he is unmanageable even as a paradigm case. He was telling jokes about Bertrand Russell at a time when the undergraduate audience scarcely knew who Bertrand Russell was, so it is no surprise to read here that he consorted with his fellow Footlights only when performing, and never came near the club at any other time. Mr Hewison's own choice for the nonpareil Footlight is Peter Cook, a judgment from which there is no reason to demur. At the time Cook's originality must have seemed devastating, and if it looks less formidable to hindsight, that might only be because his epigones have been talking in funny voices ever since. Later on, John Cleese made an almost comparable impact, in the sense that he, too, had clearly got his originality fully worked out in advance.

But for everyone else, humour was a craft to be learned, even if the talent was unmistakable. Indeed, it can be said that the realisation of the necessity to learn is one of the marks of talent, even for the genius, who seems so advanced only because, a critical capacity being part of his gift, he has managed to learn on his own. For most practitioners, collaboration and competition aren't just a help, they are a necessity. This necessity the Footlights in modern times provided, especially during that period when the club possessed its own room above MacFisheries in Falcon Yard, an alley off Petty Cury which has since passed into history along with the smell of the fish, the whole area having subsequently become an antiseptic shopping mall.

Mr Hewison is very good on the Falcon Yard club-room for a man who can't have spent much time there unless he came via Bletchley in a baby carriage. With two smoking concerts a term it would have been an intensive school for performers anyway, but the real fanatics were in there every afternoon working on sketches and songs. On smoker nights, with the audience hanging off the walls, the disco in the Yacht Club above shaking the ceiling and the smell of mackerel rising inexorably from below, you could go on and click or you could go on and die. If you died, you could give up or try again. If you went on trying again, you might find out something about putting words in the right order.

For those who never subsequently made their mark as professional performers, how to put words in the right order was the most valuable lesson they took away. Mr Hewison sensibly disavows the obligation to analyse the whole field of recent British humour, but he might have made a little more of what undoubtedly *has* been an influence stemming directly from the Footlights: the writing and production of situation comedy. He talks a lot, as he was bound to do, about what happened to the writer-performers, but tends to lose interest when they do more writing than performing, or more producing than writing. Jonathan Lynn, for example, is duly credited as a fill-in cast member for the *Cambridge Circus* touring company, but there is no mention made of the writing he has done for *Yes, Minister*, which is on a level with that of Clement and la Frenais. Humphrey Barclay is credited for *Cambridge Circus* but not for his career as an executive producer. In every ex-Oxbridge group which has made it big in professional light entertainment there are at least a couple of performers who could be replaced. Some have been just plain lucky, and some of those know it. But there is nothing iffy about writing or producing a hit sit-com. It is a craft, and it should be noted that some of the most gifted practitioners started learning it at Cambridge, by finding out the hard way that if you say things in the right order you get a laugh and some spare time in which to nut out an improvisation, whereas if you say them in the wrong order the laugh doesn't come, there isn't time even to breathe, and you sweat right through your off-white shirt into your badly chosen dinner jacket.

Unbeatable training, but Cambridge was never the only place where it could be obtained, and nowadays there are performers arriving from all directions – a much healthier state of affairs. Footlights might just conceivably have produced Victoria Wood, but it could never have given the world Tracey Ullman. Current undergraduates in Footlights might copy Twentieth Century Coyote, but it is extremely unlikely that they would take such an original approach by themselves. Oxbridge undergraduate humour is essentially a second-hand response to experience. It might eventually lead to longer-lasting things, but in almost all cases it starts slowly. It takes a literary turn, ensuring that its perpetrators have a lot of self-consciousness to get out of their systems before they go on to discover, if they ever do, that, like any other form of poetry, humour taps a deep instinct. But since for just that reason the comedian must go to school, and since the Cambridge Footlights has always been a school of some kind even when preponderantly concerned with the waxing of legs and application of false eyelashes, Mr Hewison has a story to tell which repays his efforts, and which even non ex-Footlights Committee Members might just possibly like to hear told.

London Review of Books
1–14 September, 1983

Pure Genius

Blessings in Disguise by Alec Guinness
(Hamish Hamilton, 1985)

CONCEALING itself with a squirt of ink, the octopus makes a cloud which if seen from far enough away looks like a revelation. Alec Guinness's autobiography has been a big hit in his native country. The British value their actor-knights so highly that they bought even Lord Olivier's autobiography, an obvious attempt to entangle the curious reader in the outer defences and leave him there to die of boredom. By turning on the charm instead of the electrified fence, Guinness makes himself even less accessible in his book. He comes out of it as a regular guy, just like you and me but with a measure of acting talent, and he writes well enough to make the fantasy sound plausible. *Blessings in Disguise* is a heart-warming document, a reassuring pledge of sincerity, like the newspaper which the con-man asks you to look after for him until he comes back again with your fifty dollars.

Great deceivers don't lie, they merely omit. There is no telling how much of his life story Guinness has left out. But there is a suspect docility about what he has left in. This is the tale of how life happened to a nondescript. Broke and unknown in a furnished room, he learns from the great at the Old Vic during the mid-1930s, makes his name, does his bit in the Royal Navy during the war, becomes a film star more by luck than judgment, receives high honour by a fluke, and winds up shyly blinking in the effulgence of his own apotheosis. One has had so much good fortune.

The reader might need to remind himself that the real Alec Guinness has imposed himself with a success made only more brilliant by the fact that he seemed so unimpos-ing. Whereas the other British stage stars asserted their individual styles with a verve that cried out for comment, Guinness offered little that a critic could pin down. Olivier prowled and yelped, Richardson boomed and lurched, Gielgud made mellow music. Guinness remembers in this book that the only time a critic praised *him* for making music on the stage, another critic accused him of having no music at all. Guinness forgets to mention that he first pointed out this favourite moment of critical self-cancellation in his contribution to a little symposium called *An Experience of Critics* more than thirty years ago. He was always, and rightly, pleased with his personal enigma. His colourlessness was his characteristic. On stage he used it to hold his own against those who dazzled, and on screen he used it to leave them standing – or, rather, prowling, lurching, and making music.

There is no denying that Guinness could never have equalled the nectarine sonority of Gielgud's speeches in *Chimes at Midnight* or been as weirdly adorable as Richardson in *Greystoke*. Nor is there any doubt that Olivier, besides being responsible for directing at least two of the greatest Shakespeare films, is far and away the most gifted British actor to adorn the international screen, and will probably keep that title beyond the grave. But Guinness was the film star. Before the period of the late 1940s and early 1950s known to movie historians as Ealing comedy, the British film industry, even during the heyday of Alexander Korda, was only fitfully alive. Since Ealing comedy, the British film industry has been only fitfully alive. Ealing comedy *was* the British film industry. And Sir Michael Balcon, alias the Man Who was Ealing, always insisted that the man who was really Ealing was Alec Guinness.

It was, of course, both of them: Balcon the production genius and Guinness the big draw. It was also the group of talented writers and directors who gathered around them. There were ungainsayable historical factors – television, fated to drain the film industry of creative talent by the lure of quick returns, was not yet powerful – but mainly Ealing's magic was a question of writers, directors, and actors. The story would be fascinating as told by Guinness, even if he were to tell it with bias. But he hardly tells it at all. You would have liked to hear about the strategic discussions; about the decisions on what film to make next; about how they squared the circle, creating brilliant myths in the twilight of an empire. A lot of thought must have gone into all that.

Little of it gets into the book. The anecdotes are above average for a talk-show but the level of argument is judiciously held well below what Guinness would obviously be capable of if he let rip. He is often bitchy but seldom critical. On one occasion a long-cherished regret stimulates him to an edifying tirade. He admired Tyrone Guthrie but thought his influence disastrous, since the arena theatre that Guthrie promoted merely compelled directors less gifted than Guthrie himself to be pointlessly fussy, while depriving the actor of his most cherished effects.

> The theatre, when the performer cannot make a clean entrance or exit seen by the entire audience at the same time, and is obliged to make artificial moves purely for the sake of movement so that different parts of the audience, weary perhaps of a back, can get a glimpse of a face; where, when stillness is called for, the actor must rotate through 180 degrees to reach most spectators as well as other actors, is not so much a theatre as a circus.

Such a passage, where the opinion becomes a viewpoint, makes the opinions surrounding it seem casual. Elsewhere Guinness often proclaims, but rarely illustrates, a deep distrust of what he calls 'great acting'. We are told only enough to assume that he doesn't like the kind of art that draws attention to its technique. There is an attitude behind this distaste, and an aesthetic behind the attitude. But he gives us only the distaste.

If he is too polite to tell us who hammed it up and how, he is not too polite to tell us who was drunk and when. Robert Morley, reviewing this book for *The London Review of Books*, chided Guinness for neglecting to mention, when evoking how thoroughly the ageing Ralph Richardson would get crocked, that Richardson was the superior actor. You can disagree with Morley's judgment and still regret that Guinness couldn't have employed indiscretion to better purpose. With some well-chosen bad examples, he could have told us what good acting is. But to expound his views he would have had to unfold himself. He prefers – a more guarded openness – to reminisce.

Not that the reminiscences aren't first class. Some of them sound almost candid. We learn of his fly-by-night mother, who in his childhood could be relied on for nothing except a careless liberality in allowing him to wander off to the theatres and nourish his dreams. In his young manhood, when he was playing in Shakespeare, Chekhov and Shaw at the Old Vic during the 1930s, she would show up at his flat to touch him for a loan or, if he was out, pawn his possessions. Immediately, on hearing this, we give the author extra points for the gentlemanly punctilio of his adult life. The pull of the Catholic Church, to which he eventually succumbed, becomes easily understood. Brought up in disorder, he conceived a passion for order. In the most undependable of all professions he became famously dependable. More remarkably, indeed unbelievably, he seems to have found *it* dependable. He makes acting sound a bit like working in a bank. If Guinness in *The Lavender Hill Mob* has always made you think of T. S. Eliot and vice versa, this book will do nothing to dispel the impression.

Acting, especially film acting, can offer success but no security, since the hazards increase with choice. Guinness makes risk sound marginal. In *Kind Hearts and Coronets*, his first Ealing comedy, Guinness refused to get into the basket of a balloon, despite assurances from the director that it was safe. The balloon crashed into the Thames. In *The Lady-killers*, the last Ealing comedy, he was assured that an iron rail on top of a sixty-foot-high wall was safe. The rail broke in his hand. These are good stories, told snappily enough for Johnny Carson to laugh at them before the commercials. But between those two incidents came the period when Guinness helped raise Ealing to the status of a national cinema – and, by no coincidence, to the only international acceptance which the British film industry has ever consistently enjoyed. Before Ealing, the versatility Guinness had shown in the two David Lean Dickens films, *Oliver Twist* (as Fagin) and *Great Expectations* (as Herbert Pocket), had seemingly doomed him to the list of featured players. It took Michael Balcon to see that a character actor of sufficiently protean powers could be a leading man.

But didn't it also take Guinness to see it? If so, the ambitious planning that went into his unique coup is not remembered here. And it was such a bold venture. Guinness was not the leading man of *Kind Hearts*: Dennis Price ably filled that role. Guinness, however, without unbalancing a perfectly judged film, stole the notices.' His multiple appearances were something new then, and still are now, because later attempts (most notably by Peter Sellers) to play several characters in one movie were invariably dogged by the actor's urge to step out of each role in order to demonstrate that it was he who was playing it. (Only in *The Wrong Arm of the Law*, where Sellers, firmly controlled by the director and well served by the script, was playing a character who was playing a dual role, did he manage to rein himself in.) Guinness had the self-assurance to leave himself out of it. None of his eight characterisations in *Kind Hearts* required more than an eighth of his technical resources, but virtuosity was not the point. Mutability was. He never stepped out of any of the eight roles even for a moment. As a character actor he had established the terms in which he would become a star: a multiple man, who didn't just change his tricks for a role, but changed his personality.

Guinness was at his most powerful when pretending to be someone pretending to be someone. *The Lavender Hill Mob*, *The Man in the White Suit*, *The Card* (called *The Promoter* in the US), *The Captain's Paradise* and *The Ladykillers* all comically star him as someone forced, by either external circumstances or internal necessity, to act out a new personality. Sartre in his little book *L'Existentialisme* had held that we must remake our personalities every day. Existentialist philosophers had already noted that the actor was merely the most salient exemplar of a universal human requirement. They might have been thinking of Alec Guinness, who incarnated the notion in its most pure form, carrying nothing from one role to the next except his unfettered ability to play them. Hardly any face, hardly any voice.

Or, rather, the ideal voice, through which the English language speaks itself, with no interference. Sellers, mimicking Guinness in a Spike Milligan sketch called 'Bridge on the River Wye', found one or two mannerisms to emulate, but on the whole Guinness doesn't do anything to a line except say it correctly. Olivier articulates energetically like a man whose mouth has grown younger during the night; Gielgud can never do less than a Chaliapin *mezza voce*; Richardson put the emphasis on the wrong syllable to remind you that syllables were what words were made of. Guinness just spoke English, which made him, later on, a natural first choice for a Roman Empire patrician, an old-school Red Army General Staff officer, or a Jedi Knight emeritus in huge movies made with American money. Americans would like to believe that the upper brackets of any country, time or planet speak English. But they would also like to believe, against their democratic convictions, that the English spoken is *English* English. The Romans felt the same way about Greek.

Guinness spoke English English in his transitional film, *The Swan* (1956). Ealing comedy was left behind. Big American pictures were in view. He was on the threshold of international screen superstardom. But in conventional terms it never quite happened, and *The Swan* tells you why it never could have. All he had to be was Molnár's wastrel Ruritanian prince with whom Grace Kelly declines to contract a dynastic marriage because she is in love with Louis Jourdan. But Guinness made the part too interesting. He raised questions about the prince's identity when the prince's identity was not supposed to be in question. Dramatic films made during the Ealing period – *The Malta Story* is a notorious case in point – had already suggested that Guinness could not be an ordinary leading man. Torn loose from the Ealing setting, where he had been an extraordinary leading man, he had to become once again a character actor, although an extraordinary character actor, and on the grand scale. Everyone remembers him as the star of *The Bridge on the River Kwai*. But William Holden was the star, and Guinness merely shared with Sessue Hayakawa the job of adding distinction to a hollow picture. In the floating world of international film-making as understood by Sam Spiegel and David Lean, the precise social notation of Guinness's Englishness would be decorative but rootless, like a water lily.

A reduced weight of responsibility might have been welcome. When he did carry the whole picture, and the picture flopped, he must have taken it to heart, because looking back he only too readily concurs with the critical consensus. He makes disparaging remarks about his performance in *Our Man in Havana*, for instance, and seems to think that the film deserved its failure. But *Our Man in Havana* delighted many people at the time, and in retrospect is one of the richest films of Guinness's later career. He is no doubt right to place more emphasis on *The Horse's Mouth*, for which he wrote the screenplay. But as Gulley Jimson he was stuck with the task of acting out the standard English eccentric, whose painterly genius the audience had to take on trust. As Jim Wormald in *Our Man in Havana*, the ordinary man pretending to be a spy – pretending to be a man pretending to be ordinary – he was in his element.

In Britain, where television is strong – mainly because the film industry is so weak – it is no decline for a star to work out his time on the smaller screen. The two John Le Carré adaptations in which Guinness has starred for the BBC, *Tinker, Tailor, Soldier, Spy* and *Smiley's People*, have been hailed as British TV at its most distinguished. My own view is that they have so much distinction they can hardly breathe. Their stately progress is a snail's pace. Guinness had done better: the script gives him so little to go on that for once in his life he looks guilty of Great Acting. But if Guinness's George Smiley is not, for him, good acting, it is certainly good casting. As Le Carré's unfathomable spook, who looks unfathomable even when there is nothing in particular to be unfathomable about, he attains the emblematic summation of what he has always been up to.

Why the British spy should have such a reputation in the world is a separate question. Perhaps there is a widespread belief that the country has only pretended to decline, or else that there is some secret life which a decaying surface leaves untouched. Secret intelligence. Guinness has always embodied that, and it could be said that deciding to keep himself secret was the most intelligent thing he ever did. If so, this book is in keeping with his deep-laid plan. He purports to overcome his reticence, reinforces it while doing so, and goes on cherishing the enigma of which his performances are the variations.

New York Review of Books
27 March, 1986

Boomtown Saint

Is That It? by Bob Geldof
(Sidgwick & Jackson, 1986)

THE READER who finishes this book will be unlikely to echo its title. Surprisingly solid for a showbiz rush-job, Bob Geldof's autobiography could not be more personal if he had written it himself. From the blurb on the back flap one learns that Mr Geldof was 'helped' by Paul Vallely of *The Times*.

It doesn't matter. For a journalist, Paul Vallely is unusually literate. He knows that the plural of talisman is talismans. Also he commands a deceptively simple prose style. But the rich fund of memory is surely Geldof's own, and without too much exaggeration it can be said that the evocation of his Dublin childhood has a specifying force which reminds you that Swift, Joyce and Beckett came from the same city.

The school tuck-shop sold writing materials:

All around the shelves were stacked with the paraphernalia of inscription: copy books, exercise books, graph books, notepads plain, notepads narrow feint, notepads broad feint, notepads broad feint with margin. It smelt of pencil shavings and chocolate.

Geldof never wrote much in any of those notebooks – his main literary achievements at school were forged reports, for which his father beat him. His father also beat him for embezzling his school fees.

Geldof held these punishments against his father, school, city and country. He loathed his Catholic upbringing, and conceived a fine hatred for the Irish priesthood which his later admiration for individual priests in Africa did nothing to alleviate. In the circumstances he was ineducable, and might well have been ineducable in any circumstances. But on this evidence the English language got into him anyway.

'It was a peaceful border then, with just the odd explosion and a lot of agricultural smuggling.' If this sentence were to be shuffled so that the odd explosion came last, it would be funnier. Geldof's sense of humour lacks the calculation to make you laugh. But he has an eye for absurdity. Masturbation was supposed to be evil but he couldn't stop doing it: he must have been the champion wanker of his epoch. Both on the front flap and on the back of the jacket, under the David Bailey photograph of Geldof with arms spread like a jolly Jesus, parents are warned that they might 'find parts of this book offensive'. Children might not. The fascination has probably gone out of self-abuse. For Geldof's generation in Dublin, however, it was still the perilous first step towards ruin. The second step was staved off by a total ban on condoms, which had to be imported clandestinely across the aforementioned border. While still at school, Geldof always carried one, although apparently never the same one for long.

He was precocious in a society where precocity was antisocial. But in retrospect he is smart enough to see, and humble enough not to stress, that the real precocity was in giving up some of his time to helping the Simon Community look after down-and-outs. Plenty of bright, rebellious, style-setting, charismatic young men have swilled and fornicated, but not many of them have had the urge to kiss the wounded.

The young adventurer's mad lust to get out of Dublin is remembered with a vividness which should get his book so roundly condemned in Ireland that it might have to be imported along the old condom trail. In London he wore flares, ate enough hash to get scared and was horrified by heroin without even trying. Those junkies of the period who are still alive will find his attitude to the drug question either very square or enviably prescient. He sounds like Mr Clean with a contrived dab of dirt on his nose, but he knew hard times in a youth culture gone sour. His band, the Boomtown Rats, was conceived of as a return to authenticity: the name comes from Woody Guthrie.

Geldof talks sense about pop music so it is no wonder the music Press hated him from the start. Cleverly he incorporated criticisms into the band's publicity. 'The Boomtown Rats,' said the posters, 'have learned a fourth chord.' But he not only knew that the allegedly rebellious punk bands were hyped all the way, he said so at the top of his voice. He actually *said* he wanted to get rich, famous and laid. The music journalists wanted all that too but weren't going to get it, so they were unlikely to forgive someone who was going to get it and wouldn't pretend indifference. As far as they were concerned, he had zero street cred.

The streets didn't think the same. The Boomtown Rats boomed. When a pop act becomes successful there are only two kinds of money it can earn – not as much as you might think and more than you can believe. Geldof earned only the first kind, but all his other dreams came true. The ideal woman, Paula Yates, attached herself in the role of groupie. Her progression to the status of *Lebensgefährtin* is recorded with a candour that one hopes they will not regret. Perhaps such utter openness is the best thing for both of them. If Geldof's head ever threatened to swell, Paula would be the girl to level it out again. She is a highly trained mickey-taker.

Being such modern young people they had a baby to find out whether they wanted to get married. 'One Geldof bastard is enough,' said *Melody Maker*. 'Abortion of the year,' said *Sounds*. No wonder Geldof finds Fleet Street a relief by comparison.

Touring to promote records, Geldof saw the world. He did not fall for China, where he heard stories of what the Cultural Revolution had cost in human suffering. As always, pain got his attention. When the band's popularity, as pop popularity will, started to fade, he had his own agony to contend with, but it didn't stop him noticing other people's. The idea that he started the Live Aid campaign in order to revive the fortunes of the Boomtown Rats is a kite that not even the music Press could get off the ground. Broke then and since, he did it for the starving.

Geldof has no illusions about the regimes under which famine flourishes. He knows that uncontrolled aid can only subsidise their lethal fantasies. He is very worldly, but that is no disqualification from sainthood, which would fit him awkwardly, although better than the knighthood he did not receive. Geldof is nothing like Horatio Bottomley. He is a bit like St Augustine, who (in what the theologians rather unfortunately call his ejaculatory prayer) said 'Give me chastity, but not yet.' He is a lot like St Vincent de Paul, who could have had a great career in the Church, but chose to do Christ's work instead.

Observer
11 May, 1986

～

Geldof was subsequently rewarded for his efforts with a knighthood, and for his candour with a Press campaign calculated to separate him from his wife. He allowed neither accolade to influence his conduct.

N. V. Rampant Meets Martin Amis

'THIS IS the big one,' I told myself nervously. 'The Martin Amis interview. This is the one that could make you or break you.' As I neared his front door my heart was in my mouth.

No doubt he would have said it more cleverly. He would have said his heart was palpitating with trepidation like a poodle in heat in a monastery of mastiffs. Oh yes, he had the long words, Martin Amis. And he knew how to use them. He not only had the metaphors, he knew exactly what words like 'metaphor' meant. He knew what 'trepidation' meant. They had told him at Oxford. He had the education. He wasn't going to let you forget it. I asked myself: Why not cut your losses and get out now? But no, I told myself: because you've got something to offer too. Otherwise why would the oh-so-famous Amis be available at all?

'Come in,' said a familiar voice when I knocked with trepidation. (Yes, I knew what the word meant. It was only fooling back there when I pretended I didn't.) 'The door's open. Just push it.' Yeah, *pushing it*, I couldn't help thinking. Maybe that's what you've been doing, Martin, old son. Or Mart, as your friends call you. Your very powerful friends who can make or break a reputation with a flick of the telephone.

On the hallway occasional table was a copy of the collected works of Shakespeare, left oh-so-carelessly lying around so as to impress the less well-read. Well, I had heard of Shakespeare, so no luck there, Martin. But where *was* Martin?

Then I saw him lurking behind the volume of Shakespeare. Martin Amis, the oh-so-lauded so-called giant of his literary generation, was only four inches high.

'Glad you could make it. Glad in more ways than one,'

said Martin in his self-consciously deep voice. 'Usually I drop down to the floor on a thread of cotton at about this time and start for the kitchen in the hope of getting a drink by dusk. But I've lost the thread.'

Lost the thread in more ways than one, I thought, Martin, old son. Especially in this new book of yours, *Money*. But I didn't say so. I couldn't risk the notorious scorn, the laser-like contempt of his brilliantly educated mind. And I hated myself because I didn't say so. And I hated him. But not as much as I hated his book. 'Congratulations on a master-piece,' I said non-committally. 'I laughed continuously for two weeks and finally had to be operated on so that I could eat.' It was a tactful way of saying that I hadn't been as bowled over as he might fondly imagine.

'Thanks,' said the oh-so-blasé so-called genius, taking it as his due. 'Do you think you could give me a lift?'

He stepped into my open hand and I carried him into the study, where I put him down on his desk beside his typewriter. I could see now that I had been wrong about his being four inches high. He was three inches high. To depress the typewriter keys he must have to jump on them individually, and altering the tab-set would need a mountain-climbing expedition. I began to pity him. I could see now why he had chosen literary success.

But I could also see why I had not chosen it. So I was grateful to him. Grateful to Martin Amis, the post-punk Petronius. Yes, Mart. I've heard of Petronius. You didn't get *all* the education. There was some left over for the rest of us, right?

Through the ostentatiously open door of the bathroom I had noticed that the bidet was full of signed first editions of books by Julian Barnes, Ian McEwan and other members of the most powerful literary mafia to hit London since old Dr Ben Johnson ruled the roost. When I carried Martin through into the kitchen for that so-long-delayed welcoming drink, the refrigerator was full of French Impressionist lithographs piled up ostentatiously so that the casual visitor couldn't help seeing them. 'Antonia gave me those,' said the would-be neo-Swift oh-so-self-deprecatingly. 'She said after *Money* I should write a book about Monet or Manet.' He chuckled, pleased with his ostentatious modesty. Pleased with the secret language he shares only with his friends. With his friends and the beautiful Antonia Phillips, who just happens to control the *Times Literary Supplement*.

All of Martin's friends control something but this is the first time he has married one. Perhaps he will marry them all. I began to wonder who would marry me. Suddenly I noticed that Martin Amis was now only two inches high.

'Look,' said Martin. 'I feel I'm sort of disappearing. Do you think we could cut this short?' I was only too glad.

For finally I couldn't see what it was all meant to prove. Yes, he had published a novel every two months for ten years, was talked of in the same breath as balls-aching old Balzac, and had won the hand of one of the leading beauties of the day. But so what? He had never written a profile for the *Sunday Times Magazine*. He had spent too much time locked away reading all those books to know what was really going on in the London he was oh-so-celebrated for allegedly knowing intimately. Had he read any of *my* books, for instance? So far they existed only in manuscript, but they had enjoyed a pretty wide circulation among those not too proud – not too *old*, let's face it – to pick up a *samizdat* without using rubber gloves. Had he read *The Sandra Documents*? Had he read *Offed Infants* and *Tonto People*? Would he even bother to hear about my soon-to-be-forthcoming *The Aimed Sock*?

I should never have taken this assignment. He was afraid of me. Afraid of what I represented. Afraid of someone who was better at what he had always been best at – being young. Being unknown. Once *he* had been unknown. That had been what he had been famous for. But now he was not, and it was killing him.

When we shook hands in farewell at his front door, Martin Amis was barely one inch high. There was an empty milk bottle on the doorstep. I started to put him down carefully beside it. Then I changed my mind and put him down carefully inside it. Half-way down the street I looked back. No bigger than a bacillus with delusions of grandeur, he was drumming with microscopic fists as he slid down inside the curved wall where the side of the bottle met its base. His thin voice cried: 'I need you! I need you!'

I had him where I wanted him at last.

London Review of Books
18–31 October, 1984

Part Five

DAUGHTERS OF ALBION

The Wrong Lady Diana

Lady Diana Cooper by Philip Ziegler
(Hamish Hamilton, 1981)

EITHER she was the biggest tease in the universe, or else well-born young ladies did not fall into bed quite so easily then as they are widely supposed to do now. The author of this biography favours the first explanation, writing as if the lady had told him about it herself, but he doesn't say why he believes her. She might be just *saying* that she was a tease. From my own admittedly limited experience, Lady Diana Cooper is capable of saying anything, if she thinks you are dumb enough to swallow it. Philip Ziegler has reason to consider himself astute, but he perhaps ruled out too soon the possibility that the queen of the put-on had spotted the ideal patsy. The chief lacuna in an otherwise interesting book is its failure adequately to convey the heroine's play of wit, which even today can leave everybody else in the room sounding retarded.

Anyway, there can be no doubt that before and during the First World War all the golden young men who were to be cut down in battle resolutely besieged her. The most they could hope for, apparently, was to lie chastely beside her, but they were ready to settle for that. They knew what sex was and some of them were even accustomed to getting it, not necessarily from ladies of less exalted provenance than Lady Diana Manners. It follows, if they did not get that from her, that they got something else. In this book it is assumed throughout that she satisfied nobody's physical desires, least of all those of her beloved husband, the notoriously amorous Duff Cooper. It seems a fair inference that she satisfied the imagination.

A long time later she still satisfies the imagination, or at least stimulates it. The present reviewer wasn't exactly fresh in from the sticks when he first bumped into her at dinner, but his education in the ways of the *beau monde* still had a long way to go. No doubt finding that my initial pleasantries indicated a certain chippiness begging to be put down, she volunteered the opinion that the best thing to do with the poor was to kill them. 'After all,' she assured me, 'we *are* the *best people*.' I took this view seriously enough to argue against it for the next half-hour, at the end of which she assured me that she had a phial of poison beside her bed and that when the indignities of old age became too great she would end it all. It didn't occur to me at the time that this threat might have been a comment on the forensic quality of what she had just been listening to. But here again one doubtless overrates one's own impact. She probably had her hearing aid turned off. I had made the elementary mistake of trying to impress her.

As this book reveals, men have been doing that since the turn of the century, but the wise ones have always realised sooner or later that if she puts up with your presence at all then she is impressed enough already, so the thing to do is adopt a light tone or, failing that, pipe down and listen. Even at her present advanced age she enjoys the benefit of total recall, a characteristic which has stood Philip Ziegler in good stead.

For large stretches of the book he has been faced with no greater challenge than to transcribe her memories in grammatical English. Indeed for the opening fanfares of her life the job was already done, since *The Rainbow Comes and Goes*, the first volume of her autobiography, would be hard to better as a portrait of her young self or of any other bright young thing in that generation. As a writer she had energy, verbal invention, natural comic timing and a fastidious ear which would have ruled out the possibility of her ever using, as Mr Ziegler does, such a cloddish term as 'life-style' – something he must have learned at Oxford, or perhaps at Eton. With the proviso that *suppressio veri* and *vis comica* are both ever-present likelihoods, anything Lady Diana writes or says is as transparent as Malvern Water. Whether at the start of the story or anywhere else during its long course, the most Mr Ziegler could decently add to his subject's clear stream of reminiscence was a few extra beams of light from odd angles.

One of the odd angles is necessarily the sex angle. Lady Diana Cooper can be included in few categories but one of them is undoubtedly the category of those who don't mind being gossiped about in print – a category which the professional gossips would have us believe includes everybody. Thus it is possible to read this book without feeling like an accomplice to a robbery. Not that the facts here revealed would have been particularly embarrassing even had she wanted them withheld. She is no more likely to embarrass us in the sexual department than in any other. She is never strident. What she does seem, on this evidence, is a bit unreal. Continually and chastely in love with the one man while he and all around her are successively consumed by more or less ephemeral passions, she is starring in a play by Shaw while everybody else is in a play by Schnitzler.

The libidinous cyclone of which she has perennially functioned as the calm eye was already whirling before she was born. Probably her real father was the angelically handsome seducer Henry Cust, who played tennis in the nude. Her mother, Violet, Duchess of Rutland, sculpted so well that Rodin compared her with Donatello. Watts said she drew like Holbein. But the first thing to say about Violet was that she was supremely beautiful. (Had she not been, and not been a duchess, Rodin and Watts might not have placed their comparisons quite so high, but let that pass.) It was fated that the Duke of Rutland should linger on the sidelines while Henry and Violet reproduced their kind. The result was the Platonic ideal of beauty who until very recent times held the unchallenged title of Lady Diana. Lately she has taken to introducing herself as 'the wrong Lady Diana' but it is unlikely she believes it. There were any number of princes she might have married, and the same might well have been true if she had been born without a bean.

By the standards of her class she was neither rich nor idle. To envy her as a member of the upper crust, however, is probably easier on the nerves than to appreciate her for what she was and is – the natural centre of the action. In those last years of the old world a party would have formed around her whatever her origins, and her unique personality could have come from anywhere. Class divisions can be wiped out but not even Mrs Mao was able to produce a society of such homogeneity that it had nobody left in it whom people thought more highly of than they did of her. The more society is levelled down, the more glaring the disparity between the attractive and the unattractive, the vivid and the dull. For Lady Diana's mother there could have been no question of dabbling in show business. Lady Diana found herself drawn to it by what seemed like a natural impulse. Probably it was, but it was a social impulse too. At the same time as the stars set out to acquire class, it became permissible for members of the ruling class to seek stardom. Lady Diana's knack for getting herself into the newspapers instead of keeping her name out of them, for making a spectacle of herself on stage and screen instead of taking up her natural position as a power behind a throne, might have had something to do with an instinctive recognition that high society was no longer big enough to contain her, and that her proper stamping-ground was society itself.

Anyway, Mr Ziegler does not spend much time exploring his heroine's unconscious motives, and perhaps he is right. The conscious motives are interesting enough. 'Goodbye, my darling,' wrote her future husband Duff Cooper in 1914, 'I hope everyone you like better than me will die very soon.' At the time it must have sounded like a joke. Before the machine-guns started chattering, the young men had all sat around in country houses and London drawing-rooms fancying themselves for their own brilliance. Privileged by birth, they allowed themselves the double privilege of tempering their philistine heritage with bohemian pursuits. But their puffed-up chests could not keep out bullets. Lady Diana worked as a nurse at Guy's while one by one they were killed off. After the battles the hospitals filled up with enough realism to cure romance for ever. That was how she learned not to cry. She could easily have reneged on her self-imposed duty but she stuck it out. Whatever her subsequent shen-anigans took their inspiration from, it wasn't from lack of knowledge about life. Probably she knew too much. In later years she was famous for seeming unsympathetic when friends injured themselves, but, having had to treat young children for burns during the war, she had perhaps been obliged to take a detached view of pain, or at any rate seem to. The favoured treatment for burns at that time was to pour hot wax on them.

The nightmare over, she married Duff and the party was on again, never really to slow down until his death. Mr Ziegler is obviously aware that his readers might smile at the Coopers' idea of penury. Duff had £10,000 out of a trust, a £600-a-year allowance from his mother and his Foreign Office salary of £520 per annum as a *bonne bouche*. Multiply the figures by the appropriate factor – twenty at least, I should have thought – and you might decide that they weren't exactly scraping along. But her mother was not being wholly irrational when she called Duff penniless. By the standards of Diana's legitimate expectations he was broke to the wide. It was a love-match, right enough, even if between a ram and a freemartin. Men who had missed out called Lady Diana either a nymphomaniac or a lesbian, but the truth, if that is what she is telling, seems to have been that her inclinations were simply not very strong. Such a deficiency, if deficiency it is, brought with it at least one unarguable benefit. She was without jealousy. Duff spent his whole married life running after, and usually catching up with, every presentable female in the area. Diana either turned a blind eye or, when things threatened to get out of hand, marshalled the traffic. Students of the domestic arrange-ments prevailing among the British upper orders are used to hearing about weird ménages. Here is another. Less kinky than the alliance between Harold Nicolson and Vita Sackville-West, it was even more remarkable. Very few men did not fall for Lady Diana in short order, but her devotion to her husband never wavered. The conun-drum is made even more puzzling by the fact that it is not easy, at this distance, to be sure of what it was that Duff

Cooper actually *did*, apart from being ambassador to France.

But that lay in the future. First the Coopers had to be poor in Gower Street, with nobody except Rubinstein to play the piano, while Chaliapin sang and rose-petals descended on the guests. Getting to know absolutely everybody is not as good as absolutely everybody wanting to know you. With Lady Diana the second condition always applied, so there was never any call to give the first a moment's thought. The result was complete lack of affectation. Which is not to say complete lack of histrionics: Max Reinhardt having made her a star in *The Miracle*, she showed no great desire to get her light back under the bushel, especially since Duff needed the money. Mr Ziegler is quite right when he says that even now she has the presence to command any room she is in. Some of her friends would say that he is not so right when he suggests, on the subject of cash, that Lady Diana was ruthless about extorting it from rich admirers such as Beaverbrook. Plainly she would skin them without a qualm, but it was usually for the benefit of a friend in need, not for her own. Even her biographer, who ought to be saturated with his subject's personality, sometimes seems unaware of the full extent to which she defied convention. Behind her show of independence there was real independence.

As an aristocrat with talent she was bound to elicit plaudits from successful artists making their way in the great world. They hailed her as an actress in the same way that Rodin hailed her mother as a sculptor. But there was nothing condescending about the way they admired her self-assurance, or what they thought was her self-assurance. Evelyn Waugh is the most prominent case in point. Far from being impressed by the creative gifts of well-born ladies, he wasn't even impressed by his own. He wanted to be accepted as a gentleman, not as a genius. Turning the factual Lady Diana into a fiction called Mrs Stitch, he had no lack of material to make the character vivid. But her capacity for driving small cars down the steps of public toilets is only the surface of the character. The real point of Mrs Stitch was the same as the real point of Lady Circumference – the ability to do the right thing from sheer breeding. Lady Circumference is an unalloyed philistine yet she reaches the right conclusion about Mrs Melrose Ape merely from listening to her preach. But Lady Circumference is a figure only in the early, avowedly comic novels. Mrs Stitch is still there in *Sword of Honour*, still the dotty but authoritative incarnation of *noblesse oblige*.

Mr Ziegler tells a revealing story of how Waugh tried to impress Lady Diana by misdirecting a suitcase-laden stranger so that he would miss his train. Lady Diana straightened the stranger out and then dressed her admirer down, as well she might have. The incident would probably have added itself to Waugh's towering burden of guilt even if his crime had not been pointed out to him by so telling a finger. Waugh knew all about his own interior drama. His name came up the second time I met Lady Diana, at a fancy-dress ball. Once more I was lucky enough to draw her as a dinner partner. I was pretending to be an Australian in a black tie while she was in her standard outfit as a nun. On her right she had the Arab who was financing the party. He was dressed as a sheik but that was because he was a sheik.

On my left sat the sheik's girlfriend, a Japanese model who kept saying that her favourite city was New York because on the terebision she could watch the moobies until dawn. Of necessity Lady Diana and the present writer were thrown together. She started by telling me that all the poor people ought to be killed but this time I had wits enough about me to quiz her about Evelyn Waugh. She has met almost every prominent writer since Meredith, who gave her an inscribed copy of his poems, but there is no doubt in my own mind, and probably not in hers, that her friendship with Waugh constitutes her closest involvement with genius. She told me that Waugh apologised to her in advance for Mrs Stitch's behaviour in *Sword of Honour*. (Mrs Stitch, it will be remembered, shelters Ivor Clare and tries to pull strings for him after he shows cowardice during the débâcle on Crete.) After Lady Diana read the passage in question, she told Waugh that she didn't know why he was apologising: in real life she would have done exactly what Mrs Stitch did in the story.

By her own principles, which are the only ones that have ever mattered to her, she would have been right. Perhaps Waugh guessed it and generously ascribed to her, out of his sure instinct for character, conduct that to his intellect seemed equivocal. There is no telling. But the mere existence of Mrs Stitch is enough to give us some idea of how much he got from the original. He idealised her as he idealised all the aristocracy, but it must have been a solace to him that he did not have to idealise her very much. She put as much energy into the ephemeral gestures of sociability as he put into a work of art. Artists who admire aristocrats are often unduly receptive to the aristocrat's traditional disdain for artistic seriousness. According to Montherlant, Saint-Simon left his sentences untidy because to neaten them up would have been beneath him. Waugh was too much of an artist to be that gentlemanly, but he could still dream of what it must feel like to be carefree and at ease. Lady Diana was a key figure in his dreams. Theirs was an instructive friendship, which Mr Ziegler could have made more of.

But there is not much time for social analysis when you are drowning in a plethora of upper-crust anecdotes. Another war having begun, on to Algiers, where our heroine transforms the assigned accommodation from a shanty into the social hub of the Mediterranean. Gide shows up and refuses to leave. Lady Diana arranges a meeting between de Gaulle and Churchill, tiptoeing away at just the right moment, so that they are soon canoodling. Onward to Paris, where the Coopers arrive in September 1944 escorted by forty-eight Spitfires.

As chatelaine of the smartest of all British embassies she attracted a lot of flak at the time for having Collaborators on the premises. Some of the criticism has still not died down, but it should be clearer by now that the question is one the French themselves find by no means simple. A lot of writers and intellectuals who had not been in very much danger suddenly put on berets, called themselves Resistance fighters, and pointed the finger at such butterflies as Cocteau. Lady Diana received Cocteau, perhaps recognising that he had done the Resistance a favour by staying out of it.

Meanwhile the real Collaborators were continuing their plush lives unharmed. 'Vile denouncing traitors and traitoresses,' she noted, 'get off scotters.' Her refusal to take the artists seriously while they adopted holier-than-thou postures seems like the right response at this distance. Nor did she care anything for precedence, arranging the *placement* as it suited her, which left a lot of French ladies scandalised. But scandalised people have a lot to talk about and there was soon no other subject of conversation except the permanent picnic she was running on the embassy premises. On summer nights the picnic shifted to Chantilly, where select parties of hikers, led by Lady Diana, would take shelter in a pavilion beside the lake and find it providentially equipped with a cold buffet and champagne. When Ernest Bevin came to visit he pounced on her in a corridor. All things, except that, to all men, she sang 'Wotcher, all the neighbours cried' while swerving adroitly out of reach. Both she and her husband, the book says, were in love with Louise de Vilmorin, but since only Duff was getting any satisfaction from the relationship, nerves on his wife's part would have been understandable. She sailed on, doing nothing ordinary and everything right. The only lastingly wrong note she struck was through staying on too long. After Duff was replaced as Ambassador they should have left Paris but ran a rival embassy instead, throwing unofficial parties that put the official ones in the shade and generating bad blood which is understandably still boiling.

Siegfried posed a philosophical problem which not even Nietzsche could quite settle. It is all very well to say that somebody might do all the right things from instinct, but how can the rest of us tell? Nevertheless it can be said that Lady Diana, with the glaring exception of the alternative Paris embassy caper, waived the rules to the general benefit. Arrogance is self-questioning deep down. True self-assurance has no such doubts. She suffered always from nervousness and often from severe depression, but never from anxiety about how she stood. When thieves broke into her London flat and tied her up, Evelyn Waugh said that the loss of dignity must have been awful. This time he had really misunderstood completely: by her standards, dignity was not something you could lose through mere circumstances.

As the years advanced, they made alterations to her famous face. She had the damage repaired but without pretending that time did not exist. Always to live without self-deception was at the centre of her appeal: an object of fantasy for others, she was a realist herself. She thinks, as several Roman poets thought, that life has little to offer after the senses go. Even without the contrary evidence provided by how much fun she is obviously having while saying such things, there would be reason to call this a limited view, but it would take a brave man to be certain that he will not reach the same conclusion in the end. The third and latest time I sat beside her, which was the night after I finished reading this book, I was all set to ask her about Chaliapin when suddenly a howl arose from an Austrian of advanced years sitting on her left. He had turned up the volume too high on his hearing aid, a clever means of securing her attention. She revved up her own hearing aid and drowned him out. So much for *him*. At her age, she said, only the little pleasures were left. Any time now she would have to uncork that phial of poison. Senile dementia would be a blessing but unfortunately in her case the brain was the last thing to go. Standing on your head when young makes the brain strong. Could I stand on my head?

A minute later I was upside-down. Duly clarified, my brain registered the fact that Lady Diana Cooper had not lost her ability to make men show off. Whether they are the better for it is one of the many questions this book does not settle. Mr Ziegler might have done more to analyse Britain's class structure but only at the cost of telling us less about someone who does not fit into it. Lady Diana Cooper has never represented the ruling class, the upper class or any other class, since a class is represented by its mediocrities if it is represented by anyone. An extreme case, her example might help to remind her countrymen that classes are composed of individuals.

A social class is an abstract concept. The penalty for

treating abstractions as realities is to succumb to the aberra-
tion which Whitehead called the fallacy of misplaced con-
creteness. Britain's lingering political curse, the class war is
fought between phantom armies which have real casualties.
At the moment, with the rise of a central Parliamentary
alliance, there are signs of a let-up. Ten or even five years
ago, many more of the reviews this book has received would
have been derisive condemnations of an alleged anachron-
ism. Now there is perhaps a more general recognition that a
just society can be arrived at only by correcting specific
injustices in the society we already have. Hence the welcome
new air of tolerance. Which is not to say subservience.
Indeed, it was the old rancour that was subservient, for ever
complaining about the life of uninterrupted pleasure that the
best people were supposedly enjoying. If they were, then
they weren't the best people, and if it was uninterrupted,
then it wasn't pleasure. We must judge the worth of our own
lives according to our own lights. Lady Diana Cooper has
never felt any other way, so it is no mystery that waverers
from all walks of life buck up when she is around.

London Review of Books
18 February, 1982

Out Into the Light

I T WAS the chocolate wrappers that made Joyce Grenfell an
overnight sensation as far as Australia was concerned. She
was already famous before she arrived, of course. Even in the
late 1950s Sydney wasn't *that* far away from England. We
had all seen her in the films. But most of her film roles up
until that time had been horse-faced Grand Old Girls of the
Miss Gossage type, so nobody was ready for the elegant,

self-possessed creature she turned out to be when she arrived on her first theatrical tour.

The audiences were delighted with her. So, by and large, was she with them, but she didn't like the chocolate wrappers. It was the custom for everyone in the audience to buy a five-shilling box of Winning Post chocolates during the interval and consume the entire contents during the second half. Each chocolate was wrapped individually in crinkly brown paper and there was a printed guide, also on crinkly paper, to help you identify the flavour of each chocolate by its shape. The printed guide made, if anything, even more noise than the wrappings. When the lights went down for the second half the whole audience pulled the lids off their boxes of chocolates – the lids came off with an audible sob, betokening the tightness of the air seal – and started searching through the crinkly wrappers for the chocolate of their choice. It sounded like a million locusts camping on your television aerial.

Joyce put up with it for two nights and then decided it was time to call a halt. On the third night the lights went down, the curtain went up, and they were at it. Instead of launching into her second-half opening song, Joyce advanced regally to the footlights and told the audience that if the eating of the chocolates could be delayed until the end of the performance it might be possible to enjoy both her and them, but if the chocolates had to be eaten now then she would be obliged to withdraw. The audience sat stunned, a freshly unwrapped heart-shaped strawberry cream half-way between lap and gaping mouth. There was a long, tense silence. Then from here, there and eventually everywhere came the reluctant sigh of lids being squeezed back on.

The Press next day tried to make a thing out of Joyce's queenly intransigence, but the public loved her for it. She would have been a huge success anyway, but after the affair of the chocolates she was something more – an institution. Lyrical wit and perfect aplomb made a heady compound. She would have been impressive enough as a gifted comedienne, but as a gifted comedienne who was also *toujours la grande dame* she was dynamite. At Sydney University we in the Journalists' Club took the bold step of inviting her to lunch. We were frightened stiff that she might say yes, but felt reasonably confident that she would be too busy for anything so unimportant. She double-crossed us by accepting.

On the appointed day we were all on our best behaviour. Drawn up in the carefully prepared University Union dining-room, we must have looked like a firing squad in mufti. She relaxed us by pretending not to notice. Everybody at the table either forgot his manners or else had never had any, but we coped by picking up the same cutlery as she did. Gradually it became apparent that she was prepared to hear something more adventurous than mere pleasantries. We tried to impress her with our knowledge of contemporary humorists – Peter Sellers, Nichols and May, Mort Sahl. She was very good at not damping the conversation by telling us that she knew them all personally, although when the subject switched to Ealing comedies – all of which we knew line by line and frame by frame – she casually let drop some inside knowledge about the geography of Ealing. Think of it: this woman had been to Ealing!

We made attempts to shock her. There was a good deal of swearing, as if to prove that young Australian males with intellectual proclivities were nevertheless tough, dinkum types underneath. By this time dessert had arrived. Joyce chose a pear, decapitated it, and rotated her spoon inside it, extracting the contents undamaged, whereupon the empty skin fell contentedly inwards. It was all done with such inexpressibly accomplished ease that it produced the same effect as the exhortation about the chocolate wrappers. While we sat with mouths ajar, she whipped an Instamatic out of her reticule and photographed us.

Greatly daring, several of us asked if we could write to her. She said we certainly could. My own first letter, rewritten a dozen times, was a model of lapidary prose that made Walter Pater sound like Jack Kerouac. I was staggered when she answered it, saying how much she had enjoyed meeting us all and waxing enthusiastic about the opportunities Australia offered to the committed bird-watcher. I wrote her another letter, perhaps a touch less strained. By now she was back in

England, but she answered that one too. In the next letter I enclosed my latest poem, and in her next answer she did me the honour of criticising it in specific and useful detail. This was a particularly selfless gesture, since she must have spotted that I had composed it for the occasion out of no other impulse except the desire to impress. Without letting me know what she was up to, she was once again embarked on her usual task of helping someone to become himself.

I was unpromising material, but perhaps that was the challenge. Much later I realised that there were scores of us whose spiritual welfare she was quietly supervising, but she had the knack of making you feel that you were the only one. We were all her only sons. When I arrived in London, broke to the wide, and absurdly proud of it, she was more patient with my pretension to radicalism than the occasion warranted. (So was Reg, for that matter, who in my case must have been wondering how much boredom his wife's kindness to waifs and strays was going to let him in for.) At the time I was incapable of realising that my own convictions were essentially a pose and that she was the true radical, since the values she represented were beyond the power of any government either to create or to destroy. But she never mocked me, although once or twice I caught her smiling in the middle of my most moving prepared speech. I was still asked to the Christmas party, where I had to play uncle to several enchanting children she was looking after over the festive season. Joyce describes the scene in her book *In Pleasant Places* but charitably makes no reference to my lurching self-consciousness. It still bothers me that I had neglected to clean my finger-nails.

Artistically creative people often excuse themselves from everyday obligations. But Joyce, who was artistically creative to a high degree, never did, not even once. She was very good at planning her day. Not that she ever let you know how much effort she put into fitting everything in. It all just happened. Once at Elm Park Gardens I spent an hour in hysterics while she tried out some new sketches on me – a privileged audience of one. For me it was the highlight of an idle day, or more probably an idle year. Later on I realised that she must have written a dozen letters that day, seen a dozen people, planned a dozen other days like it. Her use of time was like a classical Latin sentence – packed with meaning, nothing wasted.

As the Feldmarschallin points out to Octavian in *Der Rosenkavalier*, it isn't the what, it's the how. Joyce was an object lesson in how to behave. She never preached, and I am not even sure that she ever set out to teach by example. But it was plain even to an eye as unpractised as mine that her good manners went far below the surface, all the way to the centre of the soul. Her good manners were *good* manners. It gradually occurred to me that doing the right thing meant more than just conforming to some abstract code. The implications of this realisation were disturbing. I might have to abandon my vague expectations of the millennium and settle down to doing something about my clear duties in the present. I tried to stave these thoughts off by mentally enrolling Joyce in the exploiting upper class, but since she obviously worked for a living and was a lot better than I was at treating the lower orders like human beings, this belief was hard to sustain. It even began to occur to me that I did not know very much about life.

I am still learning and always too slowly, but like so many of Joyce's friends I owe to her much of what acumen I have come to possess. Katharine Whitehorn once said that you can tell the person who lives for others by the haunted look on the faces of the others, but Joyce wasn't like that. She never imposed herself for a second. She simply lived her life, and the way that she lived it made you wonder how well you were living yours.

In the last ten years I saw less of her than I might have, perhaps through an unacknowledged conviction that if I had her as a conscience I would never develop one of my own. There was also the danger of sunburn from reflected glory. At Cambridge I invited her as a guest of honour to the Footlights annual dinner. She did a variation on her pear routine and gave a speech that left the congregation of apprentice comedians slack-jawed with the sudden, awful awareness of how much class you had to have before you could be as classy as that. A few years later, still in Cambridge, I was married and a baby was on the way – overdue, in fact. Joyce was playing a week at the Arts Theatre before taking her show into London. She arranged for two chairs to be put in the wings for my wife and myself, explaining to my wife where the nearest loo was. 'You practically have to spend your *life* there at this stage of the proceedings, don't you?' It was complicity between mothers. You would never have guessed that this was the one happiness she had never been granted. But it was a small thing beside the happiness she could cause, as I saw and heard all over again when she walked out into the light.

Then months went by without a meeting and the months stretched into years. At the touch of a button I could see her on *Face the Music*. We talked occasionally on the telephone and more occasionally still we exchanged letters, but she knew that I had broken free. My second mother had joined my first mother as someone to grow apart from. Those of us who must learn self-possession, instead of attaining it by instinct, are often jealous of our isolation, and guard it hardest against those who taught us most. Perhaps I am trying to find a good name for ingratitude.

But in the last year of Joyce's life I somehow reached the conclusion that we had better meet soon. She gave me lunch at Elm Park Gardens. As always it seemed no time since the last time. For once doing the right thing at the right moment, I tried to thank her for what she had done for me. Some of what I had to say is in this article, which is the inadequate record of how she helped one young man to find his way. The hundreds of others whose lives were touched by her must all have stories like it. Beyond those favoured hundreds who knew her in person are the thousands and the millions who could tell just from the look of her that she had a unique spirit. There was a day when a woman who aroused as much loving gratitude as that would have been canonised for it. So far Christian Scientists have got along without saints but perhaps in her case they should think again. Meanwhile she remains an unforgettable example of just how extraordinary an ordinary human being can be.

~~~

At the kind invitation of Reggie Grenfell and Richard Garnett, the preceding piece first appeared as a contribution to the memorial volume *Joyce* (London, 1980).

The Queen in California

THE ROYAL Scuba Tour of California began last Saturday with scarcely any rain at all. The clouds over San Diego were full of water, but none of it was actually falling out of the sky as the *Britannia* edged towards Broadway Pier on the Embarcadero, just along from Anthony's Fish Grotto.

The surrounding area was heavily populated with members of the Secret Service wearing hearing aids and talking into their sleeves. Less numerous but more cheerful were the citizens of San Diego, some of whom were allowed on to the pier itself, at the end of which an honour guard of sailors and marines drilled with clattering M-14s, while E-9 Master Chief Dye conducted the orchestra and frogmen were under water checking for bombs.

As things were to turn out, the frogmen were the only people appropriately dressed for the upcoming week of official events, but as yet nobody knew that. The American media were in position and fully equipped with Canon 600-45 Telefoto lenses the size of garbage-disposal units and microwave dishes aimed at their very own relay helicopters, which were up there in the grey sky like benign vultures.

The British media were scantily accoutred by comparison but looked less scruffy than usual. Several of our photographers, though they had not gone so far as to put on a tie, had shaved only a few days before. Relations between the Palace and the British media had been strained by recent events, but with goodwill on both sides the special relationship could

still be restored. As for the special relationship with the
United States of America, the Queen and President Reagan
would take care of that later, on horseback.

A 21-gun salute crashed out as the *Britannia* tied up. You
couldn't help thinking that all the explosions might be
setting a bad example, but out on the water the voices of
dissent were limited to one small boat carrying the rubric
GOD SAVE THE QUEEN FROM NUCLEAR ATTACK. This was easily
countered on shore by such friendly messages as BODY
BEAUTIFUL CAR WASH SAYS WELCOME QUEEN ELIZA-
BETH. The lady thus addressed carefully negotiated the
gangway. Her pearly queen frock was too thin for the
weather but the pain-trained royal constitution made light of
the discomfort. As for the Duke, he was in naval uniform
with fully faded gold braid: very Falklands factor, very stiff
upper teeth.

With the Reagans saving themselves up for later, the
welcoming committee of lesser dignitaries could be rapidly
dealt with. The Royal Couple then climbed into a COMNAV-
SURPAC Admiral's barge to inspect the habour, across which
small squalls were skittering as a portent of bigger things.
Somewhere out there in the rain sat the aircraft-carrier
Ranger, with a single Tomcat parked on deck to indicate
American air power. Lunch for the Royal party would be
served below decks, but first there would be a reception on
the *Britannia* for the media, including the British media, who
had all rushed back to the Holiday Inn to pick up their
engraved invitations, clean their finger-nails and tweeze out
those ugly superfluous facial hairs.

This event was a big plus for the British Press. The ground
rules were that nothing the Royals said should be quoted,
but one of the American radio reporters nastily went on the
air straight afterwards and said that the Queen had made a
dull remark about the wet weather. Since only the presence
of a canvas awning over the deck had saved everybody
from being washed into the sea, Her Majesty's remark was
scarcely inappropriate, but that was a minor consideration
beside the fact that the American media had made the
British look comparatively well behaved.

Brimming with self-righteous fervour, the British Press from then on were Royalists to a man. Although it was too early to say that the Palace and Fleet Street were as one, nevertheless there was a palpable sense that the Brits were all in it together, if only in their native capacity to sneer at, nay revel in, the rain. The Californians, by sharp contrast, were in a panic, having counted on the standard sunshine for a number of alfresco events, culminating in the famous horse ride during which the President, an A-picture leading man at long last, would finally and incontrovertibly get the girl.

On Sunday the Royal Couple lunched in a foursome with Mr and Mrs Walter Annenberg in Palm Springs. In his erstwhile role as US Ambassador to the Court of St James, Mr Annenberg evidently endeared himself to the Monarch through his unique command of the English language, by which his house, when he had the builders in, became a domicile undergoing elements of refurbishment. The Queen must have dug Walter's act in a big way, since it now cost her a flight and two motorcades in each direction just to get more of it.

Back at the *Britannia*, which had meanwhile moved north to Long Beach, she changed clothes for the biggest event of the week not counting the horse ride, namely the jumbo dinner in Sound Stage 9 at Twentieth Century-Fox. There was more rain on the way, but her spirits must have undergone elements of refurbishment in Palm Springs, because instead of ordering the Captain of the *Britannia* to set course for England she voluntarily entered the limousine that would take her to break bread with Marie Osmond, the current Tarzan, the man who used to be Davy Crockett, and at least two of the Gabor sisters.

These and several hundred other guests arrived by limo, stepping out under an awning while the shivering media, under nothing but the wet night sky, took notes and fired flashbulbs. 'I've had the priviledge,' said Henry Kissinger, 'of meeding the Gween before, bud id's always a special oggasion.' The limos being a block long each, it took a while for all the guests to be delivered, even though Chuck Pick, chief executive of Chuck's Parking, took personal charge of the platoon of carhops unloading the precious cargo. Chuck made up in histrionics for what many of the guests were too old to manage. Fred Astaire was one of the younger luminaries present. Some of them had risen from the grave for the occasion but they had more in common than mere immortality. Gradually it dawned that they were nearly all Republicans. The Democrats were at home, seething. When Nancy Reagan finally welcomed the Royal Couple, she was shaking hands with practically the only invitees who hadn't voted for her husband.

Inside went the Royals with the First Lady attached, leaving the media out in the rain with about 1,000 security personnel and the terminally hysterical Chuck. The British media took shelter for the several hours that would elapse before they were allowed in to catch a brief glimpse of the uncrashable bash.

Your reporter found himself huddled under a wooden staircase with a tabloid gossip famous for never having written a sentence both true and literate at the same time, and a photographer who carries an infra-red lens for taking pictures of the Princess of Wales through brick walls at night. I was starting to see things from their point of view. When your subject matter is inside eating, it is not nice to be outside suffering. But when we eventually got inside it became clear that the guests had not been having much fun either.

The Royals were seated with the British filmstar colony all along one side of a long table up on stage, like a Last Supper painted by Sir Joshua Reynolds. Before and below them stretched a sea of Americans all staring in their direction. It was a stiffening circumstance in which only Dudley Moore could possibly look cheerful, although Michael Caine was also trying hard. Jane Seymour looked very attractive, which was more than you could say for Anthony Newley. Rod Stewart, clad in a black and gold John Player Special pants suit, sported an extravaganza hairstyle that left his wife Alana's coiffure looking like a crew-cut, but facially he resembled an ant-eater who had run out of ants.

The Duke was talking to Julie Andrews. In between the Queen and the First Lady sat Tony Richardson, looking very calm. Later on it emerged that this was because, having not been apprised of the *placement* until he was about to sit down, he had died of fright.

To have expired was to be fortunate, because the Entertainment now began. Emcee of the Entertainment was Ed McMahon, Johnny Carson's straight man. It is conjecturable that Carson would be lost without McMahon, but there can be no doubt that McMahon is lost without Carson, who was not present, having stayed at home because of a wisdom tooth, or perhaps because of wisdom. McMahon introduced Dionne Warwick as a Great Song Stylist. For the benefit of the Queen and other strangers, he explained what a Great Song Stylist was. A Great Song Stylist was someone who was not only a singer with Style, but a stylish singer with Greatness.

Ed took so long over the introduction that Dionne felt compelled to deliver an extended set. She was breathtaking if your breath is taken by a display of technique. She clapped her hands and swayed her hips. Gene Kelly, seated just in front of me, did neither of these things. Nor did the Queen, but she evidently quite liked George Burns, the next act on. George also went on too long, but at least he was himself. Frank Sinatra and Perry Como pretended to be Frank Sinatra and Dean Martin, doing that endless medley which is a good joke if the previous numbers have been kept short. They hadn't, so it wasn't.

The Entertainment had elephantiasis, like the evening in general. When Hollywood gets beyond energy without taste, it arrives at taste without proportion. Perry ruffled his hair to prove that it really grew on top of his head, even if it had started its life somewhere else. 'You obviously do *not* adore me,' Frank sang at the Queen, who if she didn't nod her head, didn't shake it either. The big night out was a downer, but it wasn't her fault. They had put her on display.

In fact she had been had. The evening was a pay-off for Ronald Reagan's financial backers, who would never have met the stars if the stars had not come to meet the Queen. Buckingham Palace had been hustled into bankrolling the next campaign wagon.

But if the Queen felt manipulated she didn't show it. The rain was sufficient proof that not even the President could fix everything. It fell all night and on through the next day. Sections of California began dissolving into the sea. Lady Susan Hussey, the Queen's Lady-in-Waiting, packed away the silk frocks and laid out the macintosh, the boots and the sou'wester. If necessary, flippers and breathing apparatus could be flown out from home. It was time for a show of True Brit – the truly British grit not soluble in water. Up in the Sierra Madre at the British Home for old people, the lawn squished like spinach quiche. The media stood in it ankle deep while Her Majesty met an old lady in a wheelchair and received a quilt for Prince William.

The awed *Time* reporters, all wired up like the Secret Service, talked into one another's hearing aids through their sleeves, but the Queen had already moved on to the City of Hope Paediatric Hospital, there to be met by the founders, these latter including the inescapable Zsa Zsa Gabor in a Royal purple fur coat, taken from some species of animal to which she probably represents the sole source of danger. The hospital had been specially repristinated at a cost of $100,000, much of it spent on the water-based paint which had been carefully applied to the gutters, down which it was now flowing.

On the way north to Santa Barbara next day, busloads of media shone pearly headlights through the solid white rain. The sea was full of mud and far too rough for the *Britannia* to leave Long Beach. The Queen's visit to the Rancho el Reagan was still on, but she would have to fly to Santa Barbara instead of sail and there would be no horse ride. It was a cruel disappointment for the British media but having caught the spirit of True Brit from their Monarch they were stoic in adversity. Even Paul Callan of the *Mirror*, a gossip columnist with the literary sensibility of a vampire bat, had been heard to squeal 'She is *our* Queen!' at some importunate Americans who had tried to get between him and his Sovereign. The *Mail*'s Peter McKay, compared with whom Callan writes like Congreve, had a moist glint in his tiny eyes which could only be tears of pride, since it was not yet raining inside the bus.

Behind us, the coast road crumbled into the waves and a tornado punched a large hole in downtown LA. Up ahead at the airport, the President waited inside the Tracor Aviation hangar for the Air Force DC-9 bearing the Royal Party to come sluicing in under its own power. There were several hundred spectators, all chosen by the White House for their Republican views. I was on top of a filing cabinet with a trainee cheer-leader called Tuesday Pflug. A nice girl who had already met the President ('I have Ronald Reagan germs on my hand!') she had never even *seen* a Democrat, except in police bulletins.

The plane pulled ear-splittingly into the hangar, the Reagans glad-handed the Royals, and they all motorcaded off towards the hills past the happily sodden crowds and such signs of greeting as WELCOME TO GOLETA QUEEN ELIZABETH GARAGE SALE 26,000 ITEMS NEW AND USED. The American media kept describing the onlookers as subdood but who isn't subdood when submerged?

The media contingent for the ranch climbed into the assigned ground-clearance vehicles and after a thought-provoking trip up roads like rapids they de-bussed to discover a specially installed set of outdoor telephones wrapped in polythene. They also discovered that although there was no horse ride, the President had dressed as a cowboy anyway. He looked radiant, like a man who receives a visit from the Queen of Great Britain and Northern Ireland on the very day that the Dow-Jones Index goes up nineteen points. Starting to tell the Press all about it, he was cut short by the Queen, who after jeeping 2,400 feet up a mud mountain to eat a plate of re-fried beans might perhaps have begun wondering about the point of it all. Dimly visible through the mist, the backsides of two riderless horses glistened in the adjacent field.

But the Queen and the President had ridden together in England, and if Reagan gets re-elected they will no doubt ride together again. Back went Her Majesty to spend the night in the *Britannia*, still stuck at Long Beach. Thence next

morning she commuted to San Francisco in Air Force Two,
the President's spare Boeing 707, which landed in a plume of
jetwash as the drenched media cowered on a flatbed truck.
When the Queen stepped down to meet female Mayor
Feinstein, the rain magically ceased. 'She's smiling!' cried a
local television front-person. 'That's a first!'

The merry mood intensified when the Queen checked into
forty-six rooms of the St Francis Hotel, because the media
were staying there too, although only in one room each. The
American media started interviewing the British media
about whether this sort of thing happened very often. The
British media, who were getting to like being interviewed,
casually suggested that it happened every day. Suddenly all
the limelight switched to their star, James Whitaker, who
had arrived from London and moved into the studios of San
Francisco's very own KRON-TV. Billed as Royal Reporter
James Whitaker, he immediately established a special
relationship with KRON's beautiful anchor-person Jan
Rasmusson. 'Edward VIII,' he told Jan, 'was a person who
put his own feelings ahead of duty.' The Queen, he made it
clear, wasn't like that.

Whitaker's magisterial tone sealed the alliance between
the Palace and the British media. Nothing could now keep
the San Francisco stopover from being a success, even if the
water level at the Alviso sewage treatment plant went over
nine feet and automatically dumped the raw effluent of a
million people into the bay.

When the Royals plus Nancy snuck out for a quiet dinner
at Trader Vic's, they found Whitaker already there talking
to the cameras. Next morning there was a show at Symphony
Hall that left the Twentieth Century-Fox Entertainment for
dead. Tony Bennett sang 'I Left My Heart in San Francisco',
a song that makes little sense if the singer is in San Francisco
at the time, but what the heck.

That night in Golden Gate Park there was a protest rally
involving 136 separate organisations, one of which consisted
of a bearded man in a lace ball gown, but as the Royals and
the Reagans sat down to a State dinner for 250 guests,
including Joe DiMaggio, it was clear that the Scuba Tour

had turned into a hit. The memories, as they say locally, Will N. Doer.

Observer
6 March, 1983

Dedicated Follower

F OR THE reporters and photographers of the international fashion circus, London comes between Milan and Paris. Once just an interlude, in recent years British Designer Week has taken on an importance all its own, and this year it promised to be a relief after Italy, where the big names had drowned their models in gold lamé. Choked by ostentation, the fashion circus fought to get on the planes to London, where the young designers, having less to spend, must perforce try harder to be fresh.

The first show I saw was by John McIntyre, who a few days previously had been broke to the wide. His backer had dropped out. Then a new backer stepped in. This was heavy drama, which the collection duly reflected. Inspired by Vita Sackville-West, Violet Trefusis and their passionate alliance, the clothes emphasised discipline. The riding coats were severely cut and the riding crops meant business. Jodhpurs made of unlikely materials looked floppily soft, but the high boots came down hard. It was made clear that Sissinghurst Sapphism took no prisoners.

Pretending to be either Vita sizing up Violet or vice versa, the models glared hungrily, their diamanté beauty-spots sparkling in the photo-flash. Their lips were bruised purple. Female *Wehrmacht* officers had met the Lesbos Olympic riding team and pitilessly kissed. Most of the outfits looked fairly unwearable by any woman not planning to invade a

Polish monastery on horseback, but there were some handsome long coats with crewel-work lining on the outside and the furry outside inside.

I was able to watch the next show with my legs uncrossed. Wendy Dagworthy favours a lot of lighthearted skipping and jumping by the models. The clothes, when they weren't moving too fast to be visible, seemed mainly to consist of Yugoslavian army surplus, eked out with some Korean War-vintage kapok-quilted combat jackets. The girls wore men's shoes of the type that you see despairingly offered on the bargain racks outside the shop – size 11½ yellow leather casuals with elasticised gussets to chafe the instep. The occasional ensemble of Kandinsky cotton smock over banana plaid, or *tricoteuse* cap plus 38th Parallel pyjamas, had the same allure as the layered look which has recently been brightening the streets, and which certain members of my family hope to achieve by stealing my shirts out of the drier.

Betty Jackson's show was next on the morning's tight schedule. From the catwalk tent at the Commonwealth Institute the fashion circus set off towards Olympia. The *Observer*'s contingent moved at a brisk trot. *Vogue*'s rapid deployment force went in their own minibus. American buyers rode in limousines. Everybody got there at the same time and jammed the Wedgwood-veneered venue.

Betty Jackson's overnight success has been twelve years coming, with the result that her clothes look wearable even at their weirdest. At first I saw big shoulders and thought aha! Montana. Then I saw long sweaters and thought aha! Sonia Rykiel. But Jackson has her own way, especially with wool. The black medieval student suits were cutely strict, an effect reinforced by lorgnettes and half-glasses.

Black and silver brocade pants suits with silk shirts underneath looked very classy. They were greeted by a storm of photo-flash, indicating that all the correspondents had signalled their photographers to get the snap. When the air turns white you know it's a hit outfit. The same almost applied to the black velvet pants plus transparent black lace top, but the brassière was hard to ignore in there, like an inadequately camouflaged gun emplacement.

Instead of visiting the Emanuels' show, I skived off for lunch. The Emanuels are a charming duo but I had not forgiven them for decking the Princess of Wales in a wedding dress that so thoroughly disguised her beautiful figure, or for lumbering Karen Barber with puffed sleeves in the European ice-dancing championships. Women's clothes should not fight the woman, in my view.

If my view was old-fashioned, Jasper Conran seemed to share it. His was the first show of the afternoon, and immediately impressed with its authority. Apart from a few sweaters which made the girls look as if they were auditioning for the Los Angeles Rams defensive line, there was nothing extreme. His jumbo trench coats were more roomy than threatening, and the general look of black and grey was made lush with velvet trim and purple silk scarves. Having found the day a bit shrill so far, I was glad to find that somebody could sing from the chest register.

Conran's long skinny black jersey silk shifts would have been hard to wear for any woman with ordinary protuberances. Even some of the rail-thin models seemed to have acquired an extra pair of nipples at the hip, although I was soon told that these were bumps raised by the seams of their tights. Generally, however, the clothes were user-friendly.

There was a mightily pretty yellow brocade pants suit with a deep green velvet coat and cap. It turned the air white, yet would still look good on a short girl. Too many designers make clothes that will hang properly only on Jerry Hall. Yves Saint-Laurent, a cannier operator, never designs anything that can't be worn by Paloma Picasso, who can walk between Jerry Hall's legs without ducking. Saint-Laurent's is not an entirely disproportionate name to invoke, because Conran already has something of the same knack for stamping an identity on a whole collection without resorting to optical mayhem.

Wanting the same kind of restraint from Body Map, of course, would be like wanting Tina Turner to take a vow of silence. Back at the Commonwealth Institute, Body Map's was the last show of the day, and the fashion circus, which is able to keep going only because of the mildly speedy side-effects of Feminax, was feeling pretty whacked.

Body Map woke everybody up. All the shows had featured boy models along with the girls, but Body Map also fielded small children and the designers' mothers. 'Body Map presents the half world,' drivelled the commentator in sepulchral tones. Girls raced past in black lipstick, tasselled PVC platform boots, satin acetate tart-trotter frocks with Zen stickers, and G-strings worn over the loon pants instead of underneath. The artificial fabrics were so tacky it was obviously a matter of conviction.

Shirred petroleum by-products were edged with flatworm ruffles. Boys chosen for their Chelsea supporter faces did karate kicks to reveal that their printed cling-film posing pouches were holding them in as well as up. Linoleum-look bathing suits for the girls had terraced frills at the back, a 40-year plunge into the past. Long woollies, the only clothes you could imagine even a madwoman wearing twice, were stacked with frills from neck to hem, like floppy toy pagodas.

Pushing back the limits is an activity subject to the law of diminishing returns, which in Body Map's case must surely soon set in. Meanwhile the fuss helps to keep the fashion circus on the *qui vive*, instead of just spending a dozy week pre-Paris. London's profile goes up, the buyers flock in, the rich look smart, the smart get rich and the innocent go broke.

Observer
24 March, 1985

~⌒~

Some of the designers mentioned above were out of business within the year. Foreign visitors had come to marvel, but went away without buying anything. A German fashion correspondent told me why. It wasn't because the clothes were too challenging, it was because they weren't well-finished enough. The message for the aspiring young designer ought to be plain: if you want to be Jean Muir, learn to sew.

Part Six

IN THE HALL OF
ICONS

Ugh!

I F YOUR Superbowl money, like mine, was on the Redskins, the game started to go wrong even before the Raiders blocked that punt in the fifth minute. The game went wrong before it began. It went wrong when 'The Star-spangled Banner' was sung by Barry Manilow.

How can such an intense feeling as not being able to stomach Barry Manilow put you in a minority? But such is the case. Nobody you know can stand four bars of him. Yet everybody you don't know thinks he is marvellous. Apart from those people with whom you are personally acquainted, the entire population of the world worships Barry's loose trousers just because they are draped around the jutting, bony bottom which poses and pouts on top of his pipe-cleaner legs like a second face even more impertinent than the first.

When he flutters the eyelashes on his first face in the feigned self-adoration that is really self-adoration, untold millions of people actually *like* him. They want more instead of less. How can this be? You can start finding out with *Barry Manilow in Concert* (Guild), a tape which does for the Manilow fan what the old EMI COLH Beethoven piano sonata LPs with the green sleeves did for admirers of Artur Schnabel.

An open-air crowd the size of the one at Gandhi's funeral is already roaring in a collective frenzy before a bongo crescendo brings Barry on in a detergent-blue suit with diamanté trim. 'Seems I've been away-ayy! For ever!' The fans let him know that for him to miss them is as nothing compared to them missing him. He is moved by the mere fact of this rapport. Underneath the mock-nervous self-criticism of his patter ('Ah, come on Barry, *relax*!') is the supreme confidence of a crowd-pleaser whose

239

crowd is already pleased just to have obtained a ticket.

But though the deal is all sewn up in advance, Barry sings as if the adoration of the multitude were forfeit. When he sings of the love between himself and a woman, the emphasis is on the near-impossibility of a passion so fervent being durable as well. There is a lot about givin' it a try, gettin' through, we can work it out, we can make it *last*. The enraptured fans clearly believe that they are all included. He loves them so much that there will have to be a miracle, lest the fire consume itself.

After the opening set he mimes exhaustion. Were he to quit the stage now it would be like Byron leaving town: they would be slashing their wrists. But Barry, true to his code, remains. All he does is remove his jacket, thus to reveal a dinky white waistcoat defining a chest which it would otherwise take weight-training to render visible. This is not your standard macho stud body. From certain angles this is not even your standard lamp. But it has resilience. Barry is not just skin and bone. He is also cartilage, especially in the nose.

Barry's hair, a tea cosy woven from carrot peelings, surrounds a knowing smile. Something is about to happen. The spotlight turns inside-the-refrigerator blue. He claps his hands. His long feet shuffle forward with the weird syncopation made possible by two knees in each leg. He cries 'Ugh!' just off the beat while twitching his pelvis forward, as if goosing a sheep on roller-skates. 'It's got to be the Noo York rhythm in my life!'

From then on, Barry is unstoppable. He roams the stage like a wild beast unleashed – a gerbil on the rampage. He can say naughty things because every woman out there is his mother. 'We have been rehearsing our little *buns* off, gang!' This is the rap on the move, a technique of which he is the most accomplished exponent since Sammy Davis Jr, with the difference that Barry, careful not to infringe the rule by which the only thing he can do that the audience can't is sing in tune, never says a single even remotely funny thing. 'Hoo! Hey! All *right*!' To which the audience replies 'Ayy!' As Wallace Stevens once remarked, art must be abstract.

But sing in tune Barry does. Nobody, not even John Denver, ever got to be a big star by accident, especially in middle-of-the-road music, where people know what they want, even if the rest of us find it hard to believe they want it. Further out towards the edge, there is more room for the occasional freak with nothing to offer except nausea, but even there the ability to persist is nearly always a sign of virtue.

Britain's very own Kate Bush has carried on like a dingbat from day one, but only the deaf deny she is gifted. It has to be admitted, however, that only the blind appreciate her straight away. A healthy, well-shaped girl, she dresses to frighten the horses. Her costumes, décor and dance-routines – all controlled, like her music and lyrics, by Kate herself – are well to the fore on *Kate Bush: The Single File* (EMI). The video pop single is allegedly an up-and-coming art form, but surely after Kate it can only be down-and-going. This has to be the apex.

As you might expect, Kate's monster hit single 'Wuthering Heights' is on early. Wearing a négligé which might just conceivably have belonged to one of the Brontë sisters if any of them looked like Donald O'Connor and wore diamond earrings in bed, she makes a deceptively normal start by dancing the number in multiple image to sub-Martha Graham unarmed-combat choreography.

Things warm up later on, until with 'Suspended in Gaffa' – yet another addictive tune, with yet another set of demented lyrics – we find her clad in palest lilac pedal-pushers and aluminium gauntlets, crying 'I don't know why I'm crying' while doing Kung-Fu calisthenics in a South-East Asian warehouse full of dust.

Your eyes get a quieter time with *Kate Bush Live at the Hammersmith Odeon* (EMI), since with a stage show she can't change drag for every number. But you still have to contend with the way she looks when, instead of miming to playback, she is warbling and trilling into a microphone wired directly to her skull, so that she may be free to dance herself silly in a Superman leotard, plus leg-warmers, pith helmet, flippers, etc.

Kate is full of serious messages – she has sussed out, for example, that nuclear war is bad for you – but a deep and true showbiz instinct tells her that they are best delivered *per media* the maximum possible concentration of production values. That's what she's doing upside-down in a silver bubble making mouths like Carmen Miranda: getting your attention by impersonating a yodelling embryo.

In the days when Kate was a real embryo, Elvis Presley was already getting old. As we now know, he got old faster than most people because of the various toxins he was pushing into himself. A less well-appreciated fact is that the end of his career was almost as productive as the beginning. *Elvis Presley on Tour* (MGM/UA) shows him in his dotage. The high-collared costumes designed to minimise his jowls make him look like one of his own look-alikes. A few tired passages of pastiche karate have to fill in for the body language that wowed the world when he was young. But never since his first Sun records has he made such hard-driving music. The big ballads are the usual tedium, but the Nashville guitars on the blues-based and country songs bring the melody out of him as if the spring were still clear instead of clouded. Rhythm, his sixth sense, was still there even after the other five were gone.

Observer
29 January, 1984

~~

When, after ten years, I gave up my *Observer* television column in 1982, there remained the question of how best to work out my contract. Video seemed a logical area of further interest. I started to write about it once a month, with the idea of choosing, from the already endless supply, tapes to fit a given theme each time. Really it was a chance to write about anything, but a difficulty soon emerged that I might have expected at the start had I been less eager. The reading public had not been watching the same tapes. So the luxury I had enjoyed with the television column, of writing to topics which were fresh in the reader's mind, was not there. Too spoiled to do without that, I dismantled the project before the first year was up. While it was running, however, I gave it my best attention, and the three pieces here included could have been written on no other pretext. The opportunities were infinite. That was just the trouble. There is also the possibility that I had grown soft. Making a spectacle of myself on television, I had begun to feel too much sympathy for anyone else doing the same. Not even Barry Manilow could arouse ire: just awe, and a kind of bitter gratitude, as an unfrocked priest might feel who watches an evangelis making lonely women weep.

The New Diaghilev

DISCREETLY increasing itself a few titles at a time, the 'MGM Classic Collection' (MGM/UA) has already reached the point where you need a month to take it all in. But unless your first allegiance goes to Elizabeth Taylor modelling lingerie for the fuller figure in *Cat on a Hot Tin Roof*, there can be no doubt that the musicals are what validate the word 'classic' in the collection so far. Just follow the dancing feet.

Not that even MGM had a sure-fire formula. Musicals could be either mechanical or successful, but not both. What MGM had was an inspired producer, Arthur Freed. Opinions differ about which was the very best musical with his name on it, *Singin' in the Rain* or *The Band Wagon*, made in 1952 and 1953 respectively.

Those with ambitions towards forming a library will have already purchased or stolen a video of the former, but they should note that the latter is also there for the asking, at an advertised playing-time of 108 minutes, which the first-time viewer will find is far short of how long it takes to see once. Some of the numbers will have you lunging for the rewind button before they are half over. The awful, addictive thing about video is that if you can't bear the visual high to end, it doesn't have to. *The Band Wagon* is the video drug in its pure form: cocaine for the corneas.

Freed usually made sure, sometimes too sure, that the numbers, while never clashing with the story, weren't crowded out by it. Fred Astaire is ruminatively crooning 'By Myself' only ten minutes into the picture and ten minutes after that he is in full flight with the shoe-shine dance routine, which expands into the amusement arcade production number, which in turn ends with a sight-gag so good it makes you laugh even when alone. Direction by Vincente Minnelli, screenplay by Comden and Green, choreography by Michael Kidd – everything fits together straight away because of the producer's sense of proportion. Away from Freed, no one concerned was immune from the self-indulgence that spins things out.

Even Astaire, unless advised to the contrary, would chew his dialogue ten times before swallowing. But he always danced economically even when the routine going on around him limped. *The Band Wagon* never limps, but it does sometimes swan about, especially while establishing Cyd Charisse as a ballerina, so that she can kick over the traces later on. Astaire has to do a lot of standing around flat-footed, and you would be left feeling short-changed if it were not for 'The Girl Hunt' production number at the end.

The pre-war musicals usually spaced numbers of even length evenly throughout. The post-war musicals favoured a tease-play approach by which numbers that weren't long enough led up to a flag-waving finale that went on longer than you could believe, or – as happened particularly when Gene Kelly was involved – could bear. But 'The Girl Hunt' brings *The Band Wagon* to a blissful climax. Astaire and Charisse finally get to strut their full range of stuff, including a two-minute jump-time jazz dance duet which is the most exhilarating thing of its kind on film.

It's the sequence set in the Dem Bones Café, starting from

when Astaire enters with his hat over his eyes. Charisse is perched on a bar stool with her coat done up. She sheds the coat and unfolds that marvellous figure, which would have been poetic even if she hadn't been able to dance – although if she hadn't been able to dance she wouldn't have looked like that. When the film came out I saw it over and over just for those few minutes. When I found out that her real name was Tula Ellice Finklea I only loved her more.

On the Town is earlier and less lush. Freed is once again in charge, but Stanley Donen is keener than Minnelli to cut out the fashion photography and keep things moving. This quality paid off when Gene Kelly was, as here, the star. A Kelly ballet, if left unguarded, would swell to absorb the entire movie. But in 1949 they still had the clock on him.

Since he is one of three sailors on shore-leave, and since each sailor has a girlfriend, Kelly gets, theoretically at least, only 16⅔ of the total screen time to bare those perfect teeth and/or rise slowly on *demi point* with his bottom tensed. Otherwise Ann Miller bares her perfect legs and Betty Garrett lures Frank Sinatra up to her place – a rare example, for the time, of a lady taking the lead. The way Sinatra's voice comes sidling through the ensembles tells you what tone has that loudness hasn't.

But the producer is the real hero. Five of the six leading characters are wrecking the natural history museum with a song-and-dance routine almost as soon as the picture starts. The sixth character, Vera-Ellen, is an aloof ballerina, but luckily for us she has to earn a secret living as a sideshow dancer on Coney Island, so in the fullness of time she burns the boards with the rest of the gang, and thus obliges Kelly to stop indulging in his least endearing facial expression, shy awe. 'Gosh Ivy, I mean Miss Smith, I . . .'

It didn't matter so much if he talked like that, as long as he eventually danced. In *Anchors Aweigh* he is still talking half an hour into the picture and not a dancing foot has been heard, nor has Sinatra sung a note. Freed's name is not on the credits. Once again it is the story of sailors getting liberty, but this time you want them to be deprived of it.

The Barkleys of Broadway ought to be, on paper, a better bet.

Freed is in charge, Comden and Green do the script, and Fred Astaire stars with Ginger Rogers. What can go wrong? One tends to conclude that Charles Walters couldn't direct musicals, but it can only have been the producer's fault that when you finally finish waiting for the first number it turns out to be Oscar Levant playing 'Ritual Fire Dance'. Freed had not yet made *On the Town*, but he was no beginner: *Meet Me in St Louis* was already behind him.

While Homer nods, the two stars cool their heels, no doubt remembering the blessed days of black and white. But it wasn't colour that deprived musicals of their simplicity. It was choreography. The form became so organic that only a producer of genius could keep it under control. In the pre-war Astaire musicals the dances were created by the star himself, with the assistance of Hermes Pan. Together, they knew exactly what was right for him – the routines were balletic only in the metaphorical sense of being light as air, even when he was kicking holes in the floor. Post-war, ballet took over, with *An American in Paris* providing merely the most gargantuan example. Kelly was ballet-prone anyway, but even Astaire got sucked in.

It was Art with a capital A and it spelt death to the screen musical, a tradition which had previously managed to free itself from the cold hand of Busby Berkeley, whose production numbers looked like colonies of bacteria staging a political rally under a microscope. But from ballet there was no escape. Shoes which had worn taps wanted to point their toes. The new energy fell for the only temptation that could kill it – going legit. Strangely enough it was the genius who fell hardest. Arthur Freed was the new Diaghilev until he tried to be like the old one.

Observer
26 February, 1984

Making a Whore Movie

D ON'T FEAR for your children just because someone in
Making Michael Jackson's Thriller (Vestron/Palace) keeps
saying how proud he is to have made a whore movie. He
means a horror movie. Michael Jackson's *Thriller*, starring
Michael Jackson, was the video promo of his hit single.
Making Michael Jackson's Thriller is an hour-long video about
how they made the promo, and is itself now a hit video,
available at low price so that your offspring can talk you
into buying it for them and then drive you crazy with
it.

You could do worse, although after your first look at
Michael Jackson it might seem hard to imagine how. He is
not the prepossessing tot some of us remember from the
heyday of the Jackson Five. Four of the Five having hived off,
Michael has been left older, taller and weirder. He is very
handsome in a nose-job sort of way, but a fluorescent light
has been turned on behind his eyes, making him look like an
all-night delicatessen, or Little Richard turning into a wolf.
This is a big help in the 'Thriller' number, which is all about
turning into a wolf.

The number, which is really a bit of a plod, occupies
the first few minutes of the tape. Michael sees a werewolf
movie with his girl and then, while walking her home, turns
into a wolf himself. Zombies rise from the grave and join in
the dance, their artfully tattered flesh suggesting death,
corruption and a high capital outlay.

The rest of the tape is about how they spent the money. It
turns out that Michael's features, though vulpine from the
start, were assisted in their transformation by plastic whis-
kers, yellow contact lenses, etc. There is much proprietorial
talk from the film director John Landis, who looks pretty
horrible himself, but perhaps the children will not notice.

247

What they and you will positively like, however, are the plentiful samples of Michael dancing.

As a singer he is good in the Frankie Lymon sweet-scream tradition, but as a dancer he is in the Bojangles bracket, a fact attested to by Fred Astaire, who taped Michael's performance of 'Billie Jean' at the Tamla 25th Anniversary Concert and told him next day that he was a great little mover. That same performance is included here and you will bless the rewind button for letting you see how Mr Jackson sings with his feet. All there is is him, the microphone and the band.

A better number better sung and better danced than 'Thriller', if it doesn't teach your children that a big budget isn't everything, it might at least take you back to the real magic of Motown, when the choreography was limited and sharpened by how long the backing vocalists had to spin on the spot before getting back to the mike. But you can't tell the young ones about your memories. They want their own memories, which Michael Jackson is now supplying. Watching him turn into a wolf is as delightful to them as watching them turn your money into a cheap tape is depressing for you.

After the monster success of *Raiders of the Lost Ark* as an own-your-own-feature-film video, *Flashdance* (CIC) is the next bid to work the same trick. The difference, however, is that *Flashdance* is not enough of a movie to be a bargain at the low price. Despite a large helping of Jennifer Beals's pretty if impassive face, a low price is just about right. Anyone overwhelmed at getting so much for so little will have to be a big fan of the same young lady's pretty but not at all impassive behind, which does a lot of high-frequency vibrating in close-up.

There are rumours that someone else's bottom was used for the tight shots, while Jennifer's actual fundament was in the dressing-room learning its moves for next day, but after my recent analysis of Barry Manilow's gluteal histrionics I don't want this column to get a reputation for being bum-struck. Sufficient to say that *Flashdance* is predicted on one assumption: that Ms Beals's harmonically agitated tush is a brave sight.

So it is, but perhaps its effect would be less if the rest of her had more to do. The plot is from any episode of *Fame*. A welder by day, Jennifer dances provocatively in a bar by night, but what she really wants to do is get into ballet school. She is so talented that all she need do is apply, but it takes her the whole movie to get her courage up, because of the timidity induced by social deprivation. Not, be it noted, social inferiority: this is an American movie, not a British one.

Pittsburgh is exquisitely photographed, as if it were Venice. The urban blight looks as good as in *Rocky* and similarly survives scaling-down for the small screen, but only Ms Beals's well-turned body can explain the video's chart-topping sales in the United States, where Dad's undivided attention proved that here was a show for all the family, and not just for the daughter dreaming of being a ballerina, or anyway dreaming of being a movie star dreaming of being a ballerina.

As for the dancing, apart from a few glimpses of the longed-for ballet class it is all disco, with all of disco's limitations. Ms Beals strutting about and punching the air is a lot more appealing than John Travolta doing the same thing, but the choreographic vocabulary is inherently famished. A solitary sequence of break-dancing by street urchins is the most alive part of the picture. In break-dancing, even if the music is monotonous, the different parts of the body are at least reacting differently. One of the break-dancers does a flat fall on to his back that will make you wonder if that wasn't how the style got its name. Ms Beals looks on with the mysterious smile of one who will soon throw away her lunch pail, tie on a pair of satin point shoes and marry her Porsche-driving boss, who despite owning the factory is a macho hunk.

Erstwhile macho hunks now buckling at the knees might be revived by *Playmate Review* (CBS/Fox), the latest attempt by *Playboy* magazine to repackage its ethos in video form. Its predecessors, *Playboy Video Collector's Edition I & II*, tried hard to give you something of the mag's fabled scope and sweep, including enough *obiter dicta* from Hugh M. Hefner to

convince you that he might indeed be the greatest philo-
sophical brain since Hugh M. Hegel. But the centre-fold
girls were undoubtedly the main event, and this latest
compilation, subtitled '10 Intimate Playmate Portraits',
sensibly includes nothing but.

The Playmates, like the heroine of *Flashdance*, don't want
you to think they are just pretty bodies. Called such names as
Kelly Tough and Shannon Tweed, they have deep reasons
for taking their clothes off. 'I'm excited about the oppatoon-
ity to be a Playmate. I think I've learned a lot about myself.'
She has learned, among other things, how to go big-game
fishing in the nude. 'I dew feel like I have an affinity for the
ocean.' Inevitably this affinity is best demonstrated by a lot
of lying around naked on deck, alone with the sea and with
nobody else in sight except the camera crew hanging from
the mast-head.

'I have the *greatest* family,' says Patti Farinetti. 'My
mother's behind me in everything I dew, and she's very
proud of me. Wherever we go, she says, "This is my daugh-
ter! The one who was in *Playboy*!"' All the girls have sup-
portive mothers. ('Supportive' is an American word
meaning 'insane'.) Some of them even have supportive boy-
friends, such as Kim McArthur's fiancé Cal. 'I think Kim
has *grown* a great deal because of her involvement with
Playboy.'

The emphasis on self-realisation is universal. 'Look where
I am today,' says Patti or Kelly or Kim or Shannon. 'It's
really unbelievable.' And it really is. Kelly Tough, for
example, is out in the woods, lying around starkers next to a
camp fire. 'Noodity and camping go together as far as I'm
concerned.' Kelly seems undaunted by the possibility that a
bear might eat her, or worse. 'After you become a Playmate
you learn confidence,' she says gratefully, having interpreted
the camera's unrelenting attempt to get between her legs as
an offer of assistance in her quest for fulfilment.

Clearly she is a nice girl. They are all nice girls. With the
current clamp-down on hard-porn videos, soon these nice
girls will be all that's left. It should be a comfort, but
somehow they are far scarier than the hookers, perhaps

because they find it all so natural. That's it: they have
nothing to hide.

Observer
6 May, 1984

Pictures in Silver

Camera Lucida: Reflections on Photography by Roland Barthes, translated by Richard Howard (Jonathan Cape, 1982)

T HE FLOW of photographic images from the past suggests
that what we are already experiencing as a deepening
flood in the present will seem, in the near future, like a
terminal inundation. Most of the theoretical works purport-
ing to find some sort of pattern in the cataract of pictures only
increase the likelihood that we will lose our grip. But oc-
casionally a book makes sense of the uproar. Appearing in
the author's native language just before his death, Roland
Barthes's *Camera Lucida*, now published posthumously in
English, will make the reader sorrier than ever that this
effervescent critic is no longer among the living. Barthes was
the inspiration of many a giftless tract by his disciples but he
himself was debarred by genuine critical talent from finding
any lasting value in mechanised schemes. By the end of his
life he seemed very keen to re-establish the personal, the
playful, and even the quirky at the centre of his intellectual
effort, perhaps because he had seen, among some of those
who took his earlier work as an example, how easily method
can become madness.

Whatever the truth of that, here is a small but seductively
argued book which the grateful reader can place on the short

shelf of truly useful commentaries on photography, along with Walter Benjamin's *Das Kunstwerk im Zeitalter seiner technischen Reproduzierbarkeit*, Susan Sontag's *On Photography*, John Szarkowski's promotional essays, and the critical articles of Janet Malcolm. Also asking for a home on the same shelf is the recently published *Photography in Print*, edited by Vicki Goldberg and including many of the best shorter writings about photography from its first days to now. As well as the expected, essential opinions of everyone from Fox Talbot to Sontag, there are such out-of-the-way but closely relevant pieces as a reminiscence by Nadar which suggests that Balzac pre-empted Benjamin's idea about photographs robbing an object of its aura; a stunningly dull critique written by one Cuthbert Bode in 1855 which shows that photography has always generated, as well as a special enthusiasm, a special intensity of patronising scorn; and a brilliantly turned *Hiawatha*-metre poem by that fervent shutterbug Lewis Carroll.

> From his shoulder Hiawatha
> Took the camera of rosewood
> Made of sliding, folding rosewood;
> Neatly put it all together.
> In its case it lay compactly,
> Folded into nearly nothing;
> But he opened out the hinges,
> Pushed and pulled the joints and hinges,
> Till it looked all squares and oblongs,
> Like a complicated figure
> In the second book of Euclid.

There is, of course, a much longer shelf, indeed a whole wall of long shelves, packed with commentaries which are not particularly wrong-headed. But they are platitudinous, and in the very short run it is the weight of unobjectionable but unremarkable accompanying prose which threatens to make a minor art boring. The major arts can stand the pressure.

Barthes at his best had a knack for timing the soufflé. The

texture of *Camera Lucida* is light, making it suitable for a heavy message. The message is heavy enough to be called subversive. Barthes finds photography interesting, but not as art. An awful lot of would-be artists are going to be disappointed to hear this. But before they smash up their Nikons in frustration they should hear the argument through, because if Barthes is disinclined to treat photographers as artists he is uncommonly inclined to examine what they do with an intelligently selective eye. 'A photograph is always invisible,' he writes, 'it's not it that we see.' Barthes says that what we see is the subject matter: 'the referent adheres'. Barthes airily dismisses all talk of composition. Indeed he goes a long way towards saying that a photograph hasn't got any formal element worth bothering about. He claims for himself, where photography is concerned, 'a desperate resistance to any reductive system' – pretty cool, when you consider the number and aridity of reductive systems his example has given rise to.

Barthes says that what he brings to the average photograph is *studium* – general curiosity. What leaps out of the exceptional photograph is a *punctum* – a point of interest. In Kertész's 1926 portrait of Tristan Tzara (unfortunately not reproduced in this book), the *studium*, says Barthes, might have to do with a Dadaist having his picture taken but the *punctum* is his dirty fingernails. In William Klein's photograph, 'Near the Bowery' (1954), you and I might have our attention drawn by the toy gun held to the smiling boy's head, especially if the scene arouses an echo of the Viet Cong prisoner being summarily executed in one of the most famous pieces of news film footage to have come out of Vietnam. But Barthes can't help noticing the little boy's bad teeth. Barthes is not always startled by what the photographer finds startling and is never startled by what the photographer rigs to be startling – abstract and surrealist concoctions leave him cold.

A photograph, says Barthes, does not nostalgically call up the past. Instead it shows the past was real, like now. Photography proves the past to be a reality we can no longer touch. Instead of the solace of nostalgia, the bitterness of separation. Photography is powerless as art but potent as magic. Thus his little book concludes as it began, with a confident emphasis on subject matter.

When John Szarkowski, in his 1966 critical anthology *The Photographer's Eye*, showed that for every master photographer's laboriously created definitive statement there was at least one amateur snapshot equally interesting, the photographic world had the choice of inferring either that the artists weren't artistic or else that the amateurs were artistic too. On the whole the latter course was taken, mainly because Szarkowski so persuasively extended the range of what it was possible to discuss about a photograph, so that the mere business of selecting what to shoot stood revealed for what it is – an artistic choice at some level, however diffident.

Similarly Barthes's potentially devastating re-emphasis is mollified by his willingness to concede that the selectivity involved is not just his own unusually receptive eye for the *punctum*. The photographer is allowed the faculty of selectivity too. Barthes does not seem to allow even the best photographer much more, but perhaps he just never got around to developing his argument, which nevertheless is an attractive one as it stands. If one famous American classical photographer's photograph of trees has ever worried you by looking indistinguishable from another famous American classical photographer's photograph of trees, here is a way out of your dilemma. The identity of subject matter tends to render the alleged compositional and tonal subtleties nugatory in each case. There is no reason to feel guilty just because we have got one of the Westons mixed up with one of the others.

The composition of a photograph can be analysed usefully, but not as long as it can be analysed uselessly. As with a literary work, there is a line to be drawn between the critical remark that yields meaning and the analytical rigmarole which tells you little beyond the fact that some ambitious young academic has time on his hands. Barthes's thesis is a refreshing simplification. But a fresh look doesn't always simplify. In *Before Photography: Painting and the Invention of*

Photography, the catalogue for the Museum of Modern Art exhibition which will next be seen in Los Angeles and Chicago, Peter Galassi cunningly advances the deceptively simple thesis that some paintings prepared the way for the invention of photography by manifesting 'a new and fundamentally modern pictorial syntax of immediate, synoptic perceptions and discontinuous, unexpected forms'.

Galassi's argument has already been examined at some length by Charles Rosen and Henri Zerner. I will not rehearse their analysis beyond saying that they find Mr Galassi's achievement as impressive as I do. They argue that Mr Galassi gives an incomplete account of perspective. Galassi says that over the centuries the original pictorial strategy, to make a three-dimensional world out of a flat medium, gradually reversed itself, and became the new pictorial strategy of making a flat picture out of a three-dimensional world – at which point photography, which might have been invented much earlier if anyone had really wanted it, finally showed up in order to answer the new need. Rosen and Zerner recommend that Galassi should take into account the implications of the empirical representation developed by the fifteenth-century Flemish painters. No doubt they are right, but I can think of someone else who might fit Galassi's theory even more instructively – Velázquez.

As Ortega explains in *The Dehumanisation of Art*, Velázquez was the first to look into the distance with a dilated pupil and so blur the focus of things near. That is why foreground figures in some of his pictures – one thinks particularly of 'Las Meninas' – look so strange. They are strange because they are the unexamined familiar. They look the way things look when we are looking past them, as if they were floating, *converdidas en gases cromáticos, en flámulas informes, en puros reflejos*. Converted into chromatic gases, into formless flames, into pure reflections. (Ortega's writings on aesthetics are so poetic that they constitute an aesthetic problem in themselves.)

Unless I have got it hopelessly wrong, Ortega uncovered in Velázquez a concern with focus and depth of field which presages just those aspects of the photographic vision. No doubt Velázquez developed these perceptions out of a desire to mimic how the eye actually sees, but Galassi seems to be saying that the photographic pictorial strategy developed out of just that impulse, away from conceptual ordering and towards the randomly inclusive. Ortega, who said that you could see a Velázquez in one gulp, even has a vocabulary that seems ready-made for Galassi's thesis. Ortega says that the closely focused analytic vision is feudal and that the distantly focused, synthetic vision is democratic.

Doubtless other readers of Galassi's essay will have their own ideas, not just because his argument is the kind that makes us recognise something we already suspected, but because so many of us have a head full of references. By now Malraux's *musée imaginaire*, the Museum Without Walls, has transferred itself from books of reproductions into our own skulls. But a brain which already has a few hundred of the world's great paintings arranged inside it is likely to panic when asked to take in several thousand of the world's putatively great photographs as well. Yet we can retain the notion of the photographer as artist without feeling obliged to accept his every creation as a work of art.

By and large that is what John Szarkowski does in his excellent introductory essay to *The Work of Atget*, Vol. 1: *Old France*, the magnificently produced and highly desirable catalogue volume for the first of what will be four Museum of Modern Art exhibitions devoted to Atget's work, the cycle being due to complete itself in 1984. The material will take a long time to show and took even longer to get ready. Berenice Abbott gave the museum her collection of about 5,000 Atget prints in 1968. Maria Morris Hambourg, Szarkowski's co-scholar on the project, has been occupied with nothing else since 1976. Together they have performed prodigies of research, but one expects no less. Less predictable was the way Szarkowski, while diving around among all this visual wealth like Scrooge McDuck in Money Barn No. 64, has managed to keep his critical balance, something that a man with his capacity for enthusiasm does not always find easy.

Echoing the useful distinction he established in 1966

between documentary and self-expression, Szarkowski is able to divide Atget's work up into the large number of photographs which are of historical interest and the smaller number in which the historical interest is somehow ignited into an aesthetic moment – in which, that is to say, the *studium* acquires a *punctum*. But the viewer who finds his attention not only attracted but delighted by some of these pictures will be hard pressed to decide where the *punctum* is. Is it in the plough or the well, the overhanging tree or the doorway in the wall?

It soon becomes clear that the best of Atget's photographs, while they are unlikely to hold your interest as long as paintings might do that are nominally of the same subject, nevertheless owe their aesthetic authority to much more than an isolated piquancy. They really do imply some kind of controlling artistic personality, however attenuated. The notion of *punctum*, while necessary and welcome, is too limited a critical criterion to be sufficient. On the other hand, Barthes's other and larger notion, the one about the thereness of the past and the lost reality which rules out nostalgia, is underlined with full force. Leaving aside the soft tones of the albumen process, here is Old France looking close enough to touch and as irrecoverable as the Garden of Eden – an effect only increased by Atget's reluctance to include human beings even when the exposure time would have allowed it.

On a smaller scale but still good to have, *The Autochromes of J. H. Lartigue* shows us an unfamiliar side of another indisputable artist – his work in colour. The autochrome process has the effect, when the prints are reproduced today, of making everything look like a pointilliste painting. Since Lartigue's sensibility was so like Seurat's anyway, the echo effect is often uncanny, but in fact Lartigue was no more likely than his predecessor Atget to ape painting. In his late teens when he started shooting autochromes, he kept it up from 1912 to 1927. The best surviving results are given here, prefaced by a typically charming interview with the master himself.

It is a small book but makes a substantial supplement to

his indispensable *Diary of a Century*,* which chronicles his work in black and white and proves him to have been the first great lyrical celebrator of human beings at play. In black and white the relatively short exposure time enabled him to capture movement. In autochrome he couldn't do that, but his joyous personality still comes bubbling through. He had an inexhaustible supply of pretty girl acquaintances trying out new scooters, dashing brothers who built flying machines, etc. Perhaps other photographers were similarly blessed, but Lartigue knew exactly what to include in the frame and when to press the button or squeeze the bulb. Highly endowed with a knack for what Cartier-Bresson was later to call the guess, Lartigue could see a *punctum* a mile off. He could see *puncta* in clusters. In other words, he had a self to express.

As time increases the total number of photographers and it becomes increasingly obvious that there is no room for all of them to express themselves, it may become permissible to suggest that documentary interest is a sufficiently respectable interest for a photographer's work to have, and that if a photographer can go on getting good documentary results for a long time then he is artist enough. To have such a point conceded would make it easier to save some of the masterly but less than outstanding photographers of the past from an otherwise inevitable public revulsion against the indigestibly strident claims made for their seriousness.

The Photography of Max Yavno, for example, is a book well worth having. Yavno has been taking thoughtful photographs since the 1930s. Not all of them are as striking as his famous 1947 picture of the San Francisco cable car being swung on the turntable by its balletically swaying attendants. The picture adorns the jacket of this book, is superbly reproduced in a plate within, and features in just about every anthology of photographs published in the last thirty years.

---

* Remainder copies of *Diary of a Century* were still available at the Strand Bookstore when I was in New York recently. Students who want to build up their own library of important photography books should watch the remainder shops, which tend to view such items as bulky ephemera and price them low to keep them moving.

It should be possible to allow a man a few such happily sought-out and taken chances without trying to find the same significance in the rest of his work, which the law of averages dictates will be more *studium* than *punctum*. Luckily, the mandatory prose-poem captions (once again it is hard to suppress a blasphemous twinge of regret that James Agee and Walker Evans ever got together) are largely offset by an appended interview with Yavno in which he reveals himself to be admirably, indeed monosyllabically, unpretentious. Except when generously reminiscing about his fellow veteran practitioners, he keeps things on the yep-nope level, Gary Cooper style.

Much the same applies to *Feininger's Chicago 1941*, in which Andreas Feininger, in a lively introduction written forty years later, keeps his ego perhaps excessively within bounds. Forgetting to inform us that he was a Bauhaus-trained intellectual who personally invented the super-telephoto camera, Feininger gives humble thanks that he was obliged to view Chicago with the fresh eye of the displaced European. Here are parking elevators at a time when cars were just about to lose their running-boards, Union and Dearborn stations when the silver trains still ran, Lake Shore Drive before Mies van der Rohe built his apartments, and the kind of skyscraper that Stalin copied and that now exists nowhere except in the Soviet Union. Feininger presents his lost city without any accompanying verbal elegies.

The Weston family tends to be less taciturn. *Cole Weston: Eighteen Photographs* enshrines the colour work of one of Edward Weston's sons. Like Brett Weston, another son, Cole seems to have inherited from his father a deep sense of mission. As is recounted in Charis Wilson's introduction to this volume, Edward Weston had Parkinson's disease and young Cole had to help him work the camera. It's like reading about Renoir *père et fils* – an apostolic succession. On the other hand it is not like that, since the painter and the film-maker each had a separate, fully developed artistic vision which makes their blood kinship remarkable, whereas one suspects that for photography to run in the family is no more startling than for carpentry to run in the family, as a craft to be learned rather than an inner impulse to be bodied forth. Nonetheless, here are sumptuous colour prints of California surf, Nova Scotia fishing coves, Utah aspens, and similar Americana. A close-up of rust on a water tank looks like abstract expressionism, showing that painting still has its pull despite all the disclaimers. Also a nude lady seen from the same angle as the Rokeby Venus reclines on an old stone staircase in Arizona. She looks exactly like a confession that the staircase would not be very interesting without her.

Cole and Brett Weston take you back to Edward Weston, to Paul Strand, to Minor White, to Ansel Adams – to every master photographer, in fact, who has ever gone out into the American landscape and tried to isolate a clean piece of nature within his metal frame. Some of the results are collected in *American Photographers and the National Parks*, edited by Robert Cahn and Robert Glenn Ketchum. The pictures are arranged chronologically, starting with a William Henry Jackson study of Yosemite Falls in 1898. Jackson got a terrific action shot, in colour, of the Yellowstone Great Geyser in 1902. Edward Weston's Zabriskie Point picture of 1938 reminds you of just how good the old man was at waiting for the right shadows. The Ansel Adams pictures will be familiar to most readers but still stand out. They don't stand out so far, though, as to convince you that subject matter is anything less than very important. Even for Adams, to pursue too closely the light patterns on a cactus was to court inanity. In Barthes's terms, the referent adheres. If it doesn't, you've got nothing.

Adams deserves our lasting respect for the reverent skill with which he photographed a mountain, even though a modern amateur with up-to-date equipment might fluke a picture not entirely risible by comparison. After all, Adams knew what he was doing, and could do it again. So could Paul Strand when taking pictures of clapboard houses. Nevertheless *New England Reflections, 1882–1907* features, among other things, enough clapboard houses, photographed with more than enough verve, to set you wondering whether that particular form of architecture ever needed Paul Strand to bring out its full beauty. All the pictures were taken by the three Howes brothers, who formed themselves into a commercial outfit and toted their tripods around New England persuading people, obviously with profitable results, that great moments in life should be permanently recorded. The glass-plate negatives having miraculously survived to our own day, here is the permanent record. It is a fascinating little book which Richard Wilbur honours with a foreword that you might wish were longer, since Wilbur's distinguished, visually fastidious sensibility is exactly what such material requires to give it a proper context. But Gerald McFarland provides a useful historical introduction and anyway the pictures are so rich themselves that you would be drowning in *puncta* even if you didn't know where and when they came from.

All seems in order, even the home for the handicapped, whose inmates have formed up for a serene group shot as if Diane Arbus did not exist – which, of course, she as yet didn't. Here is the irrecoverable past only a few inches away. Some of the buildings are still intact, so that inhabitants of New England who buy this book will be able to stand in the right spot and look through time. Paradoxically, the Howes brothers were just going about their everyday business, with not much thought of preserving a threatened heritage, whereas Atget, who had a Balzacian urge to register his epoch, saw much of what he photographed destroyed within his lifetime, and if he were to come back now would find almost nothing left.

If a photographer wants to express himself but fears that his personal view might be short on originality, originality of subject matter is one way out of the trap. The only drawback to this escape route is that the number of subjects, if not finite, is certainly coterminous with the known universe. Already most topics are starting to look used up. In *Man as Art: New Guinea*, Malcolm Kirk has persuaded an impressive number of New Guinea natives to pose in full warlike and/or ceremonial make-up and drag. Thus we are able to observe, in plate 74, that a Western Highlands warrior male called Nigel resembles, when fully attired for battle, Allen Ginsberg in blackface with a Las Vegas hotel sign on his head.

Some of the pictures are stunning, or at least startling, but there is no denying that the natives have shown at least as much invention as the photographer, whose skill in lighting them and pressing the button can scarcely be compared to theirs in caking their skins with clay, inserting bones in their noses, and pulling on their grass skirts. Nor, more damagingly, is there any denying that we have already seen most of this in the *National Geographic*, albeit on a smaller scale. Much of the justification for these big picture books is that they give you big pictures, but there is also the consideration that what looks appropriately dramatic when bled to the edges of a full page in a magazine starts looking emptily pretentious when pumped up to folio size. Not only is it bigger than the negative, it's bigger than the reality. In real life you would learn all you need to know about Nigel without going quite so close.

Still on the *National Geographic* beat, *Rajasthan: India's Enchanted Land* comprises pictures by Raghubir Singh which suggest that its title might not be a complete misnomer, although for at least this viewer the *puncta* which are obviously meant to be bursting out of such a picture as 'A Gujar Villager, Pushkar' remain defiantly quiescent. Far from being amazed that a man with a turban is wearing a watch and smoking a cigarette, I'd be amazed if he were not. More exciting, or less unexciting, is another shot in which all the village males, after a hard day's work supervising the women, are rewarding themselves by sucking popsicles. There is a foreword by Satyajit Ray to remind us that for Indian artists of all kinds Rajasthan is a fairly resonant part of the subcontinent, but you can see how a foreign photographer with a reputation to make might want a more jazzy angle.

In *Falkland Road, Prostitutes of Bombay*, Mary Ellen Mark shows how this can be done. She moved in with the eponymous hookers, became part of the scenery, and ended up by reaching such a level of acceptance that the girls and their clients allowed her to photograph them *in flagrante*. The results are unlikely to put you off sex, with which the activities in Falkland Road seem to have only a parodic connection, but they might well put you off India. The girls work in cubicles the size of packing crates and perform their ablutions in a bucket. Hepatitis hangs in the air like aerosol spray. For the alert customer the whole deal would be a bit of a downer even if Ms Mark were not poised in the rafters busily snapping the action. The intrepid photographer contributes her own introduction, in which she spends a lot of time conveying her deep affection for the girls without ever raising the topic of whether she, too, might not be said to be drawing sustenance from the sad traffic, and in a much safer way. Still, Cartier-Bresson photographed whores in Mexico in 1934.

Already responsible for nine books, Ms Mark was born in 1940 and graduated from the University of Pennsylvania. Susan Meiselas, author of *Nicaragua*, is a Sarah Lawrence graduate who does not give her age but can safely be adjudged even younger than Ms Mark. Both women are getting well known fast, not because either of them is Giselle Freund or Lotte Jacobi reborn but because they both know how to get in and get the story. Ms Meiselas's story is the Nicaraguan version of with-Fidel-in-the-Sierra, down to and including the berets, Che moustaches, and .45 automatics triumphantly raised in adolescent fists. 'Yet unlike most photographs of such material,' says an accompanying note from John Berger, 'these refuse all the rhetoric normally associated with such pictures.' Not for the first time one wonders how Berger, inventor of the purportedly illuminating concept 'ways of seeing', actually does see. His eyes certainly work differently from mine, which find Ms Meiselas's every second picture laden with rhetoric. But despite more recent reports from Nicaragua, one concedes that the rhetoric might be, in this case, on the side of the angels. Nor can it be gainsaid that people calling on themselves to be courageous often behave rhetorically. Who looks natural when nerving himself for battle?

Photographs, according to Barthes, never entirely leave the world of words. In *Visions of China* Marc Riboud's photographs taken between 1957 and 1980 constitute, even more than Eve Arnold's recent volume on the same subject, a reminder that if we know nothing about the background we might well make a hash of interpreting the foreground. Orville Schell's introduction makes much of Riboud's supposed ability to see past the rhetoric to the reality beneath. Certainly Riboud got off the beaten track and managed to hint that not all was harmony, but it should not need saying – and yet it does – that he got nowhere near recording the full impact of the Cultural Revolution, which we were allowed to see nothing of in the form of pictures and have since had to hear about in the form of words. Most of these words were emitted between sobs, since those victims who survived are often unable to recall their sufferings with equanimity.

This fact should lend additional significance to such a photograph as plate 89, 'Student Dancer, Shanghai, 1971'. It shows a radiantly happy girl being inspired by the mere presence of Mao's little red book. But in this case the *punctum*, instead of crossing from the photograph to the viewer's mind, travels in the other direction. Today's viewer will have heard that the Chinese ballerinas were sent by Mrs Mao to have their muscles ruined in the fields. The dancers were already suffering at the time when Shirley MacLaine, a dancer herself, was wondering, in her television documentary about China, why the Chinese looked so happy. The viewer haunted by these considerations is unlikely to look on Riboud's photograph of a Chinese dancer as being anything more edifying than a pretty picture.

But where any pictures are hard to get, all pictures have some value, even if they seem to point in the wrong direction until interpreted. So it is with China and so it will probably always be with the Soviet Union. Vladimir Sichov's *The Russians* deserves immediate notice, since the standard of photography in the Soviet Union is so blandly low that any attempt at realism looks like a sunburst. Sichov was born in 1945 and in 1979 was permitted to leave for the West. He brought 5,000 rolls of film out safely – his whole archive. The full effect is of a dowdiness so comprehensive that it becomes almost enthralling. Unfortunately Sichov seems to have concentrated on the routine dowdiness of old women in shapeless coats rather than the more interesting dowdiness of young ones in the latest fashions from GUM. The true visual squalor in the Soviet Union resides in what is thought to be chic, a fact which Sichov has subsequently had ample opportunity to realise, because he is nowadays an ace cat-walk photographer for the Paris fashion shows, a task to which he brings the hungry eye of a man raised during a famine. Photographers brought up on a visual diet in which swimsuits look as if they have been cut out of motel shower curtains tend to be especially grateful for what Yves Saint-Laurent hangs on Jerry Hall.

William Klein makes America look almost as scruffy as Russia but in the case of his collection *William Klein* much of the flakiness is due to inky printing. Klein has issued a protest about how his publishers have treated him and if later copies look like my early copy then he is right. Some of the pictures look like action shots of a black cat in a coal bunker. In the ones you can see, however, *puncta* proliferate. The snap Barthes liked of the little boy with the toy gun to his head is here spread over two pages, making the bad teeth more attention-getting than ever. But most viewers will probably still take the gun, rather than the teeth, to be the main point. Mainly because he runs forward to involve himself instead of hanging back to be objective, Klein is very good at catching the vivid moment. There are also pictures taken in Italy, Russia, and elsewhere, but really Manhattan, where he was born, is Klein's precinct. He can see the casual calligraphic symmetry of window signs offering breaded veal cutlets for $1.05. So could every American urban photographer back to Weegee and beyond, but the thereness never fails to grip.

More involved even than Klein, more involved even than Hemingway, almost as involved as the soldiers themselves, Don McCullin gets his camera into the war. An Englishman, McCullin started by photographing his own country's dark underside, but he was not alone. Covering Cyprus in 1964 he discovered his own bailiwick, up where the bullets were flying. Since then he has been in all the wars, most notably Vietnam, where his work was on a par with that of Philip

Jones Griffiths. But his eye is not so spoiled by the adrenalin of action that it refrains from dwelling on the aftermath. Dead soldiers in every variety of contortion and civilians in every stage of starvation are duly recorded.

Scanning the worst of McCullin's horrors, you find yourself wishing that Barthes were less right about the past really having been there. But anyone not capable of realising that these things happen will not be much struck by the photographs anyway, so John Le Carré's introductory exhortations about McCullin's mission to 'appall the comfortable' are themselves somewhat cozy. It is a characteristic of the English intellectual middle class to believe that the mass of the public is uninstructed in the world's grim realities and needs waking up. McCullin is too bravely independent to share so smug an attitude but it has helped make him famous – the most dazzling current example of the photographer singled out by subject.

Not many photographers would have the nerve to follow reality as far as McCullin does in search of their own territory, even supposing that there were any territory left. The alternative has always been to take the reality nearby and fiddle with it. By now I think it is becoming clear that for photographers abstraction and surrealism are a dry well, partly because, *pace* Galassi, painting always seems to exert at least as strong a pull on photography as photography does on painting. The moment the photographer starts treating the objects of experience symbolically, the referent ceases to adhere, and what he composes gravitates seemingly inexorably towards something already made familiar by the painters.

Herbert List: Photographs 1930–1970 collects the best work of a photographer with an impressive intellectual background. Trained by Andreas Feininger, List consorted with the visiting English writers in the Germany of the early 1930s and after leaving Germany in 1936 he became the leading purveyor of surrealist-tinged photographs to the slick magazines. But in this collection it is precisely the portrait photography which looks permanent and the surrealist compositions which seem to have been overtaken by time.

Barthes should give us the courage to confess our difficulties about getting interested in the artificially arranged *punctum*.

Most of List's cleanly lit and composed surrealist confections flare to life only when they include a couple of strapping young men standing around in G-strings. Immediately you get interested in the life going on off camera. Stephen Spender evokes some of it in the introduction, which like everything he writes about the Germany of the time makes you sorry not to have been there. He is much better than Isherwood at giving you some idea of the mental excitement. Isherwood, even today, concentrates on the physical excitement.

Drawing on their memories, writers can pursue their own tastes into old age. For photographers it is not so easy. List gave up after the war, feeling that once he had explored the limits of his own technique he was through as an artist, always supposing he had ever been one. Some of the portraits are good enough to make you think he judged himself too harshly, but there is no getting away from the fact that even with them the interest resides at least partly in the identity of the sitter. It is Morandi, Cocteau, Bérard, Chirico, Picasso, Montherlant, Auden, and Somerset Maugham who lend List renown, and not vice versa.

Anyone who finds it hard wholly to admire List is going to make heavy weather of admiring Robert Rauschenberg. *Robert Rauschenberg Photographs* shows what he has been up to in a medium to which he is not new, since he started off as a photographer. Having achieved fame, and presumably fulfilment, as a painter, he has recently revisited his first passion.

Rauschenberg's chief trick in any medium is to juxtapose ready-made images. I can remember wondering, when I saw his exhibition of paintings at the Whitechapel Gallery in the East End of London in the early 1960s, why he didn't juxtapose them more tightly, suggestively – in a word, wittily. I liked what he was doing but didn't think he took it any distance, and resented the suggestion, made on his behalf by eager commentators, that the grubby white space left in each of his large canvases was meant to give my own imagination room to work. My own imagination was already *at* work, wondering how much of Rauschenberg's allegedly selective creativity was doodling.

All the same doubts go double here, where there are not even a few swipes of paint to indicate personal intervention. In plate 45 a Mona Lisa tea-towel hangs over the back of a canvas chair which is also variously draped and decorated with discarded clothes and a folded newspaper. If you buy the theory that a pure response to the Mona Lisa is no longer possible, here is food for thought. But for anyone to whom the Mona Lisa is still the Mona Lisa whatever happens, the inevitable reaction is a fervent wish that Rauschenberg would paint his own pictures and leave Leonardo's alone.

'So what?' is not necessarily a Philistine reaction. Sometimes it is required for the preservation of sanity, especially when one is presented with the intentionally meaningless and told to find it meaningful. John Pfahl's *Altered Landscapes* shows us how a competent photographer can beautifully photograph landscapes in the same way as any other equally competent photographer can beautifully photograph landscapes, but pick up extra, reputation-making acclaim by 'altering' them, hence the title. A picture taken in Monument Valley includes a piece of red string squiggling along the ground, which enables it to be called 'Monument Valley with Red String'. Some of the pictures generate a sufficient frisson to make record album covers. Rock groups with metaphysical proclivities often favour the sort of album covers in which a line of large coloured spheres marches across the Sahara: altered landscapes for altered states.

Sam Haskins, it hardly needs saying, is better than competent, especially when photographing pretty young girls, for whom he has a hawk eye. But *Sam Haskins/Photographics* reveals a desire to be something more than the kind of craftsman whose output the uninitiated might mistake for soft porn. The term 'photo graphics' calls up Moholy-Nagy's photograms. Think of a Moholy photogram, add colour, focus the composition on the exquisitely lit, plumply swelling pantie-cupped crotch of a young girl lying back thinking pure thoughts about a sky full of roses, and you've got a Haskins photo graphic. You have to take it on trust that the picture bears no relation to a hot paragraph by Terry Southern. This is a meticulously produced book by whose technical accomplishment Haskins's fellow-photographers will no doubt be suitably cowed, but the sceptical viewer could be excused for wondering whether a picture of a rainbow shining out of a pretty girl's behind might not be a more direct indication of the artist's state of mind than the circumambient surrealist trappings.

With *Bill Brandt: Nudes 1945–1980* we are in another, less ambiguous, part of the forest. The model and inspiration for the young British photographers of the 1960s, the one home-grown loner they could admire without reserve, Brandt dedicated his career to photographing Woman in a way that would resolve her sensual appeal into a formal design. Hiding the lady's face and applying every device of elonga-tion, distortion, and convolution, he pushed the formal design towards the abstract. But it approached the abstract asymptotically, as if Brandt were aware that when the referent ceased to adhere the result would be not just no woman but no anything.

Brandt's hermetic commitment cost him a great deal and won him deserved admiration. Looking at these pictures, even the most clueless viewer will sense himself in the presence of a rare concentration of thought and feeling. But it is still possible to say, I think, that in treating the human body as a sculptural form Brandt was unable to avoid the gravitational pull of sculpture itself. Warm bottoms become cold Brancusis. Hips turn into Arps. Finally, in his most recent phase, Brandt unexpectedly and shockingly starts to load his nudes down with ropes and chains, as if it were his new ambition to take a studio on Forty-second Street or set up in partnership with Helmut Newton. It looks like a despairing confession that whereas a painter can signifi-cantly change the woman in front of him and make her part of something more significant, a photographer can't signifi-cantly change her without destroying her significance altogether. But with all that said, nobody should mistake this book for anything less than the work of a unique, isolated master photographer.

In the long run the photographers who glorified women individually, rather than rendering them all symbolically impersonal, stood a better chance of being called artists. The Hollywood portrait photographers rarely thought of themselves as much more than craftsmen, but John Kobal's essential book *The Art of the Great Hollywood Portrait Photographers* has no doubt given the survivors a higher, and well-merited, estimation of themselves. Likewise assembled by Kobal from his unrivalled archive, *Hollywood Color Portraits* is the colour supplement to the black-and-white standard work. Less weighty than its predecessor, it is still well worth having. Not only was colour less adaptable than black and white to subtle lighting; it was also much harder to retouch, so in this book you see some of the stars as they really looked, right down to the enlarged pores and – in Burt Lancaster's case – the five o'clock shadow of Nixonite tenacity.

Theories of the hunger towards realism suffer a setback when faced with this order of evidence. Black and white was the ideal, colour was the real, and the ideal looked realer. Bob Coburn's colour picture of Rita Hayworth in 1948 is just a pretty girl. 'Whitey' Schaefer's 1941 black-and-white portrait of her is an angelic visitation. Yet surely the black and white is the more true to the way she was. Not many of us who are grateful for her talent can look at such a photograph without feeling the bitterness of the irrecoverable reality that Barthes talks about. There was a day when supreme personal beauty was impossible to capture fully and so could fade without its possessor being too forcibly reminded of its loss. That time is past – one certain way, among all the conjectural ones, in which photography has changed the world.

For reasons of space and self-preservation I have had to leave many current books out of this survey. Nor are all the books I have included likely to prove essential in the long run. But *A Century of Japanese Photography* I can confidently recommend to any institution concerned with photography and to any person who can afford the price. Compiled in

Japan and presented for Western consumption by John W. Dower, the book is a treasure city, a Kyoto of the printed image. Barthes would have been so shot through with *puncta* that he would have felt like Saint Sebastian, or Toshiro Mifune in the climactic scene of *Throne of Blood*. Peter Galassi will find his theory simultaneously borne out and borne away, since so much of Japanese painting led up to photography (what else did Hiroshige and Hokusai do with their winter landscapes but bleach out the inessential?) and so many of the Japanese master photographers are drawn back into the established pictorial tradition.

Since the Meiji restoration the Japanese have been photographing one another and the inhabitants of every country they have invaded. They seem rarely to have decapitated anyone without getting some carefully framed before-and-after shots. The level of violence in the book is made even more terrifying by the degree of delicacy. You feel that you are at a tea ceremony with Mishima and that he might behead you and disembowel himself at any moment and in either order.

The photographs of war put McCullin's work in its proper perspective. McCullin might be trying to awaken our dormant psyches but for the Japanese, the gap between everyday tranquillity and stark horror seems always to have been only a step wide. And just as readily as they photographed the violence they inflicted, they photographed the violence inflicted on them. Elegantly judged, Pompeii-like photographs of the charred bodies after the Tokyo fire raids may be edifyingly compared with similar studies obtained in Nagasaki and Hiroshima. Proudly saluting from the cockpit, a kamikaze pilot taxis past a class of schoolgirls waving cherry branches in farewell. Words are needed to tell us where he is flying to, but once we know that, the picture tells us that he was there. Probably some of the schoolgirls are still alive and can pick themselves out in the picture. They were there too. Reality is the *donnée* of photography and sets the limit for how much the photographer can transform what he sees into a personal creation. For the artist photographer the limit is high but it still exists. To think it can be transcended is to be like Kant's dove, which, upon being told about air resistance, thought it could fly faster by abolishing the air.

New York Review of Books
17 December, 1981

Part Seven

THE ART OF SPORT

Ice-Dancers

Tomorrow in Ottawa the World Championships commence in which Jayne Torvill and Christopher Dean will defend their ice-dance title for the last time, so this might not be the only article on the subject in today's newspapers. But it will be the only article on the subject written by someone whose own talent for ice-dancing is beyond question.

It was at Peterborough last year that I invented the difficult ice-dancing manoeuvre now generally known in the sport as 'landing on the money'. The rink was crowded and I was attempting to astonish my small daughter with sheer speed. Twenty-five years had gone by since I had last skated, but all the old style was still there – ankles touching the ice, nose level with the knees, arms flailing. Tripping over some young fool's trailing skate, I took off, sailed high, and fell with my body so perfectly arched that my upper thighs were the first part of it to hit the ice. The small change in my trouser pocket was driven through the flesh almost to the bone. The purple bruise could not only be seen for weeks afterwards, it could be read: ELIZABETH · D. G. · REG · F. D. · 1976.

So what follows is essentially a tribute from a fellow-skater. But by now, however distinguished one's qualifications, there is no hope of attaining piercing new insights into the art of Torvill and Dean. A whole literature already exists. In addition to John Hennessy's excellent book *Torvill and Dean* (David and Charles, 1984) there are deeply researched magazine articles without number, down to and including *Family Circle*'s indispensable analysis of how Jayne cossets her dry skin, 'cleaning with RoC gentle milk and tonic and moisturising with Clinique'. All one can do, while quietly cosseting the embossed bruise on one's thigh, is to attempt a synthesis.

275

A big help in this department is a newly rush-released video called *Torvill and Dean: Path to Perfection* (Thames), which features all the glittering routines in which they have given us so much, plus several prime examples of the interviews in which they have very sensibly given us so little. Jayne's definition of the difference in character between Chris and herself is obviously the longest sentence she can, or at any rate wants to, utter. 'He panics and I don't.' The video thus reminds us directly of what the book and articles admit only by default: that these two speak a language beyond words.

Ice-dancing, until recent years, was barely respectable. Pairs skating, its snootier elder sister, was not only athletically more taxing but had an apparent monopoly of aesthetic clout. Indeed ice-dancing wasn't even an Olympic sport until 1976, by which time pairs skating was a full decade into the era pioneered by the Protopopovs, the Russian couple whose name sounded like a moped misfiring, but whose skating was so lyrical that you couldn't wait to see them again.

There was no problem about seeing them again because they won everything for years on end, but in fact the epoch they inaugurated had them as its apex. Ten years or so onward, another pair of Russians, Rodnina and Zaitsev, similarly creamed all opposition, but their awe-inspiring athleticism was no more lyrical than two mastiffs fighting on a flat-bed truck moving at 60 mph. Zaitsev was Rodnina's second partner and it was easy to believe rumours that she had eaten the first.

If anyone was going to top the Protopopovs it would have been two young Americans wonderfully called Tai Babilonia and Randy Gardner, but injury cut short their career. Even had it continued, they would have been obliged to expend much of their energy on aerobatics. That was and is, in too many senses of the word, the catch: in pairs skating the man lifts the woman up, drops her and catches her. Or he throws her away and she does three turns in the air before landing on one blade. Or three and a quarter turns before landing in the audience. In pairs skating the stunts are there for the doing and time spent on just looking beautiful costs points.

But while waiting in vain for the spirit of the Protopopovs to be reincarnated in the pairs skating, the dedicated voyeur gradually noticed that ice-dancing had outgrown its original jokey status. British couples had always been prominent in this branch of the sport but their approach, to the art-hungry eye, looked strictly *Come Dancing*, with lots of hand-posing from both lady and gentleman, the cat-suit-clad buttocks of the latter tending to be flagrantly salient. The Russians, once they put their collectivised minds to it, rapidly took over the rink, principally by fielding some sensational-looking women with long legs joined to short waists. The man's job was to show the woman off. Called something like Bustina Outalova, she was exuberance personified, obviously having been raised in a luxury one-room flat full of bootleg Beatles records.

Jazz and rock, still forbidden fruit for the Russian ballet dancers, were allowed for the ice-dancers, who, like the gymnasts, were judged to inhabit an idea-free realm in which Western influence was tolerable. Besides which, no Russian ice-dance couple ever dreamed of uncorking a hep-cat sequence of steps without following it up by a homage to the Soviet folk-dance tradition involving a lot of heel down, toe up, and arms folded. Anyone who has sat through an all-Soviet folk-dancing display in the Kremlin's Palace of Congresses knows how a single evening can seem like an entire five-year plan, but when the jollification took place on ice it was redeemed by bounce. Also the heel-kicking fervour of the quick bits favoured languor in the slow bits by way of contrast, with the world champions Moiseyeva and Minenkov looking particularly classy. Among their awed admirers in the late 1970s were the new young British couple from Nottingham, Torvill and Dean – he a policeman, she an insurance clerk, but they, in their double heart, already a single conduit of artistry.

Artistry was what they were after even in their first endeavours, although for a while it took a keen eye to spot it. They did well from the start, but with a lot of pace-changing razzle-dazzle like the Russians, while their costumes were still in the fine old British tradition of crotch-catcher cat-suit for him and bumfreezer frilled frock for her. Their new trainer, Betty Callaway, was eventually to make all the difference, because she had the international connections which could secure for them what all artists demand by right – ideal conditions. But at the beginning the Callaway Connection manifested itself mainly in a comprehensive neatening up of what they could do already.

As research now shows, however, the two-person revolution was already under way. In 1981 Torvill and Dean became European and World Champions with what looked like a refined version of the conventional fast-slow-fast free dance programme, but with hindsight it wasn't a finished product so much as a whole new heap of raw material. Sandwiched between the usual bravura displays of quick footwork there was a smouldering rumba to 'Red Sails in the Sunset'. Here could already be seen some of the pay-off for the investment they had put in by taking instruction from Gideon Avrahami, a Ballet Rambert teacher who helped them make their arms and bodies part of the total picture.

The moment the pace dropped, Torvill and Dean looked different from any other couple. It was the same in the days of be-bop: playing flat out, the great names all sounded equally bewildering, but in the slow numbers Charlie Parker emerged as the unmistakable genius. You can dazzle people with technique, but you can't move them. Torvill and Dean's first all-conquering free dance programme was stunning in the fast bits, but in the slow bits it was better than that. The idea of making the whole thing slow, however, was still too daring, or too obvious, to be seriously entertained.

Torvill and Dean's big idea snuck up on them, and on the world, through the OSP – the Original Set Pattern. As the experienced watcher of television ice-dance competitions has long been aware, this necessary preliminary to the free dance not only counts for a high proportion of the total marks, it absorbs a high proportion of the total inventiveness. Torvill and Dean made this more true than ever, to the point where their OSP began regularly transmitting a unified aesthetic charge which their free dance couldn't match until the following year, if at all.

From 1981 onwards they were competing mainly against themselves, winning everything except the 1983 European Championships, from which they were forced to withdraw after a training accident in which Jayne fell flat on her back from shoulder height, with results even more painful than those engendered by the present writer's famous thigh-dive on to the bunched coins. But they competed with themselves the way artists do, growing impatient with the merely spectacular, pushing the original to extremes, joining the intensities together.

Their first fully-thought-through free dance was the 'Mack and Mabel' routine, using undoctored music from the show of the same name. Here was the embodiment of their new prosperity. The Callaway Connection had by now won them a home-away-from-home in Oberstdorf, southern Bavaria, where they could get six hours' unhindered ice-time a day on three different rinks, one of them with mirrors. The Labour-controlled Nottingham City Council had imaginatively granted them four years' sustenance up to the 1984 Olympics. A few demented voices protested that they should therefore be training in Nottingham instead of Oberstdorf, but nobody sane wanted to see them condemned to the old, punishing, late-night sessions at the local rink. It wouldn't have been enough.

Their gold costumes, on the other hand, were too much. Poised to begin, they looked like two packets of Benson & Hedges cigarettes in a refrigerator. But if the colour was garish, the cut was a distinct improvement on days of old. Erstwhile champion ice-dancer Courtney Jones had taken command of their general appearance. Jayne's hem-lines were lower; contrariwise, her knickers were cut higher at the sides; the combined effect being a greater length of leg more decorously revealed.

Jayne is ten inches shorter than Chris and must stretch to match him on the long edges. She looks good doing so and never looked better than in the slow sections of 'Mack and Mabel'. There was a central, essentially T&D moment when she, after describing a wide circle using him as pivot, pulled him towards her as if her strength was temporarily in the ascendant. The fast sections featured comparably witty moments – there was a celebrated passage where she lay across his back doing little weightless steps sideways – but your attention was not allowed to linger. The emphasis was on breath-taking, not heart-touching.

In their slow blues OSP to 'Summertime', however, the pace was cut back to the limit the rules allowed. This wasn't dancing on ice – it was ice-dancing, a different thing. The tempo never varied but everything else did, with the movements forming an unbroken sequence which made you grateful that the rules said it must be repeated twice. Torvill and Dean, who admire Astaire and Rogers, with this routine achieved something comparable to the great Fred and Ginger dance duets in the RKO musicals of the 1930s. Dean, as Astaire was, is the innovator, and Torvill, as Rogers was, is the ideal partner, but a more instructive element of comparison is in the drive towards unity, a linking of highlights. Astaire simplified the photography until the whole routine could be filmed in one shot. Dean controlled the tempo so that there was no break in the emotional tension. Seeing the results, Fleet Street couldn't believe that Jayne and Chris were not in love. Even more unbelievable was that this miracle of compressed visual eloquence was being accompanied by the mouth organ of Larry Adler, regarded by many experts as the most verbose man in England.

Their free dance for 1982 was 'Barnum on Ice'. It was rabble-rousing stuff but struck at least one fan as several hundred intricate steps backwards. The tempo was mixed but that was only to be expected: an all-slow free dance was still inconceivable at that stage. What grated was the mime. Michael Crawford was brought in to advise on how to imitate jugglers, wire-walkers, etc. They did all this very well, but for those of us in the audience who had been brought up in film societies it aroused terrible memories of Marcel Marceau. Also it transferred the source of the action to the upper body, instead of leaving it where it belonged, in that mysterious space between the boots and the blades, the inch of air through which you can see the speeding ice. The speed is transformed upwards into beauty, which the hands can do a lot to express, but not when they are pretending to juggle.

The white and ice-blue costumes, though, were an improvement on the gold fag packets, and there was an increased use of rubato, with no fixed intervals between the two skaters – they were always catching each other up and passing, sinking only to rise, rising only to sink again. They made the stiff-backed Russian couples look like sentries. The face-freezing moment, once again in a slow section, was when she, stationary on the toe of one skate, leaned on him while he drew a circle of maximum radius around her. Wanting a whole routine of beauty-spots like that was probably like wanting a whole meal of desserts, but it was hard not to be wistful.

They granted the unspoken wish in double measure, with the *paso doble* OSP and the free dance to Ravel's *Boléro*. Each routine, in my opinion, is better than the other. The *paso doble* has a theme but it is not obtrusive. The 'Mack and Mabel' theme was a bit obtrusive because you had to know she was a comedienne; the 'Barnum' theme was very obtrusive because you had to know they were in a circus; but in the *paso doble* all you have to know is that she is not the matador's girlfriend, she is his cape. It is not hard to guess this because she is dressed in a cape, a crêpe creation carefully weighted so as to drape properly at all angles. In the properly draped crêpe cape, she is flung about by the strutting matador. The moment of truth comes when he, trailing her behind him, takes three enormous strides down the long axis of the rink, stops on one skate and goes backwards.

But the *paso doble* OSP was the same thing three times. The 'Boléro' free dance is just the one thing, steadily developing all the way through, the tempo constant but the variations manifold, the full organic wow. Once again there is a theme – something about two lovers chucking themselves into a volcano – but you don't need to know the details. The opening sequence is enough to tell you that this is a story about two kids in trouble. They are running away from something. Perhaps it is their costume designer, who has gone mad with the blue paint. But no: the silk drapes lovingly, a big advance on the days when their outfits cost them every penny they didn't have.

If the camera is in the right spot – and it is, in the version recorded on the *Path to Perfection* tape – you see a delicious moment not long after the start, when they come towards you with his arms folded around her from behind. She is wrapped up in him, head bowed. Then she seems to wake, slowly spreading her arms wide, which opens his arms too, because they have been holding hands. While this is going on they are picking up speed. At such a moment, which turns out to be the precursor of an unbroken sequence of moments equally expressive, Torvill and Dean look like figments of a love-sick imagination.

But they would be the first to admit that it is all an illusion. Jayne has a nice face but it is Princess Anne's drawn by Charles Schulz. Chris, apart from his watchful eyes, has an indeterminate set of features betraying nothing of the immense physical strength with which he can wrap Jayne around his little finger while balancing on a metal edge not much bigger than the one he shaves with in the morning. Off the ice, they are beaten hollow by the average Russian couple: a rink-minx from Minsk toting a white mink muff, backed up by a tank commander built like Lenin's mausoleum. On the ice they are transfigured from within.

And appreciated from within. Everyone gets the point. The international judges showed little resistance to this new British monopoly – not even the Russian judge, whose marking had been a point of interest ever since the night he or she gave six for technical merit after Zaitsev dropped Rodnina on her bottom with a thump that cracked the rink. More interestingly, ordinary people everywhere spontaneously decided that these two were the straight goods. While I was preparing this article, two men cleaning my office window knocked on the glass and indicated that they would like me to screen the 'Summertime' routine all over again. It was evident that their head-shaking appreciation had no element of ogling. Only Fleet Street feels cheated at being left out of the secret of whether Torvill and Dean go to bed together. ('On St Valentine's morning,' wrote *The Times* correspondent from Sarajevo, 'Dean gave his partner an orchid. We cannot know of what it spoke.') Ordinary mortals, from the Queen to the window-cleaners, are responding to a deeper secret than that. Not many artists in any field can unite a nation.

And not even Torvill and Dean can do that for more than a few minutes. After the World Championships they will presumably turn professional; a move which has so far meant, for the great skaters, the loss of their grip on the public imagination. John Curry and Robin Cousins have mounted imaginative professional ice shows, but you have to go to see them – apart from the occasional television special, they don't come to you. Also it is hard to believe, despite frequent protestations from the newly wealthy ex-champions, that to be freed from the artificial restrictions of the sport is to be released into the untrammelled possibilities of art. More likely it is the sport's strict rules which provide the obstacles inspiration needs.

Torvill and Dean have level heads and will survive their success. Whether the sport will survive their success is another question. Women's figure skating never fully recovered after the reign of Peggy Fleming, who set a standard of expression which left everyone who came later straining for effect. The same applies to John Curry's impact on the men's figure skating, which Robin Cousins could reproduce but not exceed. As for what the Protopopovs did to the pairs skating, it was all summed up in one moment, when she floated towards him in an arabesque and he, with a flick of the fingers, sent her, her stately pace unchanging, all the way around in slow wide circle and back to his extended hand. That, without leaving the ice, was as high as pairs skating ever went, although in the years to come every lady competitor learned to balance her pelvic girdle on the gentleman's upstretched finger and pretend to be an aeroplane, usually a MiG 21.

Which was why Torvill and Dean chose ice-dancing instead of pairs – because you didn't have to spend half the routine just gathering speed for a lift or a jump. But even in ice-dancing there might be a limit to expression. It is the fate of all the art-sports that the period in which they are more art than sport is restricted to a few years.

Only the innovator makes art, and the great innovator tends to exhaust the opportunities he creates. As Torvill and Dean rest in Oberstdorf before their final challenge, the rest of us are doomed to follow in their footsteps, of which the most memorable, surely, were those three long *paso doble* strides down the ice to stop on one skate. At Peterborough next Saturday afternoon I might try that myself, if my thigh is better.

Observer
18 March, 1984

～∾⁓

Scarcely was this piece irrevocably published before Bestemianova and Bukhin revealed themselves as Torvill and Dean's worthy successors, not just for technical merit but for artistic impression as well. I was, moreover, unwarrantedly deterministic about what happens to ice-skating after it turns professional. The following year, the World Professional Figure-Skating Championships were shown on television in Britain for the first, and so far only, time. It immediately became clear that the Protopopovs, to take only the most salient example, had in no way lessened their lifetime commitment to an art writ in water. If one is to age with dignity, on ice is no doubt the place to do it, but to do that and to create new beauty at the same time merits applause.

The Sound of the Crucible

WHOEVER called snooker 'chess with balls' was rude but right. As I prepare this article for the press, the semi-finals of the World Professional Snooker Championship have not yet been decided. For Dennis Taylor things must look bad through his headlight-sized glasses, which give him two big pictures of Steve Davis moving elegantly ahead. Jimmy White and Kirk Stevens, however, are still stuck with each other, frame for frame. When you switch on the TV set you can hear the tension before the picture forms. It is a hiss that clicks – the sound of the Crucible.

The Crucible is a perfect name because the World Snooker Championship, like Wimbledon, takes high ability for granted and puts character to the test, heating it up to find out when it melts. The champion is the man who can stay incandescent longest without losing shape.

Over the forthcoming two-day final we will see which of two men with a comparable ability to control the cue-ball can control himself better than the other. Before they start, perhaps it is time for some philosophical reflections. This will be pretty deep stuff, but one is not entirely without qualifications. I have always found it ridiculously easy to hit the cue-ball with the cue.

Making the cue-ball hit the ball I am aiming at, on the other hand, has for some reason always proved ridiculously difficult. If the target ball is close, there is some hope of contact and – even if neither it nor the cue-ball ends up anywhere in particular – one can always pretend that the shot is part of some subtle plan. But if the target ball is farther away than about an arm's length, it is possible, not to say likely, that it will be missed altogether.

This often-repeated experience can be a salutary one for the would-be writer on the sport, because it reminds him that

285

snooker is a bit like the saxophone, out of which you can't get a sound to start with, and which you must first learn to play before you find out whether you have any particular gift for playing it.

Hence the fellow-feeling among snooker players, so like the fellow-feeling among musicians: they all labour long and hard before finding out whether they are anything special, and if it turns out that they are, they give credit to the fates and not to themselves. Tributes to one another's craft are common. There are some powerfully developed egos at championship level, but that essential modesty always shows through the conceit.

Nevertheless, even in a sport where you need so much schooling to perform at all, there is such a thing as outstanding talent. It shows most conspicuously in those players with hyped-up reflexes. Alex Higgins and Jimmy White both have the nervous system of a fighter pilot on amphetamines. White actually moves around the table even faster than Higgins: the only reason he seems a touch slower is that he does not, like Higgins, knock down the referee.

Kirk Stevens usually ranks as a quick player but when matched with White he seems sedate, sometimes pausing for thought before pointing his famous bottom at the expiring young ladies in the audience. You can tell when Kirk is thinking. When he is not thinking, he looks like an Easter Island statue with a sinus problem. When he is thinking, he still looks like that, but licks his lips.

None of which means that Jimmy White is not thinking. But he thinks on the move. Inconsistency is his weakness, yet he would not necessarily overcome it by slowing down. Higgins didn't get eliminated through being hasty. The champions lose when they miss the easy ones.

Ray Reardon, the great strategist of the game, the man with the most comprehensive positional sense, has still got all that, but nowadays misses the easy ones. The snooker player, like the ballet dancer, sadly attains his fullest knowledge just as his body begins no longer to obey him.

Or like the golfer. The difference between Jack Nicklaus and Tom Watson is that Nicklaus has begun to miss the easy ones. Otherwise, they are the same sort of champion, finishing high up even on an off-day. Steve Davis is the snooker equivalent. Compared with him, Jimmy White and Kirk Stevens are like Severiano Ballesteros: obviously brilliant, but just occasionally – say, once per round – sending an approach shot into the car park.

Davis, in addition to a strategic brain ranking with Reardon's, has the physical and/or mental ability not to miss the easy one at the critical moment. For as long as he retains that capacity, he will win more often than not. To the superficial eye this makes him a bit dull, like Bjorn Borg or Billie-Jean King. But really the self-discipline of those great champions when they were ahead was the most exciting thing tennis had to offer.

Steve Davis has Rod Laver's knack of staying sharp while in front. 'When you've got your man down,' said Laver, in his only recorded public statement, 'rub him out.' Davis's formidable PR entourage would never let him say that, but that's what he does. Perhaps this time he won't. Perhaps he won't even get to the final. But the chances are that he will get there and win.

Dennis Taylor lost it in the thirteenth frame of the semi-final, when he was only 7–5 frames down. He was 64 points up with a possible 65 left on the table. He cracked open the remaining reds and was all set to be right back in the match, possibly with the highest break of the tournament. But he went for an only mildly tricky red into the left centre pocket and hit it thin. It was a crushing psychological blow. Fifteen minutes later, he was 9–5 frames down and going blurry at the edges. The Crucible had melted him.

For a while his eyes were hard to see behind his front windows, but he played on. Disappointment is built into snooker and those who lack equanimity must learn to feign it. Not even Higgins, under such a provocation, could have allowed himself to do more than swear at a reporter, or bite a piece out of the side of his pint.

Letting your children watch Wimbledon unsupervised would be like leaving them alone with a video-nasty. Yet from watching snooker they can only profit. Snooker has no room for a Nastase or a McEnroe. A snooker match lasts too long, makes too many demands on inner resources, not just of the will but of the spirit. It is more like a war than like a battle. It is more like life.

But nobody's whole life takes place on television – not yet anyway. A snooker match not only fits into a television screen, it seems specifically designed to do so. Down at the scruffy end of Fleet Street, where envy of television verges on psychosis, they are doing their best to rob the sport of its purity, but for most players and spectators snooker will remain a dream come true.

It is also a dream come true for the sponsor, whose interest in the fine alignment of mind and body might seem questionable. But even though Steve Davis is a non-smoker, from the sponsor's point of view it is always, when he wins, an almost perfectly blissful moment.

And if a smoker – a really *intense* smoker, like Jimmy White – should happen to beat him, the rest of the dream would come true as well.

Observer
6 May, 1984

~∂~

Already drained by his last-ditch victory over Kirk Stevens, Jimmy White ended the first day of the final trailing Steve Davis by eight frames. But he came all the way back on the second day to only one frame behind before Davis took it.

Close Thing in Portugal

I

THE PORTUGUESE haven't played host to a Formula One Grand Prix for more than twenty years, so they can be counted as beginners. They have had beginner's luck. This afternoon's race is not only the last of the season, it will also decide the world championship. Usually the matter is settled earlier on. This time the main contenders are racing right down to the wire, and the wire is made in Portugal.

To make things even more excitingly comprehensible for the locals, the main contenders number precisely two: Niki Lauda and Alain Prost. Lauda is from Austria, Prost is from France, and they are both driving McLaren cars powered by TAG-Porsche turbo engines. But there is no real need to remember any of that stuff. All anyone needs to grasp is that, of the two cars which look like packets of Marlboro cigarettes with a wheel in each corner, number seven is driven by Prost and number eight by Lauda.

Lauda, nicknamed King Rat, is a scarred old rodent who has been world champion twice before. Prost is the fresh-faced broken-nosed young challenger reaching for his first title. ESTORIL DECISIVO! Let's get started.

But not so fast. Grand Prix races are held on Sunday, with the Friday and Saturday for qualifying. This time, however, an extra Thursday of familiarisation has been tagged on the front, because nobody has previously seen the Estoril circuit, which the Portuguese were still constructing on Wednesday evening. On Thursday morning not all the large pieces of earth-moving equipment had left the perimeter and there was wet paint everywhere.

But the police were ready. The Portuguese gendarmerie are a high-profile body of men and here was a chance to strike paramilitary attitudes in a macho atmosphere. Here was a chance to stop people with insufficient credentials from going through gates. The lower ranks, of whom there were hundreds, had truncheons hanging from their belts. Their senior officers toted swagger sticks.

The top cop of all had a grey uniform that looked as if Mussolini had designed it personally in 1938: forage cap peaked high at each end, dark glasses, shaped battledress fitting tightly over the corset, high spurred boots and a riding crop. The horse to go with all this was nowhere in sight. Probably it was back at headquarters watching the show on television – always supposing headquarters *had* a television. In my hotel there was only one TV set, occupying a room of its own.

On this evidence, Estoril was a bit of a back number. But the Formula One teams have the high-tech wherewithal to insulate themselves from almost any environment on earth. Behind turrets of piled tyres, the giant transporter vans open up directly into the pits. In the middle of each team's enclave sits the car, cocooned from the world. In the car, cocooned even from the enclave, sits the driver, who can be contacted only by a radio link plugged into his helmet.

Outside his car Alain Prost looks like Charles Aznavour's even smaller brother being pursued by a hundred photographers. Inside the car he is just a pair of eyes. So is Lauda, but his eyes chill you: left browless by the fire that so nearly killed him, they look like agates set in ivory.

Before Thursday's practice started, their eyes and numbers were the only things that made the two front-runners look different. Then it was only the numbers. When the turbo engines started up, it was a brave policeman who didn't blink. The circuit has a longish straight past the pits and the rest of it is kinky. The first cars out went around the two miles of kinky bits in not much more than a minute and then headed back down the straight towards the blinking policemen. Accelerating hard in top gear, they shrieked past at about 180 mph with plenty of urge in hand.

Even if you have experienced it before, a shock wave of that size breaking a few feet from your nose makes you want to go home or at least crouch behind something solid. The humbler policemen showed signs of wanting to stop guarding the edge of the track and move back a bit to start guarding the grandstand, but their officers, far in the rear, frowned at them.

Familiarising themselves with the course, some of the drivers got very familiar indeed, especially Prost, who got more familiar than anybody. But Lauda wasn't much slower by the time the session ended.

More police having arrived during the night, Friday dawned to grey clouds overhead, disgorging rain on a grey cloud of law enforcement at ground level, including a lot of dog-handlers and their dogs, which had all been to snarl school. By this time there was so much security that only the racing drivers could move about unchallenged. Not even they were allowed to move without their cars, and the cars weren't allowed out because of the wet track.

To while away the delay, some of the mechanics started to play football on the straight in front of the grandstand. The police drew truncheons, moved forward dramatically and confiscated the ball. The Lotus driver Nigel Mansell vaulted the pit wall to demand the ball back. A police dog panicked and bit its handler firmly in the behind, to loud cheers from the Portuguese punters. Then all the cars went out on rain tyres for another hour of non-qualifying practice. Bolder spirits changed to slick tyres and duly spun off, collecting in small shy groups around a corner still full of water.

At lunchtime the glum sky was partly cheered up by a lone light aircraft pulling a sign saying VEHICULOS USADOS GARANTIA. In the McLaren team's mobile restaurant, three well-bred female chefs called Liz, Sally and Heather dished up a cordon bleu meal to Prost and Lauda who sat chatting amicably while the media locked outside invented stories about their bitter rivalry.

When the afternoon's qualifying session started, more rain started with it. This was serious, because whoever put in a fast lap before the track was wet might nab the pole position if it stayed that way. 'Queek! Queek!' squealed Nelson Piquet in the Brabham pit. He was calling for a set of qualifying tyres – thin, sticky slicks. These were hastily bodged on but it was too late. Berger's ATS rammed a fence and knocked out a marshal with a flying stone. The cars came back to the pits and an ambulance went out instead.

As things stood, all the new boys who had tried hard early on were in the top positions. When everyone got going again on the damp track the aces, hampered by rain tyres, couldn't get their times down to match the rabbits. But the sun having peeked out as the end of the session neared, Piquet changed to slicks and warmed them up for a few laps so as to be ready if the track dried. It did and he put in a quick one. Prost and Lauda also switched to slicks and got out in time to go faster still, but Piquet would have gone fastest of all on his last lap if he had not steamed into a hairpin and found one of the Renaults parked neatly across it.

Harder to fathom but even bigger than the Prost/Lauda story has been the story of how Piquet would have been world champion for the third time this year if only his Brabham hadn't kept coming undone. Two wins have been small reward for eight pole positions. Either Prost or Lauda must win the championship in Estoril, but if Piquet keeps going he could easily win the race. This might puzzle the Portuguese, but since Piquet is a Brazilian and therefore practically one of their own, no doubt they will soon understand.

Yesterday the sun shone bright. Piquet went straight out on one of his two permitted sets of qualifying tyres and notched up a time that only Prost could beat. Lauda went backwards with a sick engine. Then Piquet put on his other set of qualifying tyres and pipped Prost, taking his ninth pole for the season.

The pretty 18-year-old Milanese who hands out a motor scooter for every fastest qualifier gave him his ninth motor scooter. They have seen a lot of each other this year and she also holds his can of Pepsi after he puts on his helmet. With his helmet off, he looks like Dudley Moore at death's door. It's the adrenalin: the thrill turns him pale.

II

BEFORE dawn last Sunday the vendors of cakes and fizzy drinks were already in position beside the roads leading to the circuit at Estoril. They had built their *tabhernas* out of tatty canvas and trestle tables, unpacked their not very appetising goods and made fires from the empty boxes. They weren't rich, and in the morning most of the people who bought what they had to sell weren't rich either. A lot of people came by car but almost as many came on foot, looking bedraggled and stepping carefully, because not all the mud had dried to dust.

Slogans daubed on walls exhort the Portuguese to live always in the spirit of some day or other in April. It's a worthy sentiment, but the occasional splurge can't hurt. The international Grand Prix circus is the biggest splurge there is. 'Blam blam!' yelled an outlandish engine being tested in the distance. Money was being burned. The traffic jam inched impatiently towards it. The pedestrians shuffled dust. The police were outnumbered – always a sign, in Portugal, that the crowd must be very large.

Sustained by the drinks and cakes bought at the road-side – the cakes, in particular, were evidence that the wonderful Portuguese folk traditions need to be supplemented by soulless modern merchandising as soon as possible – the punters filled the grandstands to be regaled by one last morning of untimed practice. Grid positions had already been decided but here was an indication of how fast the cars would go in race trim. Lauda needed this practice because the engine of his McLaren had been giving no end of trouble and if he finished more than one place behind his team-mate Prost the World Championship could still slip away. Prost, on the other hand, seemed to have the race sewn up, unless the unlikely occurred and Piquet's Brabham held together.

Those among the spectators who did not already know could now receive valuable training in how to tell the cars apart. They all look like a bobsleigh being humped by a lawnmower but luckily they advertise different things. The red-and-white McLarens are mobile hoardings for Marlboro cigarettes. The blue Brabhams plug Parmalat sliced ham and the yellow Renaults remind Europe about the virtues of Elf petrol. Only the Ferraris look exactly like themselves – bright red and very pretty. They even make a pretty sound, loud but sweet like an apocalyptic coffee-grinder.

The Renaults were loudest and not sweet at all. Punters without earplugs found their knees turning to jelly. Derek Warwick and Patrick Tambay drove the Renaults very quickly but nobody believed they would hold together. The Renault team has a bigger fuel refrigeration plant than anybody else, more radio links, more computers, more of everything. But it has made life too complicated for itself. The Renault organisation is mighty in committee but when the driver is alone in the car there is suddenly nobody out there he can depend on.

All this determinism was academic, however, because fortune, in Formula One Grand Prix racing, has no tides that can't turn as fast as dice can roll. It is true that you can do everything right and everything will still go wrong, but it is equally true that even the best laid plans sometimes work out. Only two years ago the Williams team had been so dominant that they had lingered too long before switching to turbo engines. They would know how to deal with success if their recent marriage with Honda suddenly came right. The Williams pit was full of Japanese mechanics wearing the green and white overalls of the Saudi sponsor.

The Williams drivers, Jacques Lafitte and Keke Rosberg, are French and Finnish respectively. The car is still not quite all there but Lafitte had been going fast and Rosberg faster still, although his car had done all it could to stop him. Between the two qualifying sessions it needed to be rebuilt. All through the second session it misbehaved and with only a few minutes to go it conked out completely, leaving Rosberg the only non-qualifier and with a long cross-country run back to the pit so that he could jump into the spare car and put in one desperate last lap against the clock, the odds and common sense. To qualify at all in such circumstances would have been an achievement. But he snatched fourth place on the grid – clear proof that the erstwhile world champion was fully capable of becoming that again, if only they would give him the wheels.

Practice ended and the cars came in to be either confidently polished during the lunchtime hiatus or else frantically rebuilt. An RAF Harrier performed prodigies of mid-air dressage to help take the onlookers' minds off the traditional cakes they had been eating. The policemen looked up longingly at such a potentially definitive instrument of crowd control.

When the cars came out of the pits after lunch, Nigel Mansell's Lotus had 'Good luck Nigel' chalked on its tyres. Next year he drives for Williams but he looked keen to depart in glory. They all parked on the grid and settled down for the mandatory half-hour of being swamped by the media. Tunnelling through the legs of photographers, I arrived at the side of Piquet's pole-position Brabham to find the still-current world champion strapped into the cockpit and being consoled for the pressures of fame by Emanuela, the girl who has by now given Piquet so many motor scooters that she has become part of his life. She gently caressed one of his BMW driving gloves and stared deep into his tinted visor.

The silver foil spread over the Brabham's fuel tank would have kept off sunlight if the scrum of media had allowed any through. The French media, as always, focused on Prost to the exclusion of the world. For him it was a dubious privilege, because those chaps would have woken up Napoleon for an interview on the night before Waterloo. Much farther back, Lauda said the necessary but not a word more. Mr Minimax long ago found the secret of hiding without running. You can get near him, but you can't get to him.

Twenty-six engines fired at once and the field toured round the circuit while the Portuguese fans told their girlfriends by sign language that this wasn't the race, it was only the warm-up lap. Then the green light shone and it was the race. The clutch dropped on a grand total of at least 15,000 unmuffled horsepower. Piquet was slow off the mark and Rosberg came belting through behind Prost, then beside him, then past him into the first corner. Trying hard to restore his squandered advantage, Piquet overdid it and spun on the first lap. By the time he had straightened himself out he was far down the field, which was led for the early laps by Rosberg, Prost, Mansell and Ayrton Senna, a young man who has made the Toleman look fast and might stun the world next year when he goes to Lotus, always provided that they get their act together.

Lauda was a long way back, stuck in the traffic. Up at the front, Rosberg's turbo spat flame in Prost's face but the dream couldn't last. Prost's McLaren was simply less of a handful and he took Rosberg without trouble at about the same time that Mansell put in the fastest lap and got set to take Rosberg in his turn. This manoeuvre, however, proved to be not so smoothly negotiable as Mansell would have liked. Rosberg had not forgotten how Mansell held him up in Dallas. Nor, reputedly, was the Finn exactly thrilled by the prospect of having the abrasive Englishman for a team-mate next year. When Mansell moved out to go past Rosberg he found Rosberg behaving as if Mansell wasn't there. Mansell had to drop back smartly or face totalisation at 190 mph plus. Really the two of them should try to have a drink together this Christmas.

Eventually Mansell got past Rosberg and established himself not all that far behind Prost, who was romping along an open road. Lauda was back in eighth position behind Johansson's Toleman. Johansson, a London-based Swede with a big blond smile, was under no obligation to move over. Lauda was up against it. The gap between him and Prost lengthened to 27 seconds. More important than the distance between them was the number of cars filling it. One car was enough to screw Lauda's chance and there were six of them.

The race was more than a third over, a dozen laps went by with Lauda still stuck, and Prost's lead over him stretched to 33 seconds. On every lap at the same spot, Lauda pulled out beside Johansson but couldn't outbrake him. In a similar crisis at the Nurburgring, Lauda had got impatient and spun, but not making the same mistake twice is one of the secrets of his mastery.

Precious time went by while he waited for his chance. Things happened to other people – Alboreto's Ferrari went past Rosberg, Lafitte came into the pits, Warwick went up a slip road, the mortified Piquet got lapped by Prost – but nothing happened to Lauda. Then it did: he saw some daylight and went through it. By now he was 42 seconds adrift from Prost but he was a place closer. Then Alboreto went backwards, de Angelis's Lotus did the same, and Lauda was three places closer: Prost, Mansell, Senna, Rosberg, Lauda.

Mansell, however, was still running strongly only half a straight behind Prost. Standing at the pit wall while Mansell went past down the straight was a character-building experience, because to dodge the bumps on the grandstand edge of the track he came booming down the near side right under your nose, obviously with every intention of winning the race. If he did that and demoted Prost to second place it would be OK by Lauda, but for Mansell to finish *between* Prost and Lauda would give the championship to Prost.

None of this would apply, of course, if Lauda couldn't get past Rosberg and Senna. But Rosberg by now had done the impossible too long, which left Senna. Lauda went past Senna and that made Mansell the key man in the world championship. Lauda, 4½ points ahead of Prost, needed the six points awarded for second place if Prost got the nine points for winning. Only if Prost came second could Lauda take the championship from third place. So Lauda must have been willing Mansell onward even as he chased him. The statistics said that Mansell's Lotus would fall apart, but what if they weren't right?

Lauda was 27 seconds behind Mansell with about that many laps to go. If he chased Mansell too hard, Lauda might break something. If he didn't chase Mansell hard enough, and Mansell's car failed to disintegrate as expected, the championship was lost. Both boldness and caution were thus Lauda's enemies. He held steady through the mental turmoil. Under far less pressure, Alboreto spun off and stirred the dirt.

Standing at the pit wall and bracing myself for the usual

shock of Mansell's transition down the straight, I suddenly discovered him arriving in the pits behind me. The piston in one of his front brakes had jumped out of its calipers and his race was over. He stepped out of the car and disappeared under an avalanche of media. When the Lotus mechanics dug him out I asked him, perhaps tactlessly, for a one-word interview. He gave it to me.

At 60 laps with 10 to go, it was Prost, Lauda and the rest. Lauda was 40 seconds behind Prost but it could have been 400 as long as his car held together. Both of them turned down the boost to save fuel and avoid stress. The Grand Prix year spiralled gently to an end. Prost won the race and Lauda won the championship. The new boy won the battle and the old hand won the war.

On the victory dais, which advertised Portugal's SG Export cigarettes, Prost, Lauda and Senna spurted champagne over one another's overalls, which advertised Marlboro cigarettes in each case. None of them actually smokes but the advertiser is no doubt confident that the consumer will fail to draw the relevant conclusion. Prost, a gentleman though French, behaved impeccably, smiling with a mouth full of aloes.

Rosberg, the only heavy smoker in the field, was eighth. Piquet finished a lap behind. Mechanical unreliability had cost him the season but losing this race might for once have been his fault. He looked sallow, but then he always does: not just from adrenalin poisoning but because of danger from young women.

The last I saw of Piquet, he had taken refuge in the back of the Brabham team transporter while the Portuguese young ladies came at him three deep. Not three deep one behind the other: three deep one on top of the other. He was still *their* world champion. While Piquet signed the programmes, T-shirts and bared wrists of the lucky ones, Portuguese policemen dressed as paratroopers threw the unlucky ones out of the van into the struggling mass below. Crowd control had at last come into its own.

Observer
21–28 October, 1984

Holders of the Golden Cross

I

BEAUTIFUL but dangerous, Rio is a city where you can be mugged in broad daylight. Wise citizens enrol in Golden Cross, a scheme for medical assistance. All over town this past week there have been huge posters featuring the handsome face of Brazil's darling, ex-world champion Nelson Piquet, looking more than ever like a combination of Jesus Christ and Dudley Moore.

'For me everything goes well,' says the face in Portuguese, 'I hold Golden Cross.' It is a hefty endorsement. Nelson Piquet does something almost as dangerous as walking along the esplanade of Copacabana Beach with an exposed Rolex.

Thursday having consisted entirely of rain, the first effective practice for today's race – the first Grand Prix of the new Formula One season – happened on Friday. The previous evening, quondam racing driver Innes Ireland, still a familiar face around the Formula One circus, had gone walking along the esplanade of Copacabana Beach and been duly mugged. The familiar face was in bad shape. There were a lot of nervous puns about the muggy weather.

This year the cars are basically the same as last year. The petrol ration is down a bit, which imposes stricter fuel management and theoretically should lower the speed, but mechanical refinements have upped the power to compensate, so it all evens out.

Some of the star drivers, however, have switched teams, in the understandable desire not to waste even one precious year of their youthful reflexes in an uncompetitive car. Star drivers are less like star actors than like star actresses, choosing their roles under the constant threat of fading looks.

At Williams, Nigel Mansell, who rose to complete stardom at the end of last season by winning some races, now finds his limelight crowded by the aforesaid Nelson Piquet, who has won many more races and might well be joining the team just in time to get himself a car that will put him back on the winner's dais where he belongs. Brabham, the team he left behind, couldn't do that for him consistently enough to give him back his championship.

Last year's Brabham kept falling apart. If this year's Brabham falls apart, the pieces will have less distance to go before they hit the ground. The only radically new car of the season, it is Gordon Murray's masterpiece, an elegant projectile which looks, in its blue livery, like a Lilo for the Royal Navy.

But new means untried, and Riccardo Patrese and Elio de Angelis will be testing as much as racing. 'We haven't done enough running,' Gordon Murray told me in the pit lane as the whistle blew for the first period of untimed practice. All the engines yelled for dear life. 'The shit starts again,' mouthed Murray philosophically. It would have further to fall before it hit the Brabham.

Off went the cars and Ayrton Senna of Brazil in his Lotus immediately started lapping quickly. Anything under 1 min 30 sec is a fastish lap – about 125 mph average speed – and Senna was down around that time straight away.

Simply because of Senna's presence, Lotus is the third big story of the season. Part of the price of Senna's presence was Derek Warwick's absence. Senna insisted that Lotus did not have the wherewithal to look after two proper drivers, so if Lotus wanted him they would have to keep the spare car for his exclusive use and give the second car to a slave. There have been loud chortles about Brazilian high-handedness, but really Senna has a point. If Lotus want him to win the war they must give him the tools.

Meanwhile the choice of slave has brought forth the most romantic story to hit Formula One since a Siamese prince raced under the name B. Bira. Yes, Johnny Dumfries is actually the Earl of Dumfries. Or is it the Earl of Greystoke? You can't imagine what this is doing to the foreign press. If

Fergie were driving the car they could not be going crazier. Mobbed in the Lotus pit by photographers and TV crews, the hapless Dumfries has to find his car by feeling around for it, and can't tread on the gas until he is half-way down the pit lane, or else he will cripple half a dozen shutterbugs from *Wochenende* and *Ici Paris* who are running backwards in front of him. It is a tough scene for Dumfries, on top of the already burdensome assumption that he is only along for the ride.

After only seven minutes of practice a Lotus was off the track and on fire. It was Dumfries. His one consolation was that Thierry Boutsen's Arrows caught fire at the same moment. Golden Cross personnel raced towards the scene but nobody was hurt. The fire in the Lotus was a nice clean one which wouldn't have done much damage if the Brazilian marshals hadn't added enough foam to destroy the car completely. When Dumfries got back to the pits he was not allowed to use the spare car. It had been set up for Senna and would stay that way.

When practice resumed after all the foam-drenched wreckage had been cleared away, Senna justified his star treatment by getting his lap time down even lower. But the Williams cars soon showed their form. Mansell, enjoying his new-found authority, was quickly up to speed, and Piquet worked his old trick of going out late to put in one magisterial, mind-bending lap that would blast everyone else's morale. With Piquet going straight down to under 1 min 29 sec the whistle blew for a thoughtful lunch.

In the timed practice session on Friday afternoon it was the same pattern, although this time it counted for positions on the starting grid. Piquet, Senna and Mansell, in that order, employed their thin qualifying tyres to appropriately sensational effect. The first two got down under last year's pole position time and Senna in particular was a sight to behold on the long straight, the undertray of the Lotus bottoming so often that the car left a continuous trail of sparks, like Halley's Comet. Short on PR skills but long on talent, Senna is a Mercury with only one message to deliver: his own brilliance.

II

THE DAY before the Brazilian Grand Prix it was hot in Rio. Down from the cliffs towards the beach at Ipanema, hang-gliders circled like vultures. Above the valley of the Auto-dromo, vultures circled like journalists. Beside the highway from town, huge billboards paid for by JPS, the cigarette company sponsoring the Lotus team, said VAI FUNDO, AYRTON, as if Ayrton Senna needed any more encouragement.

He had the whole of Brazil behind him. The only question was whether the whole of Brazil would include his senior compatriot, Nelson Piquet, or whether Piquet, who also had the whole of Brazil behind him, would contrive matters so that the whole of Brazil included Ayrton Senna. The Brazilian fans were in the ecstatic position of having two heroes, either of whom, in their view, could be defeated only by the other. Delirium was therefore compulsory.

A morning of untimed practice gave way to an afternoon of qualifying. The race was still an endless day away but the stands were full of fans madly cheering Senna's every appearance. On his first set of qualifying tyres he was soon down close to Piquet's fastest time of the previous day. Piquet thought close was too close and with ten minutes of the session left he took his Williams-Honda out on its second and last permitted set of quallies to put in a fast one. Fast was too fast and he spun off. This left Senna with an easy chance for a dramatic last-minute flying lap to grab pole position, which he duly did, arriving back in the pits to be mobbed so thoroughly by the media that he was invisible for ten minutes.

None of these histrionics meant much because Mansell (Williams) had also done well and neither Prost nor Rosberg had pushed his McLaren to the limit. Their studied cool recalled Lauda's old habit of qualifying the car in race trim and winning the event from half-way down the grid. Between Piquet's *faux pas* and Senna's flying lap, Prost's MP4 squatted patiently in the pit, while one of the Marlboro hospitality girls – a Brazilian beauty pageant winner and university student reading economics and the history of flamenco – sat on it posing for pictures. Nobody was in a hurry. The McLaren team had great drivers, a proven car, the most efficient fuel management system, and Miss Flamenco Economics. That the whole of Brazil minus Miss Flamenco Economics was behind Nelson and Ayrton could only be a side issue.

Piquet's Williams was an acknowledged threat to the McLarens, but Senna's Lotus, even if it held together, had dodgy fuel management and would have to run the race with the boost turned down. So pole position scarcely counted. Nevertheless the fans, who either couldn't tell a fuel management system from a management training course or else didn't care, went back to town happy, swarming back up the coast road by every form of transport including bare feet, some towards the garbage tips they call home, others to the beach for a last swim under a darkening late afternoon sky split by the rancid flash of Dayglo helicopters.

But the main means of transport was the small car. There is no other size of car in Rio. The Ford Escort is regarded as a luxury vehicle and Brazil must be the only country left in the world where the classic Volkswagen Beetle is still manufactured. On the highway, all these tiny cars travel flat out. Their drivers change lanes constantly without looking in the mirror, so the only way not to get swatted sideways is to floor the accelerator and keep up with a stream of traffic going as fast as anything can while all its components are continually changing position, as in a particle beam. It is very good training for late braking and probably the chief reason for the abundant supply of Brazilian Formula One drivers.

Nelson Piquet's phrase for the despised activity of putting on the brakes is 'open ze legs'. Both he and Senna operate on the principle that when disputing the right of way into a corner the other guy should be persuaded to open ze legs first. Whether the two Brazilians could do this to each other, however, remained to be seen.

Sunday was race day and hotter still, as if the temperature had been only practising. The race wasn't until one o'clock but at eight in the morning the stands were already jammed and shouting. Though not surprised that the people who

produced Carmen Miranda should go bananas, I was start-
led to see such heat being generated in an atmosphere which
was so humid already that all it needed to resemble a hot
bath was the addition of plastic ducks. In previous years, I
was informed, the crowd had to be hosed down by a fire-
truck before the race, but this year was comparatively
cool – scarcely 100° Fahrenheit – so a douche would not be
necessary.

At that moment a fire-truck went speeding down the
straight past the stands, the crowd cheering it to the echo. I
thought that this was because they were hoping it would hose
them, but then a sanitary cart full of cleaners with brooms
held high went speeding down the same straight and the
crowd cheered that too. The driver braked late for the
notorious South Corner, just like Ayrton or Nelson, except
that he opened ze legs at a rate somewhat less than the full
200 mph. But he was a Brazilian driver so they cheered him
anyway.

Grid positions already decided, there was a last session of
untimed practice with the cars in race trim. McLaren,
Williams and Lotus, the three teams in contention, all
circulated religiously in search of problems that might need
fixing. The Brabham team knew its problem and could do
nothing about it. Gordon Murray's beautiful new car, knee-
high to a carpet snake and theoretically faster in top gear
than a streak of lightning, just won't accelerate. Murray told
me that the team would stay on after the race to test the car
and find out why it had no poke. The BMW engineers
were on their way down from Stuttgart with a full set of
tools.

For now, there was nothing Patrese and de Angelis could
do except lower their heads in shame. This was easy to
accomplish, because except for its rear wing the Brabham is
lower than the Armco barrier. You'd swear it was flying
along through a slit trench.

At the scorching crack of noon the cars were out on the
grid. Senna's Lotus, Piquet and Mansell in the two Wil-
liams, Arnoux and Lafitte in the two Ligiers sat there in that
order, buried by media. The Ligiers weren't really supposed

to be so far up front but this could partly be ascribed to the fact that the McLarens were so far back, all according, no doubt, to their secret plan. Some of the cars had mini-computers plugged into them right up to the last minute, feeding the onboard electronics a program to fit the heat.

Several girls from the Oba Oba Club – Rio's version of the Crazy Horse Saloon in Paris, with sliced pineapple as an optional extra – looked on with broad smiles held in place by the pressure of tiny costumes and fishnet tights. Their high heels would come in very useful if they needed to go to the toilet. All the toilets had been blocked for days.

A warm-up lap was scarcely necessary in such heat, but it gave the marshals time to chase the media off the Armco, and the grandstands a chance to rehearse going berserk at the mere sight of Senna and Piquet. At the green light, Piquet was slow on the clutch as usual. Mansell skated past to go neck and neck with Senna all the way round the loopy north part of the circuit and back down the long straight, where they both generated a spectacular display of sparks as they headed for the South Corner at 190 mph plus, with no detectable opening of ze legs by either party. This is where Mansell usually likes to come off and he did it again, removing half the interest from the race at one blow. Mansell is on the verge of being a great driver but the first require-ment for the aspiring Hamlet is that he shall not fall into the orchestra pit during Act One.

Piquet, with a bigger margin of fuel due to smarter electronics, cranked up the boost, went past Senna and pulled out a lead. Alboreto's Ferrari was well up and the Ligiers were not yet fading in accordance with the script, but everyone knew that it was only a matter of time before the McLarens would take over as per plan. On lap five, however, Rosberg was in the pits and out of the car. If that was part of the plan it was pretty risky, because it left Prost holding the bag.

Prost chased Alboreto down the long straight but had to open ze legs. Several laps later he kept ze legs closed a bit longer, put Alboreto behind him and set about catching Senna. This was more like it. Piquet came in for tyres and

Prost trimmed Senna's 3-second lead to about three feet. This was a lot more like it.

Prost went ahead of Senna, but Piquet was only 17 seconds behind both of them and had new wheels. Senna came in for a quick change. This should have left Prost unchallenged, but Piquet was shrinking the discrepancy at two seconds a lap. For the grandstands it was too much to bear. When Piquet went past Prost the screams of the crowd could be heard above the bedlam of the engines. It was a stirring sight even if you weren't Brazilian, but on a sober view it could only mean that Prost's tyres were going sour.

Prost came in for a very quick stop, letting the prudently soft-pedalling Senna past him into second place, but surely not for long. With half the race to go, though, Prost came back in for keeps. As with Rosberg's car, the famously reliable fuel management system had fouled up, burning the pistons and slightly denting the mystique. It is traditional that McLarens run like Swiss trains, but in Formula One it is a long tradition that lasts a season. The McLaren team would have work to do.

Piquet, his handsome head held on one side to compensate for the wearing left-hand turns of the anti-clockwise circuit, lapped steadily away under a sky filling with smog. There was nothing Senna could do about it but the crowd forgave him. Just as long as a Brazilian won. Dumfries in the other Lotus would have finished a promising fifth if his car had not gone sick. Lafitte was a worthy third, and Arnoux fourth. If the Ligiers can keep that up, and BMW can breathe on the Brabham, there will be at least four teams in the picture for the most interesting season in years.

The locals, however, didn't care about the future. Rio, where the fruit rots on the vine, is a city of the present. 'Bra-ZIL!' they screamed. The two fastest drivers in the world belonged to them.

Observer
23–30 March, 1986

Riviera Daydream

I T WAS a tough assignment. Could I go to the South of France for a week, hang about the Monaco Grand Prix and the Cannes Film Festival, and pick up enough high-life atmosphere to evoke the fun-in-the-sun tang of the Côte d'Azur functioning at full throttle? Reportage, I was sternly told, would not be enough. I would actually have to get in there among the champagne, the expensive restaurants and the exposed women. You will appreciate why I hesitated for so long – a full microsecond.

I left behind me an apparently defeated country. Little did I know that a week of British triumph lay ahead. In Wardour Street, David Puttnam and Roland Joffé were even at that moment assembling the one and only, unfinished print of *The Mission*, which would conquer all at Cannes. But the last thing I heard as I boarded the aircraft was an announcement that the Government had found a way of relieving the unemployed of their houses, presumably so that they could support the hotel industry.

Short of time, I took a taxi from Nice airport to Monaco. Issued with only a certain amount of cash, I had been told that a taxi would not be expensive. It would not be expensive for Adnan Khashoggi, whose yacht *Nabila* turned out to be in the harbour when my driver, clearly ambitious to be a Grand Prix star himself, crested the hill above the port and screamed to a halt so that I could admire the view and show my appreciation in his tip.

Still frightened by the horrible velocities he had attained on the autoroute, I was pleased to be looking down on Monaco. The sun was bright, the sea was blue, and all the upthrust geology led straight down to what would have looked like a tub full of toy boats, if they had not been so obviously very large. There were hundreds of whoppers parked all around the harbour crescent and along the breakwaters. *Nabila* dwarfed them all, and was dwarfed in her turn by *Atlantis II* – Niarchos's destroyer-sized home away from home, complete with helicopter perched on top.

Yachts arouse envy among ordinary people and Niarchos's helicopter arouses envy among yachts. Plenty of yacht-owners have helicopters at home, but Niarchos has his on his yacht. In the next few days I was always able to put a cocky yachtsman in his place by slyly referring to Niarchos's helicopter or simply asking outright, 'Where's *your* helicopter then?' They can't take that. They look at their shiny teak deck as if it has all turned to ash.

I checked in at the Mirabeau, which overlooks the circuit just where it dives into the tunnel under Loew's Hotel. Too late for Friday's last practice session, I could see nothing of the racing cars except a sticky stain of rubber on the road. Most of the year the track is just the ordinary roads of Monaco. For the race, a whole kit of parts – miles of armco barrier, grandstands, bridges – turns the roads into a circuit theoretically fit for Formula One cars to race on.

In fact, it isn't. An 800-horsepower racing car really has no business lapping at an average speed of less than 90 mph. The driver, if he is occasionally to get the gear-stick into top, has to stir it like a pestle for two hours as though trying to make talcum out of granite. Also there is scarcely room to pass. You could run a horse race through the corridors of Buckingham Palace and there would still be a winner, but most likely it would be the horse who got the best start.

Pole position therefore means a lot. So far Ayrton Senna's Lotus was fastest. Nigel Mansell, driving a Williams Honda, hadn't even qualified yet. Tomorrow he would be in a hurry. Meanwhile I walked the empty circuit around to the harbour. Half my cash had been blown on the taxi so I was saving money. There were plenty of people, most of them young, who were doing the same. The town abounded with British fans toting backpacks. They looked as if they might be sleeping in the open that night, with only beer for insulation.

But they were well behaved. Football-type hooliganism is

not fashionable among motor racing enthusiasts anywhere except Italy, where it gets worse the longer that Ferrari does not win. Britain does well in Grand Prix racing. Except for Mansell there is no British driver on top at the moment, but the three leading marques – McLaren, Williams and Lotus – are all manufactured in Britain.

Exchanging pleasantries about Japanese television with sunburnt Brits as I made my lonely tour, I sympathised with their determination to see the big adventure on a shoe string. But there was no blinking the fact that we were outclassed. The rich, some of them British but all of them really belonging to the international community of tax avoidance, were omnipresent. Along the harbour wall, their moored yachts backed right on to the track, so that from their deck chairs, with a tall glass of champagne held to their pursed lips, they could get a good view as I trudged past. It wasn't as exciting as watching the racing cars would be, but it was probably more satisfactory. It was, after all, what owning a yacht was all about.

Muttering 'Where's *your* helicopter then?' to myself, I was glad to note that the men were almost unrelievedly bloated of aspect, which took the edge off the fact that their womenfolk, chosen to tone in with the ship's fittings, looked impressive at certain angles. The women are even better than the men at adopting a facial expression which says, 'I'm on a yacht and you're not.' Some of them can convey this attitude even through sunglasses. In Toytown it is hard not to become childish, and I was feeling pretty vindictive until I got all the way around the harbour and found a lovely yacht – a proper one, with sails – on whose deck John Watson and James Hunt were making inroads into lager.

They invited me on board and immediately my whole attitude changed. What could be more agreeable, more *sensible*, than to be afloat in such a setting, in such company, with a cold glass in one's hand? 'I *hate* all this,' said Watson. He does, too: he'd rather be given a car to drive. But failing that, there were worse fates than just being there. Hunt, an ex-world champion turned philosopher, just grunted at the setting sun.

Next day was hot and the cars were howling. By now I am used to the noise an F1 racing car makes and what it looks like going flat out. Television can tell you neither of these things: the sound operator can take in only a tenth of what he hears and long lenses slow the image. On a wide-open, purpose-built track the commotion is frightful enough, but when confined to the Monegasque streets, hemmed in by houses, hotels and cliffs, the clamour curdles the inner ear.

In the pits during the morning session of untimed practice, I had my earplugs in but managed a few shouted conversations. Gordon Murray, designer of the new low-profile Brabham which so disappointingly lacked urge when I saw it in Rio, was now confident that the traction problem had been solved. 'Cured the initial lack of response,' he mouthed. 'Getting better. HALF WAY FIXED.' Elio de Angelis, dauntingly handsome in his white overalls, put on his helmet and got into the Brabham. It was like getting into a sleeping bag. Senna was still fastest, but as the rest of the stars came in and out of the pits to have their machinery tweaked they, too, began to go quickly.

To find out what that meant, I threaded my way under the crowded grandstand and climbed the hill towards the Casino, with only the armco separating me from the cars. Near the top of the long shallow hill I could look back down towards the pits and watch the cars come snaking up along one of the few top-gear, full-bore stretches of the course. At scarcely 175 mph they still weren't going as fast as they could, but they were accelerating as hard. For how hard that is, you have to remember the fastest you have ever driven. Even in one of the most powerful production sports cars it would have taken you a certain time to reach that speed. The F1 cars reach that speed in the time it took you to insert your ignition key.

When a pair of knee-high cars racing side by side gather speed that fast towards you, putting 200 horsepower into the road through each wheel and a noise into the sky that sends the birds into exile, you will ask yourself, with any brains you have left, what it must be like *doing* that, if it feels so awful just watching it.

In the afternoon's timed practice, the top boys raced for the pole. Senna was still quickest for most of the session but then Mansell and Prost both turned up the wick. Mansell went straight through from non-qualifier to second spot, while Prost, seemingly with no sweat expended, ended up ahead of everybody. There was a sneaking suspicion that the next day's race had already been decided, since Prost's McLaren was the car least likely to fall apart. But before the day of the Grand Prix of the racing cars there was still the heady excitement of the night, and the Grand Prix des Poseurs.

In Monaco a lot of posing goes on all the time, but the night before the Grand Prix it reaches a frenzy. Cheapskate poseurs wear T-shirts with American words on them. The American words have usually been put there by somebody whose grasp of that language does not equal his insight into the allure of US cultural imperialism. Last winter in the Dolomites I saw an Italian ski hat that said NO STOP ACTION FOR SKI MAN. I thought there was no topping that, but in Monaco on the night before the race I saw a T-shirt that said PRO DESIGN FOR TURBO MANHATTAN.

The more up-market poseurs adopt white suits, white shoes, Miami Vice half-shaves and small gold ingots worn in the medallion position. They tour the town in cars to boggle the mind: pastel Rolls-Royce Camargues, Lagondas with digital dash-boards, replicas of the AC Cobra with an exhaust note like a flatulent buffalo. In front of Loew's, only Lamborghinis and Ferrari Testa Rossas are allowed to park. A mere Ferrari Dino has to go around the back.

Casino square towards midnight is where the posing reaches a climax. Out of the fabulous car and up to the front door of the Casino goes the poseur and his amazing woman, invariably looking as if she has just teleported from the catwalk of a Paris couture collection. How the men can look so crass and the women so elegant is a mystery. Or maybe it is not a mystery, and you and I are idealists.

Race day was perfect. The principality, a natural amphitheatre, was full to the rim. The steep grassy slopes among the cliffs were jammed with people who had all paid to sit there. Ex-world champion Jackie Stewart told me that he had once checked out the cliff-dwellers and found half of them wearing Rolexes. Jackie represents Rolex and will not rest until the other half are wearing Rolexes too. The schedule was meticulous. Prince Rainier reached the start line at 15 hr 10. At 15 hr 15: *Hymne Monegasque*. At 15 hr 17: *Fin de l'Hymne Monegasque*. The green light shone at 15 hr 30 and Prost led away, never to be headed except temporarily when he stopped for tyres. It was a procession, as forecast. But there was nothing dull about it if you were standing close.

The character-building spot to be is just after Casino square. Arriving in the square after the high-speed climb described above, the cars go light on their wheels as they dive downhill into the avenue des Spélugues – which sounds like what would happen to you if one of them crashed. Short in the chassis, the cars twitch visibly. So did the crowd, the first time Nelson Piquet came through in his Williams Honda. The inverse aerofoils on a modern GP car are supposed to hold it on the ground no matter what, but Piquet's car was airborne. I could see daylight under all four wheels as the car came towards me like a contour-flying jet fighter whose low-level radar was playing chicken with its pilot. Seconds later there was daylight under my feet as I retreated down the hill to my hotel, where I watched the rest of the race on television, with the window open for authentic background noise.

Outside my window the cars were going past in real life. But on screen I could make some sense of who was going to finish where. Prost had it in the bag, with Rosberg second in the other McLaren, followed by Senna and Mansell. All as safe as a fairground roundabout. Then, outside the hotel, right next to where I had just been standing, Patrick Tambay's Lola did a barrel roll at head height and landed on its wheels, upright but a write-off. Very glad to have seen this on television, I scuttled downstairs to take a look at the reality. They were cleaning up the junk. Tambay walked away, a lucky man. One of the old cars would have killed him. The new ones crumple and burn less easily, but the force contained within them is so violent that they can never be quite safe. There will always be less hazardous things to do. Looking at the spilled oil, I could see how the Cannes Film Festival might be less of a worry.

After an unbeatable train ride along the beaches, Cannes loomed, full of movies. Billboards bulked large along the Croisette. The American stars had stayed at home but their faces had made the trip. Only Sylvester Stallone's face looked shrunken. Outside the Carlton Hotel a cardboard cut-out of Stallone was pretending to be someone called Cobra, who apparently outguns Rocky and Rambo combined as a force for justice. It was easy to laugh at this, but more difficult to imagine the scale of security precautions that would have been necessary if Stallone had turned up. Those grenades on his belt would have been used up in the first five minutes. They would have needed the Sixth Fleet out there.

Martin Scorsese wasn't present either. But then he doesn't fly anywhere, because people might be smoking somewhere on the aircraft. It's cigarette smoke he's afraid of, not terrorism. His *After Hours* was the first film I saw and I could scarcely have made a better start. A surrealist nightmare descended from Buñuel, it has the demented coherence of *The Discreet Charm of the Bourgeoisie*. I watched enthralled from high in the plush gallery of the high-tech main cinema in the Palais, and thought that if it took all the nonsense of Cannes to support an experience like this, it was worth the price.

The nonsense is pretty intense, however. If you're pushing a movie called *College Boys Go Nutsoid* or *Monster in the Closet* (IT'S COMING OUT!), you need a big girl inside the T-shirt to get attention. Down on the beach, startlets bared their breasts to the cameras, but since all the other girls on the beach had bared breasts anyway, it was coals to Newcastle, or cupcakes to Cannes. Upping the ante, Grace Jones, a kind of black Arnold Schwarzenegger without the femininity, kept postponing her first appearance, and completed the tease-play by actually *keeping her clothes on* – a communications breakthrough.

The magnificent prop ship from Roman Polanski's film

Pirates was anchored out near the lighthouse. Polanski himself was installed on the first floor of the Carlton but left for Paris when it became clear that the flick had not clicked. Having interviewed him for television when the film was still a dream, I was granted an audience as he moved out. 'See it in Paris. They like it there. Here the atmosphere is all wrong.' He could have been right. There were too many other pirates in town.

Not that Yoram Globus and Menahem Golan are pirates. The GoGo Boys are above all that. Their company, Cannon, still churns out programmers. In *P.O.W. The Escape*, David Carradine carries a bigger gun than Rambo on a smaller budget, proving that Cannon doesn't make lousy movies – it makes derivative lousy movies. But Cannon's profits are nowadays being ploughed back into higher ground. Their prestige picture for the year is Zeffirelli's version of Verdi's *Otello*, for which the GoGo Boys staged a press conference that Verdi could have set to music.

Zeffirelli, Placido Domingo and Katia Ricciarelli were all present, answering questions in four languages. A beautiful blonde Spanish journalist quizzed Placido about *las dificultades* of singing opera on film. Placido explained that all the difficulties were sorted out by Franco – by which he meant the director, not the dictator.

Franco himself was a bit overhung with gold bracelets but eloquent in praise of Cannon. 'The blood of cinema today.' Golan sat silent through all this but when his cavernous mouth finally opened he stole the show. 'Franco will direct *Aida* in Egypt. Not even he yet knows this.' Zeffirelli looked suitably stunned. 'It will be a gesture,' added Golan, 'for peace.' The whole Middle East crisis solved by a movie! What a concept!

British independent producers are worried that Cannon will take over their whole film industry before long. The GoGo Boys are their own producers and don't need anybody else. But the world needs the British independents, as this festival has proved. I could have done without *Sid and Nancy*, a reconstruction of punk rock nihilism which tries to shock all the time, as if shock, by definition, were not a variation on normality. Presumably I was meant to hate it. Nor was *Mona Lisa* the masterpiece it has been cracked up to be. But Bob Hoskins deserved his best actor award, and low-life London never looked more seductive.

The world is fascinated by the self-proclaimed decadence of Britain, perhaps because of a suspicion that it might spread, and will need art to make it tolerable. *The Mission* could not have been more welcome. Everyone wanted it to do well. There is something appealing about the way the British film industry gets through on a wing and a prayer. The whole of Goldcrest riding on one movie – it's like the Battle of Britain, with David Puttnam as 'Stuffy' Dowding.

The lonely airfield analogy was furthered by the British Pavilion, a marquee on the beach which became a home away from the hotel for British film people. Imagination had once again made up for lack of funds. The tent was open to the sea and sky at the back, an effect widely applauded as a theatrical coup. Actually the gap was meant to be glassed in, but the cash ran out.

Luckily it didn't rain. But things can't go on like this. Next year the Australians will undoubtedly have their own pavilion set up, sponsored by Foster's or Castlemaine. Their industry, however, was reborn not through sponsorship but through tax relief. Britain should do the same. Some of the money that would pour in would come from those medallioned characters whose yachts had tied up for the party, but at least it would be flowing in the right direction.

Just once I hitched a lift to Antibes for lunch at Eden Roc, where a young American producer, who was staying at the adjacent, laughably expensive Hotel du Cap, said, 'There's no *point* staying in Cannes.' He had come to Cannes to stay out of it. Defiantly I picked up the enormous bill with a credit card, which the waiter handled as if it were radioactive. I had to borrow some cash. From then on I ate sandwiches in the Britpav.

There is a lot to be said for travelling light. But the British can't have a snug, self-contained industry like the French, whose big movie of the festival was an opus by Claude Lelouch about what has happened to the lovers of *Un Homme et Une Femme* during the past twenty years. It turns out that they have spent the whole time preserving their personal appearance.

Britain speaks the same language as America and can't have a closed market. Like the racing cars, the films must take on the world. The bravery is already there. From the indy producers all the way down to the girls who run the Britpav, everybody in the British film industry works like stink. All that's needed is enough money to absorb the law of averages. As the racing teams know, there are some you must lose if you want to win.

As I left Cannes, Elio de Angelis lay between life and death after a shunt during testing at the fast Paul Ricard circuit. He was a rich boy whose need for accomplishment came from within. Nothing else but work can give fun in the sun its full savour. It was a thought to hold on to, as the handsome racing driver's plight proved that the difference between the poseur's glitter and the real glamour of achievement comes from risk. But the time I landed at Heathrow he was dead. Back to reality.

Observer
25 May, 1986

Nearly Mansell

IF THE sun had shone, last Sunday's big race in Adelaide would have been the perfect last Grand Prix of the Formula One season. If Nigel Mansell's left rear tyre hadn't blown out, he would have been world champion. But the sun didn't and the tyre did, reducing the Adelaide Grand Prix to the status of merely wonderful and depriving Mansell of the championship. Since the same shunt might well have deprived him of his life, however, Mansell had cause to bless his fortune while he cursed it.

Last year's first-ever Adelaide Grand Prix had mightily pleased the Formula One circus, which travels the world constantly and thus had global standards of comparison. Everyone was impressed with the effort, enthusiasm and prodigious amount of money that the Australians had put into the event. All these things were once again available on an even larger scale. The chief sponsor, Foster's Lager, enticed by the prospect of a worldwide television audience of 700 million people in forty-three countries, did not stint the outlay. The viewing public totalled almost three-quarters of the population of China. Even after you sub-tracted the under-age and allowed for those countries in which the consumption of alcohol is discouraged for religious reasons, it still added up to an awfully big potential fan club for the amber fluid. Foster's duly painted out the whole town in yellow and blue, affixing a huge letter F to anything or anyone that could not fight back.

Not even the America's Cup would be so identified with one product. Sporting sponsorship had reached an apotheosis. But no amount of hype can fix fate. Chance had been kind to bring the world championship all the way down to the wire. Having just failed to clinch things in Mexico, Mansell needed only to finish in the first three in Adelaide and he would be champion no matter what anybody else did. But if he didn't, either Alain Prost, driving for McLaren, or Nelson Piquet, Mansell's co-star in the Williams-Honda team, could snatch the championship by finishing first. Prost was the reigning champion and would like to stay that way. Piquet had been champion twice before and after several frustrating years in cars that broke down he would like to be champion again. Our Nigel was up against it.

Or perhaps I should say your Nigel. He is a nice man on top of being a terrific driver but when in Australia the present writer reverts to being an Australian and is much drawn to Alan Jones. Jonesie was yet another erstwhile world champion, but after a premature retirement he had now spent more than a year guiding the chassis of the Lola while the Ford engine behind his shoulders either failed to develop any significant power or simply fell to pieces. When the car worked he drove as well as ever, but it seldom did. The Australian Press has by now learned something about Grand Prix racing, but the idea that the local star driver might lose because his car couldn't win is a pretty subtle concept for the average media man to grasp, especially with so much free Foster's on tap. Jones was therefore under heavy pressure. From Day One of the meeting he was interviewed almost out of his mind.

So were they all, of course. In Australia, too much coverage chases too few stories. When a really big story crops up, the stampede is not to be believed. The Grand Prix drivers hardly dared leave the Hilton. Ayrton Senna, the brilliant young Brazilian respected for his hot shoe even' by those drivers who don't like his one-track mind, was badgered in the lift by Press and lit up like Christmas by portable television lights as he stepped lithely into the lobby. The lobby was jammed with race fans, autograph hounds and groupies, but so was the whole city.

Adelaide is a very pretty city. Laid out spaciously on flat land with the hills in the background strictly a backdrop, it is mostly only one storey high. Two storeys rate as imposing and any public building with a clock tower counts as a landmark. Flowers cascade over wrought-iron balconies. Outside of Grand Prix time, not a lot happens except the Adelaide festival, which has won international fame in the literary world but understandably doesn't generate the same fizz among the local girls as handsome young men dicing with death, etc. No doubt Julian Barnes, guesting at the festival next year, will set hearts beating, but he would be the first to admit that when reading aloud from one of his books he doesn't crank out as much aura as Nelson Piquet doing 200 mph, or even two miles per hour. Piquet just has to stand there and the young ladies bite the backs of their hands.

They are also very fond of Gerhard Berger, Andrea de Cesaris, Alessandro Nannini, Stefan Johansson and almost anyone else with his face in the official programme, including Murray Walker, the BBC race commentator who knows everything but gets it mixed up in moments of excitement. The Grand Prix circus, knowing that Murray loves the sport, is collectively very fond of him, but from Murray's angle what makes Australia so remarkable is that the fans are fond of him too. Murray Walker is a big star in Australia. When the sunlight bounces off that bald head, he gets mobbed.

Alas, raindrops bounced instead. This year it had not rained even in Monaco. Rain in Adelaide seemed like an insult. On Friday morning, the first session of untimed practice for the Formula One cars took place in an atmosphere of threatening downpour, periodically relieved by an actual downpour. Winding, as it did last year, through the city streets, with a detour into the racecourse for horses, the track, as it did not last year, either gleamed with rain or, worse, pretended to be dry. Greg Norman was a guest in Mansell's pit. Mansell had spent some time during the previous week playing golf with Norman and admiring his accomplishments. Now it was time for Norman to admire Mansell. Such, at any rate, was the surmise of several cynical motor racing journalists when Mansell, after howling away in an impressive manner, almost immediately clouted a wall, thereby dislocating the Williams-Honda FW11's precisely calibrated pull-rod rear suspension.

This indelicacy paled, however, beside what Patrick Tambay did to his Lola. Whacking the wall sideways at considerable speed, he reduced the car to abstract sculpture. Johansson did roughly the same thing to his Ferrari but in a more detached manner. He looked at the wall for a long time while the Ferrari was sliding towards it, as if he were picking out the nicest place to hit it. Derek Warwick (Brabham) was fortunate merely to skid off into a sandpit and get stuck. When a crane picked the car up he stayed strapped in, thinking that the crane driver might put him back on the track. Instead, he was lifted over the fence. He took this in good part, although after a frustrating year he would have been justified if he had shaken his fist at the sky, the car and the cruel world.

The word 'tragedy' is used too often in sports reporting. It was a tragic year for Brabham only to the extent that Elio de

Angelis, while testing the car in France, lost his life. But for Warwick and Riccardo Patrese, though nothing worse happened to them than disappointment, it was certainly the kind of season that reminds the racing driver, by wasting it, of how little time he has at the top. Gordon Murray's revolutionary low-profile design just never came right. The BMW engine was immensely powerful but the back end of the car floated. Here, at the last race of the season, Warwick was still getting wheelspin in sixth gear on the straight.

It hurts to see such a marvellous driver nobbled by the machinery. In sports car racing, Warwick is right on top. At Le Mans I saw him drive the Jaguar through the Mulsanne Kink at 240 mph in the dark. As I shivered with terror behind the armco barrier it occurred to me that a man who can do such things should be pleased with himself. But for Warwick, what really counts is F1. If the Grand Prix cars don't quite reach the top speeds of the sports cars, it is only because the straights are short. The speeds they reach, they reach faster. They do everything more quickly. Formula One is the ultimate test of a driver's reflexes and to waste a year in a duff car hurts like being locked up for something you didn't do.

Lunch was announced by a mass drop of parachutists out of the clouds. An aerobatic biplane performed between the cloud base and the ground, making the space available look generous by looping the loop sideways. Outside the hospitality tents it rained on the barbecues. Then the hooter went for an hour of timed practice, which lasted for forty-five minutes before a sudden cloudburst washed it out. Mansell, Senna, Piquet and Prost were fastest in that order. They had really been hurrying, because although there would be another qualifying session next day, it might rain even harder. Adelaide is closer to the South Pole than its citizens care to admit.

After practice a pair of Royal Australian Air Force F-18s arrived overhead with a bang, slowed down and stunted about under the cumulo-nimbus, which was almost touching the ground. They did a last pass with their afterburners on and the thumping blast was answered from the car park by the yelp of 100 alarms. The track was then occupied by Superkarts, which look like toys but go at 140 mph when they are not being rained on. This time they were not rained on. They were hailed on. In the paddocks behind the pits and the grandstands, the clay was churned to gunk. The Ligier team freely employed the word 'merde'.

Friday evening there was a ball under a marquee in front of the Hilton. This was the hottest ticket in Australia. Those whose applications for tickets had been successful – apparently money wasn't enough, you had to own land – turned up in 1920s costumes on the assumption that they would be doing the Charleston in close proximity to George Harrison and Mark Knopfler, not to mention all those fabulous-looking racing drivers. And indeed Harrison and Knopfler were nearby, but had other plans. So did the drivers. Only Jones put in an appearance. He had to. It was his turf and his sponsor. Bravely he kept smiling, but would probably rather have been getting his beauty sleep like the others. This rain thing was no joke. You could hear it on the roof of the tent.

But it was during this very night that the race organisers showed their strength. The impossible had been allowed for. Many tons of wood chips were schlepped into position and spread on the mud. The *merde* was converted to muesli. Tramping through this stuff, you still got your trainers caked with glop, but it looked no worse than breakfast food with a high bran content. Saturday morning was thus given an air of defiance. As if charmed, all the water stayed up in the sky for the solitary hour of timed practice on which starting positions would depend.

With only two permitted sets of qualifying tyres each, the top drivers like to put in at least one of their quick laps towards the end of the session, when they know what mark their rivals have set. This final session therefore usually boils down to a rush to be last. With so much rain waiting to fall, however, there was an equal imperative to get in early.

Mansell dealt with the problem by setting a fast time early on and consolidating it with about ten minutes to go. The Williams-Honda was a thrilling sight as it hurried. For qualifying, the F1 cars carry only a cupful of fuel and the engines are up-rated, to various degrees depending on the circuit.

At Hockenheim the Honda engine had been set to deliver about 1,100 horsepower. Here at Adelaide it was presumably asked to do a bit less, but whatever it did was enough to be going on with. All the fastest cars were averaging about 130 mph but Mansell was perceptibly faster, golden poplars of sparks suddenly growing behind the car as its undertray bottomed on the long straight at a speed of about 215 mph, give or take a breath. His pole position would have seemed secure, except that Senna had one set of qualifying tyres left and was notorious for the last-minute scorching lap. More often than not he snatches the pole and more often than not he subsequently loses the race. The Lotus-Renault is a thirsty beast, apt, during the race, to collapse from neurosis while trying to reconcile two contradictory urges – to go fast and to save petrol.

When qualifying, however, the car has only one thing on its mind. Like the tyres, the engine is built to last only a brief time, and some say that even the chassis is meant to be thrown away afterwards. Rival teams make disparaging remarks ('They're wheeling out the cheap car for Senna' was one variation I overheard) but perhaps this is partly their way of dealing with the consideration that Senna is a driver talented beyond earthly measure. It has been said that he tries too hard, but the same was said of Michelangelo. Anyway, with about two minutes left in the session, he dropped from the jacks, circulated once to warm up, and then started a lap which scared people who saw only a part of it. In the Channel 9 control room, from which the race would be transmitted to the world, I saw it all.

Through the screens of twenty-two television monitors, like a message being passed by a sequence of bonfires, the Lotus slid and twitched, with Senna's lemon-yellow helmet wagging from side to side with the G-force and the sparks spouting up in columns behind him as if the road had been split by a burst pipe full of liquid gold. On the long straight the camera helicopter panned with him but he left it nailed to the sky. He would have taken the pole for sure if he had not been balked near the end by a broken Zakspeed parked in the racing line. Thwarted, he eased right off and let his previous lap count. He was still well up in the grid.

Nor, with so much room to overtake, did grid position really matter that much. Senna had merely been following his personal quest to see everyone else off. Mansell and Piquet, on the other hand, had demonstrated the clear superiority of the Williams-Honda in its present form. Perhaps a little slower over two flying laps, it would be a lot stronger over two hours – strong enough to fulfil Niki Lauda's famous precept for the racing driver, to win as slowly as possible. McLaren, the dominant team before Williams edged them out, would still be in contention. Keke Rosberg, due to retire, was eager to go out with a repeat of last year's victory, and it is only Prost's lack of histrionics which keeps making him a surprise winner, when really he wins so often that he should only ever be a surprise loser. But Mansell and Piquet were sitting pretty for the race, and Mansell was sitting even prettier for the championship, since he didn't even have to finish first.

Grand Prix drivers take a long time to mature because they must strike a balance between two opposing forces – competitiveness and patience. Mansell by now, after ten years of effort, was the master of his own mind and unlikely to succumb to complacency. But a lot of other people were being complacent on his behalf. Nigel, they thought, would do it with a gear to spare. That night the streets were full of revellers. A total of forty-nine people were busted for inebriation, which meant that thousands of others, some of them drunker than anybody I have ever seen, got away with it. The drivers wisely took room service. To emerge from the lift would have meant ambush in the lobby, whose decorative clumps of potted plants had autograph-hunters hiding out among them like bands of partisans. When the lift doors sighed open, anyone who looked like a celebrity went down under a scrum. There was a Rosberg look-alike – a photographer from Belgium or somewhere – who simply found it less exhausting to sign Rosberg's name than to run away.

On television there was Adelaide Grand Prix on every channel. You couldn't switch the thing on without seeing Jackie Stewart. Leaving aside the question of his strange compulsion to sell everyone in the world a Rolex watch, Jackie is an admirable man on several levels. Not only did he win more Grand Prix races than anybody else ever, but his long and unremitting campaign for safety has ensured that the men drawn to the sport nowadays will most likely live to talk about it afterwards. If they want to talk about it the way Jackie does, however, they will need their own television station.

In the rain-washed shopping malls, dancing fans wore paper hats shaped like racing cars in Foster's colours. They wore the scarlet letter, and it was F. In the Hilton lobby the autograph hounds, like veteran revolutionaries growing beards in the hills, shared the long vigil that might yield them George Harrison. The drivers, lulled by Jackie's bag-pipe drone, slept early. The rest of us watched the sky. It was all cloud. Not a star to be seen.

Race day dawned with the sky still dark. Rain spat occasionally right up to and through the morning warm-up, during which Teo Fabi totalled his Benetton. Jones was down to his last engine, all the others having seized up or disintegrated. Back again at the start of two days' hard work, he had no hope. Everyone else spent the time driving in race trim. After the frenzy of qualifying, this was a return to realism, and immediately Prost started looking more of a threat. But the Williams-Hondas didn't miss a beat. Their only problem was everybody else's problem too. Would it rain a lot, or just a little bit? What if it didn't rain at all? There were piles of different tyres to choose from, but once they were on the car they couldn't be changed without losing time.

At lunch, there were not only historic cars but historic drivers. Shipped out to Adelaide at huge expense, one of the ten examples of the Mercedes Benz 300 SLR ever made went by with a stately old man at the wheel. It was Juan Manuel Fangio, five times champion of the world, and nobody doubted that if he chose to put his foot down the *Rennsport-*

wagen would depart from sight like a startled hare. Behind the big Mercedes came the smaller but prettier C-type Jaguar with Stirling Moss at the wheel. Never world champion, Moss deserved to be many times over. When he drove for Mercedes in the days of team orders, he was obliged to come second to Fangio even though he might well have won. Here he was coming second again, and still not complaining.

Behind Moss came Sir Jack Brabham, the Australian expatriate who first demonstrated the disproportionate influence his country could have on this strange sport which would be like an art if it were not like an industry. Three times world champion, he won his third championship in a car he built himself – an extraordinary combination of talents, never now to be repeated, because the technology of car design has become too specialised. It was a Wagnerian experience to see these heroic figures burbling gently along in cars which once frightened the horses. You got the impression that Valhalla had gone into the used car business. The purple and grey clouds billowing up from the south did nothing to dispel the effect.

As the time to start engines approached, everything happened in the air except sunlight. Parachutists dropped in swarms, helicopters charged each other, an F-18 came back and started all the car alarms again. It was like a war up there. You would have thought that all the noise would pull rain out of the clouds the way a gunshot can start an avalanche.

But somehow the track stayed dry. Perhaps Foster's had even more clout than we imagined. The cars rolled out on slick tyres, to be inundated by media as they sat on the grid, but by nothing else. Incommunicado inside their helmets, the drivers were safe at last from being interviewed.

At the start, Mansell was slow to get going, but that might have been wise. While Piquet, Senna and Rosberg broke away, Mansell settled into a nice steady fourth, content to let a certain amount of self-destruction take place up ahead. Rosberg, using all the road and most of the kerb, got past Senna and set off after Piquet in a boom-or-bust effort that probably didn't bother Mansell as much as it thrilled the spectators. It also seemed possible that Piquet was over-doing the boost, which would slow him down later. Senna was already slowing down, with something broken. Mansell slid past him without effort into third place. Rosberg went past Piquet in spectacular fashion but for Mansell the real news was how his mirrors were suddenly full of Prost, a mobile Marlboro billboard breathing down his neck.

Prost went by and Mansell was fourth again, but there was a long way to go, although not for Jones, who finished a miserable season in a stationary car, the Foster's can painted on his helmet staying all too still for the TV cameras. The ambitious brewery was learning the hard way that the sponsor, too, must take a chance. Their driver was out. Their Grand Prix, though, was getting lucky at last. The sky didn't exactly brighten but the air was turning dry. To prove it, the cars kept on speeding up.

As Prost closed on Piquet, the Brazilian spun out, which might have said something about the state of his tyres, but more likely meant that he didn't relish the idea of having Prost ahead of him as well as Rosberg. The Honda engine has an awe-inspiring amount of grunt, but it can stall like any other. Piquet kept it going all the way through the spin, gunned it at the right moment and got back on the road, having shown why he earns $64,000 a week. He now had both the McLarens ahead of him and Mansell as well. If Piquet's tyres had gone sour, it looked as if Mansell's hadn't. It was a large assumption but seemed reasonable.

Nearing half-way, Prost got a puncture and came in early for his tyre change, which a surprised pit crew fumbled. So it was Rosberg, Mansell and Piquet, with things looking rosy for your Nigel, whom, with Jonesie out of the running, I was now once again thinking of as my Nigel too, although Piquet was refusing to be shaken off.

Piquet tucked in behind Mansell for a tow down the straight, one Williams-Honda travelling in the other's vacuum at 200 mph. Piquet overtook and Mansell didn't fight – a sensible reticence. Rosberg was 35 seconds in front, but a bigger worry was Prost, only 12 seconds behind despite everything that had happened to him. While Rosberg, variously described by Murray Walker as 'the moustachioed Finn' or 'the virtually chain-smoking Finn' hurtled on, the race behind him came alive.

Should Rosberg do the unexpected – i.e. stay in one piece and win the race – then Mansell could still win the championship, but not from fourth position. He couldn't afford to let Prost get by. For several laps that must have seemed like several years, Mansell had Prost on his back like a knapsack. Some of the pressure was eased by the departure of the moustachioed, virtually chain-smoking Finn, one of whose tyres unravelled like a liquorice strap. Tyres were turning into the story of the race, although for a few minutes more nobody knew just how exciting the story would get. Prost went past Mansell and neither Mansell nor his general staff in the pits felt inclined to mark the occasion with a stop for new wheels. Controversy will rage for ever about whether this should have been done, but the short answer is that at the time there seemed no reason.

The whole Williams-Honda operation is state of the art technology. The car carries telemetry which enables the crew in the pit to consult all the same read-outs as the driver. In their collective wisdom they decided to let him stay out there, all unaware that one of the four rubber balloons holding that miracle of advanced engineering an inch off the ground was about to go pop.

Racing tyres are advanced engineering in themselves and are built to do almost anything except burst, but this one did, while the car was travelling at the full 200 knots. The instant effect was for the undertray in the left rear corner to smack the ground, sending up a gusher of sparks which would have caused Mansell, had he been facing the other way, to give up the ghost out of sheer fright. But he was fully occupied facing forward. The front right wheel lifted off the ground and then came down again as the undertray bounced up. Mansell had either two front wheels to steer through or only one, depending. Instead of locking his arms rigid, cramming on the brakes and yelling for help as you or I would have done, he drove the car all the way down to a standstill. Luckily this had plenty of room to take place in. If the straight had been

shorter, or he had blown the tyre farther down it, he would
have spun into the wall and out of this world. When the car
came to rest, the ragged rubber casing looped around the
empty silver rim gave a last vicious twitch, like a conger eel
dying on deck.

Prost won the race and his second championship in a row.
In his acceptance speech he was generous to Mansell, having
known disappointment himself. Late next morning Adelaide
woke with a cracking hangover to find that the clouds were at
last going. The Grand Prix circus had already gone, but not
before booking the same rooms for next year. Rain or shine,
they like Adelaide almost as much as Adelaide likes them.

Observer
2 November, 1986

Part Eight

LEAVE FOR CAPE
WRATH TONIGHT

Campaign Down the Drain

O<small>N MONDAY</small> morning the Michael Foot bandwagon was loaded up at its starting-point for the week's festivities. The news conference at Transport House took place in a large room entirely full of jostling media, except for the Labour Party spokesmen up on the dais, who sat in front of a backdrop dipped in the standard blood-stirring shade of radical crimson.

The backdrop also featured some radical grammar, to help remind you that this is the party of change. **THINK** POSITIVE **ACT** POSITIVE **VOTE** POSITIVE. This is more quickly said than **THINK** POSITIVELY **ACT** POSITIVELY **VOTE** POSI-TIVELY but one doubts if it is more quickly understood. Substituting adjectives for adverbs doesn't necessarily galvanise the act of comprehension.

As subsequent events were to demonstrate, Mr Foot, while placing great emphasis on the importance of your listening to what he is trying to tell you, has not always the knack of putting it in a way the normally equipped human being can unscramble. But at least his suit conveyed a clear message. The suit, which settled approximately into position with Mr Foot leaning at various angles inside it, was blue. It meant business. It also meant wrinkles, but not even the redoubtable Jill Craigie can keep her husband pressed and brushed when he is on the move. For now, it was enough that he looked less like a minor Georgian poet than usual.

Even bluer than the suit was the tie. Mr Peter Shore's tie, which was also present, showed you how red a Labour big-wig's tie can still be. But Mr Foot's tie was at the opposite end of the spectrum. Just around the corner, the Conservative Party news conferences were being staged in a deep-space blue ambience like a NASA briefing room. Without laying overt claim to the cold-eyed slickness of Tory PR,

Mr Foot had borrowed something of that atmosphere and got it into his tie, plus those parts of his suit which were visible above the podium.

But the borrowed clothes reached no higher than the neck. There was nothing crisp or glossy about his opening remarks, which even those reporters with good shorthand were finding it hard to get down. The remarks were often accompanied by the Little Laugh, the laugh which says that the question you are hounding him with has been answered often, and with exemplary clarity, before. Almost invariably it hasn't, but the laugh is meant to arouse the sympathy of the onlooker. Almost invariably it doesn't, but that doesn't mean that Mr Foot has lost faith in the technique. It has served him ill in the past, so he sees no reason to abandon it now.

Mr Foot's Little Laugh, however, is the merest distraction when compared with his syntax. He doesn't just say that 'this election is about jobs'. He has to add that 'this is the number one issue we raised at the start of the campaign and shall continue to raise until the end'. He says that he has said it before, as indeed he has, at the beginning of the sentence. Then he says he will say it again, as indeed he does, at the end of the sentence. Except there is no end of the sentence. The most you can hope for is that the sentence will get back to roughly where it started, so that the man uttering it will be struck by some recognisable phrase which he will pause to savour. This he does by nodding his head vigorously, in full agreement with himself.

But while the echo of his voice was still travelling in circles among helpless reporters comparing notebooks, Mr Foot's body was now lunging in a relatively straight line towards the waiting black Rover 3500 radio car which would take him out for the day's stint of stumping the country. The media had been issued with a cyclostyled itinerary listing the venues in which Mr Foot would arouse enthusiasm with his renowned oratory. But wheels were not supplied.

To follow the unscrupulous Mrs Thatcher it was merely necessary to climb aboard the bus which had so cynically been provided, but to follow Mr Foot required acumen, maps and a current Access card. Luckily the first destination was an easy one. Through fields of rape which looked as if the low hills had been thickly spread with Colman's English Mustard, it was possible to reach Leicester town hall by 125 mph train just in time to see the candidate ascending the stairs of the double-decker open-topped bus which would take him on a tour of the city through ecstatic crowds.

Largely due to the presence of the dishevelled media, there were more people on the bus than were detectable lining the streets, either at any one point or considered as a total. Lack of publicity was held to be the cause. It was also recalled that Sir Harold had spoken to sparse audiences and won. Meanwhile, the media massed tightly on the top deck of the bus did their generous best to point their cameras at the greatest concentrations of people they could find. Wherever two or three were gathered together, the image was captured. 'I'll just get a cutaway of these demented hordes waving,' said a cameraman, as two women in saris stood looking puzzled in front of the GANGES SPORTING CLUB (Members Only).

Stuck in the stairwell with an earphoned sound-man who had his rifle mike up on a stick like a periscope, I got a close-up view of the heels of Mr Foot's tractor-tread shoes as he stood at the front parapet of the bus, ducking his head under low bridges and waving to the assembled children of the proprietor of Shabir's Takeaway. The Central TV crew got off the bus to snatch an action shot of it moving. They got the shot of it moving but then they couldn't catch up with it. They were last seen sprinting along the traffic island as the bus arrived back at the city centre, like one of Mr Foot's sentences returning to its point of origin after the maximum possible waste of energy.

A Press conference then took place at which Mr Foot, given the opportunity to clobber the Tories' patronising poster about blacks, said *inter* a lot of *alia*, 'another of their wretched posters . . . thought up by Saatchi and Saatchi who haven't got the slightest interest in the politics of the matter. What the Labour Party is going to do and is pledged to do and will most certainly do . . .' Sludge without nuggets. The

TV cameras picked it all up but you could tell that the producers would find it impossible to edit. Tough on the Asians, who could have used a few memorable phrases to help keep them warm through the next five cold Tory winters which the polls were insisting stretched ahead.

Overland to Nottingham went the black Rover with the media Grand Prix in pursuit. Nobody wanted to miss the thrills and spills of the afternoon walkabout in the Broad Marsh shopping centre. The excitement was intensified by an element of secrecy, since the public has obviously not been forewarned, lest they congregate in too great numbers and impair the candidate's progress. 'Ooze iss?' said a woman in zip-fronted felt bootees. 'None of um's any good,' opined her morose companion. By now several members of the public had attached themselves to the frantic half-moon of media in whose brightly lit cusp Mr Foot lurched forward like a floppy toy on Benzedrine. He has an impressive turn of speed at those moments when slowness is what's called for. But when a baby was presented to be held, he stopped and held it. The baby hated him.

Mr Foot, although patently a very nice man, handles objects in the real world as if they ought to be books, and a baby can tell when the pair of encircling hands would rather be holding a copy of Hazlitt's *Dramatic Literature of the Age of Elizabeth*. It was also possible that Mr Foot's hands would rather have been holding the neck of the local organiser, who in theory was a different man in each place, but in practice seemed to be the same chap moving one day ahead and making sure that no posters were put up, or, at best, that the word was spread by a single clapped-out Ford Escort with a defective bull-horn.

Tuesday started in Birmingham, with a public meeting in St Agnes Hall, Pershore Road, Cotteridge, out past the Stirchley 10-Pin Bowl and Fred's Frocks, just across from Richelle Frozen Foods (12 FISH FINGERS 55p). The church hall itself had a wooden vaulted ceiling, a stripped pine floor and the proudly displayed, yellow-tasselled banner of the Eighty-seventh Birmingham Company of the Boys' Brigade. The walls resounded with the unmistakable forlorn echo of generations of pimply boys in forage caps numbering off from left to right.

But by the advertised time the place was full, and not just with media, who were soon uncomfortably aware of being in possession of that increasingly precious thing, a salary. Most of the 150 or so people in the audience were unemployed, including the convenor, a stout man in a brown suit who called out, 'Reg! Reg! Is there any chance of a joog and a couple of glasses?' Mothers in anoraks cuddled already fractious toddlers, one of whom, a militant in the making, held the string of a pink balloon. Here were the converted waiting to be preached to.

The preacher arrived to a standing ovation, which was certainly not for his clothes. Grey instead of blue, today's suit was a reversion to type. If he didn't precisely look like a minor poet, he did look like a minor essayist. After sitting down and pretending to be riveted by an introductory speech of death-dealing tedium from the local candidate, Mr Foot rose to remind the local candidate that when it came to the handing out of boring speeches the champion was now in town.

'Friends may I. First of all thank you for your. WELCOME, and I . . .' The full stops, as always, were seldom at the end of the sentence, but today were cropping up with remarkable frequency during it. For an audience to whom good words would have been bread, here came a whole cargo of stones. There was passion in his heart, but he couldn't say what was on his mind. 'I know that reports appear in the newspapers about the polls but I say that they should. Report faithfully mass meetings like this.'

Reg having neglected to open the windows of the tiny hall, the mass meeting began to heat up under the television lights. Babies with dummies breathed smoke through the nose. 'Year after year after year the curse of unemployment hitting people harder and harder.' He believed it, but said it as if he didn't.

The next event was an intersuburban media motocross to Redditch, for Mr Foot's scheduled walkabout in the new Kingfisher Centre, a hardened ICBM silo masquerading as a shopping mall. On the upper level of a precinct, or the upper precinct of a level, was the Labour Party district office, where Mr Foot paused for tea and a brief interview with ITN, all other media in attendance. When Mr Foot's noble forehead is lit up by a sun-gun the veins show through the skin. Venerable and vulnerable, he looks what he is, an intellectual in a false position. But on the matter of nuclear disarmament the false position now began to sound untenable. 'Stage by stage ... move towards ... along the lines ...'

Stage by stage along the lines of the upper lower precinct level, Mr Foot moved towards Sainsbury's between glass shop-fronts and under tropical foliage gròwing in suspended concrete pipes. With Jill Craigie and Dizzy the wonder-dog in hot pursuit, he proceeded in a sun-gun halo to run tight circles around a grove of palm trees. Once again the security blackout had been almost totally successful. Apart from the local candidate and some ladies Knitting for Peace, few seemed interested. To those who might be, Mr Foot promised 'a thumping majority for Dick'. A blind lady asked, 'Dick who?'

Dizzy, a 2½-year-old Tibetan terrier who looks like an astrakhan tea-cosy soaked with shampoo, and who will instantly attack any other dog threatening to cramp his style on national television, moved on, towing everybody else with him.

Wednesday started at Transport House, with Mr Foot back in the blue suit but wearing a red tie with white polka dots. Overnight a new word had entered the nuclear debate. The new word wasn't peace, but pace. 'I think in five years we will be able to. To move towards ... the *pace* must be judged by the government that is there.'

Then into the Rover and away to Peterborough, for a public meeting in the Wirrina arena, a roller-skating rink with yellow walls and a sign saying Beadle Roller Skates PERFECTION ON EIGHT WHEELS. The joint was the size of an airship hangar and there were scarcely 200 people in it. The Labour Party's cunning policy to wear out its leader with meaningless, botched engagements had reached fruition.

'What I believe,' said Mr Foot to the reverberating void, 'is going to be decided on July the. On June the 9th.' The cameras had already drooped, the sound-men as usual had not bothered to re-load, and no producer would screen such slips anyway. Although Mr Foot finds it hard to believe, television is not out to cross him up. He does that all by himself. He is a man who has been mastered by the English language. It can do anything with him.

At the Thursday morning news conference, in the presence of Norman Mailer, the effluent finally hit the air-conditioner. Speaking about the allegedly crystalline clarity of Labour's position *re* Polaris, general secretary Mr Jim Mortimer put Foot in it. The question about whether the party hierarchy still had confidence in Mr Foot's leadership was answered by Mr Mortimer resoundingly in the affirmative. Unfortunately, he answered the question before any of us had asked it. As it happened, the first reporter to ask the question that had just been answered was myself, but that was only because I was too naive to realise the full import of what Mr Mortimer had said. Everybody else, with the possible exception of Norman Mailer, was thunderstruck. The party wise men looked as if they just received word that a Soviet SS-20 was about to arrive at Labour headquarters in Walworth Road, SE17 1JT.

Mr Foot spent the rest of the day being worn out by eventettes in South London. The grey suit came into contact with the hot pants of Michele, billed as a professional photographer's model and non-operative chimney sweep. He cuddled a convalescent fox cub, which was more than Dizzy would have done. He told a hospital that he would replenish its funds. It was the right promise, but given out of turn. On *Nationwide* that evening he was pressed flat on the Polaris issue by Sue Lawley.

The sentence he started on *Nationwide* was still going when I switched on *TV Eye* three hours later. Then, for once in a blue moon, he paused for breath. Alastair Burnet asked him whether there was dissension in the leadership, and before he could get started on the next interminable evasion a tiny, glowing chip of candour popped out. 'We *have* got trouble . . .'

He had forgotten to think positive and given a straight answer. It is a weakness to which good men are prone.

Observer
29 May, 1983

~~~

As the book which he later published reveals, Michael Foot took particular exception to the above piece, which he believed typified the way in which the media framed him. But really he received, from the up-market papers anyway, a fair press, and the men responsible for his shambolic campaign a better than fair, because they threw him to the wolves and were called nothing worse than fools for doing so. My one lasting regret about guying an honest and considerable man is that the piece contributed, I hope in only a small way, to the general impression that the Labour Party lost the election because of bad public relations. Actually they lost because of that and their defence policy, a point made more obvious by the general election of 1987, when Neil Kinnock's presidential-style campaign ran like clockwork but the vote scarcely increased.

Underdog at Overlord

AT DAWN last Tuesday, 5 June, D-Day Anniversary Minus One, I was at Waterloo station with all my equipment – notebook, two felt-tips, spare socks – and looking for my train to Portsmouth. A BR man in one of those caps that look so like the head-covering of a Second World War German NCO carefully loaded me on to the train for Bournemouth.

Panicking just in time, I was directed by another BR man on to the train for Weymouth. Finally, I was on the train to Portsmouth and arrived in time for the day's first Townsend-Thoresen ferry to Cherbourg. It was full of sane old soldiers dressed as civilians and insane young civilians dressed as soldiers.

In contrast to the way it had behaved forty years earlier, the sea was calm, but as we headed south on that historic route, my stomach was in a turmoil. A media man on the anniversary of a big battle runs only one risk, but the risk is great: that he will mistake the tone. He wants neither to be hangdog at the farce, nor to giggle at the funeral. The old Americans had paunches, white shoes, low-slung pink tartan golf slacks, globular wives and funny caps. But the funny caps said 29th DIVISION ASSOCIATION, meaning the men wearing them had been at Omaha Beach, the abattoir of the invasion, where too many of those who got ashore stayed young.

You had to be careful about the angle at which you smiled while these doddering survivors, loudly and without listening, addressed one another concerning junk food and heart failure, two phenomena whose intimate connection they seemed unable to detect. 'The nurse comes in, she's got my chart, it's peaking at seventy beats per minute, so they put my pacemaker back on the machine . . .' 'Where did she get that Diet Coke? I didn't see where she got it. Where did you get that Diet Coke?' 'It's not Diet. It's regular. It's regular Coke.'

Once they had been young GIs. Looking at them with sidelong glances of envy were a lot of young GIs who turned out to be British. Members of the Military Vehicle Conservation Group, or MVCG, they each wore immaculately pressed US Army surplus clothing. Down on the car-deck were the jeeps and trucks they had refurbished. A storeman with a computer firm had spent £150 on his uniform and £2,000 on his jeep.

In the critical regard of today's warlike British youth, the fighting services of their own country rate low for glamour, not just because of the low-quality cloth – in the Second

World War the American other ranks were far more snazzily dressed than our officers – but because of the paucity of accessories. As an ordinary GI in the MVCG Surplus Army you can wear dark glasses and chew gum. Even if you were dressed as General Montgomery, the most you could add to the dreary old battledress would be a pipe and a stick.

As if to prove this point, some veteran British cavalry officers were present, talking quietly together. Red berets were their only tribute to the past, and these, I was told, were the wrong colour, having been purchased at the last minute. These men rather gave the impression that any incipient urge to dress up and play silly buggers had been knocked out of them some time previously by their repeated encounters with the 12th SS Panzer Division.

We reached Cherbourg with no casualties except one diabetic American veteran who was so drunk he couldn't remember whether he had taken his insulin. As the jeeps and trucks rolled down the ramp for the re-invasion of France, I teamed up with some media types on the wharf and shared a taxi to the Press centre in Bayeux, where we were to receive the essential accreditation without which it would be impossible to move on the roads next day, because the French CRS, with seven Heads of State to protect, would have the whole area shut down.

Rommel had once tried to do the same but failed. On the highway heading east through the *bocage* country, it began to seem likely that it wouldn't work this time either. Every road and lane was stiff with the long-obsolete but magically spanking wheeled transport of the all-American Surplus Army. There were military ambulances with the canvas tops rolled up so that you could see the wounded lying bravely there inside, a Lucky Strike gummed to the lower lip and a bloodstained bandage around the forehead. A half-track went past us going the other way with the driver's eyes blacked out behind dark glasses. He had a Steve McQueen haircut and was chewing a cigar. Surely all these people couldn't be British?

They weren't. A convoy of jeeps had Dutch number plates. One of the trucks had German number plates. There was, of course, no particular reason to think that the teenage Germans now riding around in old US vehicles were of the same stamp as those cold-eyed young beauties who had once crewed the Panther tanks of the *Hitlerjugend* SS Panzer formations. That lot had admired Adolf Hitler and Sepp Dietrich, whereas this lot had plainly awarded their allegiance to George Segal and Ben Gazzara, pending the time when age and experience would make them plausible imitators of Robert Mitchum. *Doppelgänger* is, after all, a German word.

At Bayeux, I picked up my ID tag and was assured that for journalists there were no beds left in Normandy. In expectation of this, I had brought a sleeping bag, but what I needed was a floor on which to spread it. As an old media man, I was aware that in this scale of operation a journalist ranks lower than the infantry. The television units get all the facilities. BBC *Breakfast Time* was based down on the coast at a pretty house in Arromanches. I got there to discover the next morning's D-Day Dawn edition of *Breakfast Time* in an advanced stage of planning.

Selina Scott, looking military in a sand-coloured jacket and sensible shoes, was interrogating some veterans. Frank Bough was test-riding a British infantryman's collapsible bicycle. The back-up personnel moved purposefully between chattering visual display units linked to London. David Dimbleby, duplicating maps on a Gestetner 2002R, said, 'It's a weapon we're very glad to have.' Presumably he was on attachment to *Breakfast Time* for the big day. *Breakfast Time* is the Beeb's spearhead unit. It goes in ahead of everything else. It goes in ahead of the cornflakes. It goes in ahead of the orange juice.

The BBC had everything except a stretch of floor for a mere journalist. They didn't even have room for one of their own, Guy Michelmore, who gave me a lift to Caen so that I could look for ITN. Dodging past columns of Surplus Army conserved vehicles, Michelmore – second generation media, born to this sort of campaign – dropped me off at the Novotel, where ITN were supposed to be based. But they had moved out, swamped by the influx of old soldiers.

It looked like being a cold night under a hedgerow until Jacqueline, the organiser for Townsend-Thoresen tours, took one look into my war-weary eyes and offered me a room, but I would have to share. You can imagine that I was quick to smile my assent, and not long afterwards I was sacked out beside Georges, a French bus driver who snored like a sick horse.

Dawn on D-Day was H-Hour for BBC *Breakfast Time*, transmitting live from the Arromanches esplanade with the ruins of the Mulberry harbour in the background. With the sound of Georges still ringing in my ears, I went back down that beautiful winding road, now remarkably free of conserved vehicles, and hit the beach just in time to see Vera Lynn and Selina Scott profiling together against the pale blue cyclorama of sky and sea, Selina in a black cape arrangement as modern as tomorrow and Dame Vera in complete wartime kit right down to the khaki stockings and the silk scarf of the Dutch Airborne. There they were, the finest of British womanhood from two generations: Why We Fight. And there were the conserved vehicles of the Surplus Army, all down on the beach lining up to file past the BBC cameras on cue: the jeeps, the trucks, the half-tracks and, unbelievably, a Sherman tank.

'Everything's going according to plan,' said producer Rachel Atwell. 'But we haven't got autocue.' There was a lot of talk-back radio traffic between the technicians. 'All the veterans are in position.' 'Has Selina got that bit of paper?' 'She's got it and she's happy.' The vehicle convoy started to move. Three DUKWs came in from the sea, firing pink flares at the beach. One of the flares hit a French spectator, who was carried to the infirmary: the first casualty of the D-Day anniversary, not counting the paralytic diabetic on the ferry.

The hiccup was smoothed out by the Gang, whose piano was in position on the same spot it had occupied when they came ashore on D-Day + 16. 'We were the first electric guitars ashore in France,' explained one of the Cox twins, either Fred or Frank. Cardew Robinson did a stand-up routine that made me laugh so hard some of the French onlookers laughed too. They didn't understand, but they trusted us. It was generous of them, considering that one of their number had just been shot. 'Why are we doing the thing that we do?' sang Vera Lynn, and the heart of every man listening held the unspoken answer: to keep the world safe for you and Selina.

Just as Dame Vera and the British veterans got started on 'We'll Meet Again' (Selina joined in as if unsure of the words, the way Harold Wilson used to sing 'The Red Flag' at the Labour Party Conference) I was speeding across country to Caen railway station, where a train was due to leave for Carentan. A luxurious all-first-class express laid on free for the media – France can afford such gestures, even under Mitterrand – it carried hundreds of calmly drinking journalists westward behind the beaches, while the morning sky thickened with police helicopters supervising the roads, the hedges, the corn fields and the ruminating cows, any one of which might be Colonel Gadhafi in disguise.

From Carentan there was a fleet of buses to Utah Beach, where there was a Press tent featuring open-door *pissoirs* and an opportunity to buy a sandweej or an ert derg. With an ert derg in each hand I trudged over the dune to be gently dazzled by a sea as flat as unrolled silk with one fold about twenty yards out and the dove-grey silhouettes of warships painted on it at the far edge.

But an old media campaigner doesn't waste time admiring the view, until he has taken his position and dug in. I got right up against the front fence of the Press enclosure, with an angle on the dais, so that I could see the row of little gold chairs on which the seven Heads of State would be sitting. There was a staircase of terraced sand leading up to it from the beach. In preparation for the feet of Mitterrand, the Queen of England, Ronald Reagan and the rest, some men were assiduously sweeping the staircase, but sweeping sand free of sand is never easy. Security frogmen were operating off the beach in case Yasser Arafat attacked from under water.

A French Army officer was doing the bilingual commentary. His French was Neo-Classical, his English impressionistic. 'You can see in the offing about three or four

343

nautics . . .' Hundreds of media people from every nation including Germany, Italy and Japan were now in the enclosure or the camera tower beside and behind me. A short Arab reporter tried unsuccessfully to infiltrate my position. The Red Devils dropped from a C-130, but I had seen something more impressive at ground level.

It was Paul Callan of the *Mirror*, leapfrogging through from the Irish campaign in which the President of the United States had rediscovered his Irish ancestry – a remake of *The Quiet Man* with Reagan essaying his greatest role, that of John Wayne. Callan was sick with flu and fatigue but still on his feet. The *Mirror* had laid on a whole house for its eleven people, but ten of them were photographers who had booked themselves into hotels so as to ensure bar facilities. This had left Callan sole occupant of a château whose walls were dripping with Monets and Cézannes.

Parachutists of all nations kept on coming down, blown about by a breeze now freshening. Ranged along the beach, the military bands of the seven nations successively uncorked their party pieces. Of the twenty-eight soldiers from the seven nations standing in readiness at the flagpoles, twenty-seven were men. The only woman was in the French colour party. She fainted, perhaps in ecstasy at the music made by the French band. One of the many stretcher teams moved in and took her away. A camera crew leaned in over my shoulder to get the shot. It was ITN!

A cluster of helicopters dropped from the sky, and one of them disgorged Mitterrand. This was the big moment. You could feel even the most experienced journalists tensing up. The Japanese wire service reporters restrained the impulse to wrap white scarves around their foreheads, but I saw with my own eyes an American girl radio reporter brushing her hair. Mitterrand approached the dais, followed by our Queen, President Reagan, Pierre Trudeau and the King or Queen of Belgium, Norway or the Netherlands – few of us were sure which and it was hard to concentrate under the opaque gaze of the American Secret Service, who were now standing everywhere and looking at us through their dark glasses. One of them had his fawn mackintosh folded over his right arm with the hand hidden, meaning he had an Ingram sub-machine-gun under there. It seemed misguided at the least to be putting the hard stare on a pack of media while the countryside was stiff with nutters driving their own tanks.

Also an old media footslogger is hard to frighten. As the crowd of journalists stood transfixed, I saw Peter McKay of the *Mail* infiltrating effortlessly from behind. A Taiwanese reporter carelessly moved aside from his position on the fence and McKay was in. Today the British media were showing the world.

So were the British aircraft conservationists. A Lancaster, a Spitfire and a Hurricane paraded slowly past overhead. Slower still came a Swordfish torpedo biplane, watched with appreciation by our Queen. Seated beside Mitterrand, she turned to him and made a rotating movement with her finger, as if telling him what a propeller was, or else saying, 'We sank the *Bismarck* with one of those. Where were you?'

But Mitterrand was in the Resistance. Everyone up on the dais was a veteran, no one more so than Ronald Reagan, who was in army movies, air force movies, submarine movies: Combined Operations. His military training shows in the way he puts his hand on his heart when the national anthems are playing. All the Heads of State stand straight, but Reagan stands straighter, practically taking off backwards while his right hand says, 'Look! No pacemaker!' Once again you can see how the British play things down. The Queen, even while they are playing her song, does no more than look thoughtful and feel her own pulse while the handbag dangles. Reagan has a handbag too, but it is carried by an officer and can start an atomic war.

The Alphajets of the Patrouille de France come in low from the horizon, trailing *tricolore* smoke. They do a bomb-burst breakaway in front of the dais. The Duke of Edinburgh, seated in the second row today because he is not a Head of State, likes this bit and takes a quick shufti through a little pair of binocs. But now Mitterrand speaks. He speaks well, generous even about the Germans, *l'ennemi redoutable*. Perhaps the Germans will be invited next year. But not this year, with the security aspect such a nightmare. The CRS in their dark glasses are already worried about the US Secret Service in their dark glasses. A bunch of old *Waffen* SS men in *their* dark glasses would have been too much.

Mitterrand having concluded, the Heads of State move down the swept-sand staircase to inspect the honour guards and shake hands with the actual D-Day veterans camped almost out of sight, along the sand in both directions. Mitterrand points out the abundance of sand to the Queen. He seems very proprietorial about the sand. His gesture says, 'This is our sand.'

And suddenly it was all over. The Heads of State dispersed into the sky like bees quitting an old hive. The veterans would stay on until the next morning, but for the media it was time to get out. Threatened by another night of bunking up with the stertorous Georges, I cadged a lift with Tim Graham, Terry Fincher and a couple of other photographers from the old outfit which had covered the Queen's amphibious tour of California. Typically the boys had a four-seater private plane waiting for them at Caen airport. At the price of helping them talk their way through the CRS roadblocks, I could tag along.

The job made fierce demands on my rudimentary French, but the great secret in dealing with a detachment of CRS is to realise that there is always one guy they don't lobotomise, so that he can tell the others who to hit. '*Nous sommes,*' I explained, '*les photographers personales de la Reine d'Angleterre.*' At never less than 100 mph, we zoomed along back roads that had once cost a life a yard. At Isigny, the famous butter factory is now owned by the Germans. At Caen airport, it turned out that not even the faithful Jacqueline had been able to talk my bag through the roadblocks.

My team had to be back in England with their film before last light. Their plane left without me. Then my bag arrived in its own taxi. First a plane but no luggage, now my luggage but no plane. An Andover with the Queen on board taxied out, but they didn't offer me a lift.

Then Max Hastings turned up. To celebrate publication of his excellent book *Overlord*, he had been touring the battlefields with his publisher, his agent and two beautiful blondes. This was a media command unit, outstripping for cachet even the Selina Scott First Airborne, which had already gone back to England, but on a plane serving only BBC coffee. Max's little twin-engined Cessna had champagne and cigars.

Poised on my rolled-up sleeping bag between two seats, I looked down at the beaches as they retreated into the distance. And into the past, despite all that the toy soldiers of the Surplus Army can do to hold back time. They were still down there, pretending to shoot one another, pretending to be dead – a pretence true to every detail of the reality except its essence. Half-way through a cigar, I started to remind myself of General Patton, so I stubbed it out.

Observer
10 June, 1984

Nothing Can Hold Back the March of History

NEXT YEAR, if Cuba can make the deal it wants to with one of the big British tour operators, there will be a direct charter flight from London. For now, we had to catch the regular Cubana flight from Madrid to Havana.

By 'we' I mean a small party of British travel journalists whom the Cuban government tourism department Intur wanted to tell about the glittering prospects for diversion which their readers might not normally, unless promped, associate with the home island of Latin-American Socialism. People have somehow got the idea that Cuba is a mass meeting which Fidel Castro has been addressing continuously for twenty-seven years. We scriveners would disabuse them of that impression, after first having been disabused of it ourselves.

If that was the plan, it worked. When you can get there without hassle, Cuba will be worth going to see. Bits of it will, anyway. Other aspects are not so enticing, and lest, in describing these, I seem ungrateful to my hosts, it is best to say at the outset that I look back on the experience with gratitude. Cuba's bid to make the world welcome should be welcomed in its turn, even if the locally prevalent bureaucratic inefficiency leaves your nerves in shreds. As an island, Cuba has a lot going for it. As a State, it has a lot going against it. Classical Marxists will recognise that a thesis and antithesis have been stated here, from which a synthesis will duly emerge.

Classical Marxists would also have recognised our airliner, a hulking Russian Il-62M whose front passenger compartment was full of crated radio equipment from Copenhagen. Actual passengers, in addition to their rolled-up bullfight posters, carried Japanese stereo equipment purchased in Madrid. They all drank Cuban rum as if there would be less of it when they got to Cuba. Clearly we were heading towards part of the consumer goods vacuum known to history as Socialism.

Havana had much to teach. The lessons started with billboards at the airport. NO SOMOS UN PAIS RICO PERO SOMOS UN PAIS DIGNO. We are not a rich country but we are a dignified one. My mastery of the language, acquired from a tape called Lazy Spanish, had passed its first test. It failed the next one, however. Our Intur guide was a charming young man who spoke excellent idiomatic English. His Spanish, on the other hand, sounded like my teach-yourself tape stuck on fast forward. There went my free Spanish conversation lessons.

Built before the revolution, the erstwhile Hilton Hotel is now called the Havana Libre. The carpets are stained, not everything works first time, and room service rarely arrives. To compensate, the hit-men and pimps of olden times are no longer on the scene. It's a toss-up. Which do you like, clean carpets you might end up as a dead body on, or a run-down room in which your personal safety is guaranteed? The shops in the hotel were run by Intur and wanted our US dollars. They wouldn't take the local money. Having predicted that US dollars would be useless, I had armed myself, immediately upon arrival, with a fistful of Cuban pesos. Luckily the shops, however desperate for foreign currency, could offer, apart from rum and cigars, very few things worth buying, so it didn't matter that I had no dollars to buy them with.

My pesos I took out to La Rampa with the intention of buying an ice-cream to offset the immense heat. La Rampa is the show street of modern Havana. Everybody makes the *paseo* there in the evening. They look at each other and queue to eat ice-cream. At the most famous ice-cream parlour the queues were endless. I joined the shortest one and grew old waiting. By the time my turn came there was only one kind of ice-cream left. I began to suspect that from the economic viewpoint Cuba might be just the Soviet Union plus humidity. Some of the waiting girls, however, were very pretty, in a neatly turned-out way that made it look as if the revolution would be good clean fun to join.

Next day we were shown old Havana, consisting of historic fortresses, historic government buildings and historic Intur shops the locals aren't allowed inside. Take away the towering palms and it could have been Leningrad, a resemblance emphasised by the number of Russian oil tankers in the harbour. Russian tankers provide 95 per cent of Cuba's oil and 100 per cent of the oil slick that surrounds Havana.

The bookshops were full of party-line Soviet books translated into Spanish. More surprisingly, nearly all the books of local origin looked as if they were ready to be translated into Russian. The literature of the Spanish-speaking heritage was absent from the shelves. Marxist-Leninist tracts prevailed.

Of these, the least deadly looking were by Fidel himself. I bought a book-length interview called *Nada podrá detener la marcha de la historia*. Nothing can hold back the march of history. It sounded promising. Fidel's picture on the cover brought back memories of the heroic age when he and Che were two beards united against injustice everywhere. *Cuba sí!*

Indeed, I was hoping to find a few old revolutionary posters in the shops. At the risk of indulging in radical chic, I would have liked a good wall-sized Che to take home so that my daughter could supplement her plaster bust of Lenin with a portrait of a better man. But the old colonial building which had been converted into an Intur shopping precinct was not in the business of peddling rebellious mementoes. Apart from the brandy and cigars, the main item on sale, replicated a thousand times and stacked in heaps, was a rural scene of toiling peasants preserved in the form of a brown ceramic wall-plaque that looked like a cow pat and was heavier than a discus.

Melting in the humidity, my wrist sprained from test-lifting a wall-plaque, I was glad to be led into Floridita, the famous bar in which Ernest Hemingway drank daiquiris. The barman built him a jumbo daiquiri in the biggest glass that could be filled with frappéd ice without the ice congealing into a berg under its own weight. Having been on the wagon for twelve years, I fell off in order to bring you an authentic report of how it feels to drink one of these concoctions in an air-conditioned, dollars-only bar while the rest of Cuba is sweltering outside. I was fairly certain that it felt good, but I wanted to be sure, so I ordered another. It felt very good. You can definitely put a daiquiri in Floridita on top of your short list of things to do in Havana after you've watched a Russian tanker unloading.

The cold truth, or rather the hot truth beaded with sweat, is that most of Havana is falling apart. The streets are free of pot-holes but otherwise it looks like Nairobi. The inhabitants are fit – Cuban health statistics are as good as ours – but it takes all the native genius for mechanical improvisation to keep the capital functioning. Citizens of Havana have the extensive facilities of Lenin Park to make them feel wealthy, but they go home to a city which is essentially a pile of old American junk, a predicament exemplified by the number of superannuated Detroit cars still miraculously on the road. Heirlooms from the 1950s, made fat by amateur resprays, their quondam chrome trim now frosty with silver paint, Oldsmobiles, Buicks, Dodges and Plymouths bulk proudly in the streets of Havana as if it were a tailfin-era copy of *Collier's* advertising next year's models. Harbingers of a forgotten future, they make Cuba look like a hangover.

It's a false impression. Next morning we were out in our minibus rolling east on the *autopista*, and the country's beauty began to unfold. Well kept, busy with Russian trucks, it was as green as green can be without making you want to lean forward and adjust the colour control. Mangoes hung fatly. There was also a rich crop of revolutionary slogans. A succession of roadside billboards welcomed us to each town. VIVA LA AMISTAD SOVIETICA-CUBANA. Long live Soviet-Cuban friendship. Perhaps it was better not to translate them. 'Ideology is, above all, consciousness.' They didn't sound quite so stirring in English.

Finally we arrived at Varadero, the seaside resort which counts as Cuba's main thrust at the world tourist market. Significantly, there were few billboards. The emphasis was suddenly switched from struggle to relaxation. For tourists, that is. The Cubans would be doing the catering.

At the Hotel Internacional they do it fairly well, on a self-service basis that at least lets you pick and choose among the two main dishes on offer, instead of ordering one of them from a waiter and getting the other. Energy restored, we walked out of the back door and on to the beach, which was simply perfect. The sand was soft and stretched for a mile each way. The sea was clear and blue and the bottom shelved so gently that you could walk to Florida. What would happen, goes the old joke, if the Sahara went Socialist? The answer is: nothing, for the first ten years, and then there'd be a shortage of sand. At Varadero it hasn't happened yet. When the airport is extended and there are direct flights from Gatwick, you will be flat on your back without ever having found out that Cuba is a Communist country.

Water-skiing and wind-surfing were available if we couldn't conquer our Protestant work ethic. I conquered mine. For a day and a half I did nothing between swims except burp about on a Honda moped. At $2.50 per hour, without licence or crash helmet, I buzzed all over Varadero, which turned out to be a long promontory only a couple of hundred yards wide. At the far end was the Dupont mansion. The American tycoon who opened up Varadero used to bring his friends there by yacht and private plane. Now his house is the Restaurante Las Américas. The food is dull and the tiles blown off the roof by the last hurricane have not been replaced, but you can't object when the playground of the élite becomes the collective recreational amenity of the masses, especially if the masses include you. There were even a few Cubans present, blowing their precious dollars on a big day out.

The East Germans, with whom each Varadero hotel was stuffed to the rafters, no doubt get an assisted passage. But the Canadians go there because it's a hop, step and a jump and costs peanuts. 'I've never seen such a wonderful place as Varadero,' said a woman from Niagara Falls, who had previously been to Barbados, Nassau and Puerto Rico. 'Everything in Barbados costs at least *twice* as much.' She was especially pleased with the low price of the brown ceramic wall-plaques, of which she had bought two, presumably so as not to develop asymmetric shoulders.

With blue water glittering in the background I did in-depth research into daiquiris and the different lengths of Havana cigar. The girl reporter in our party collected material for an important suntan. Intur needed only to have left us alone and we would have written reports they could have used as a brochure. But our guide had his orders. The prepared itinerary said that we must see all the major installations of tourism.

So off we sped through the heat and cane-fields. No *autopista* this time: just a two-lane blacktop, but in good repair. The slave shanties of 100 years ago now all have television aerials and look like desirable architecture. Cane on undulating ground still has to be cut with machetes. Agriculture is hard work, but today everybody gets a taste of it. There are schools out in the fields where Cuban children spend two weeks getting a tougher version of what our children call Work Experience. Billboards remind all concerned that their arched spines form the collective backbone of the economy. Everyone a worker and everyone a soldier. 'Commander in chief, go into combat! Your rear is secure!'

My own rear was aching by the time we reached Trinidad, an old colonial town with a lot of old colonial buildings. The heat was sensational and there was no relief except beer. It was a Spaghetti Western set begging for Clint Eastwood to ride in and open an ice-cream parlour. Even the most up-market British tourist would have to be pretty interested in natural history to come all this way just to faint in front of the same house where Alexander von Humboldt once dissected a few specimens.

Gladly we doubled back to the coastal city of Cienfuegos, whose installations seemed to consist of only one hotel. The bay of Cienfuegos was famously beautiful up until the day we got there, when a Russian tanker, instead of delivering 1,000 tons of oil into the refinery, pumped it straight into the water. On television that night there was a frank admission, or rather a frank accusation, of incompetence. Those responsible would be disciplined. There were pictures of a man in uniform poking a long stick into the bay, pulling it out again and gazing learnedly at the high proportion of it which was covered with goo.

What we would have done in Cienfuegos if the bay had not been converted into a sump I never discovered, but I did discover someone who was selling old revolutionary posters. She wasn't running an Intur shop. She was in business for herself – one of the free market merchants grudgingly allowed to operate for a while until they become too success-ful and have to be clamped down on again. Cleverly she had guessed that what the hip visitor really wanted was pictures of the men who had dreamed up the utopia in whose interstices she now scratched to make an extra buck. If she is really smart, she may even rake together enough dollars to live like a tourist.

'My city, happy and beautiful,' said a large sign as we left Cienfuegos, its oilslick gleaming in the dawn. Pressure from us, plus some admirably persistent phone-calls from our guide to his headquarters, had expanded our schedule beyond the envisaged touristic limits and into the realm of politics. We were heading for the Bay of Pigs, so called because of the large numbers of crocodiles, parakeets, crabs and flies in the area.

Playa Larga, one of the several beaches around the Bay of Pigs, turned out to be very pleasant, with a nice restaurant full of real Cubans. Crabs crawl out of the sea and march a long way inland – much further than the invaders ever did. Slower crabs which get no further than the restaurant can be eaten while you contemplate the CIA's folly.

You shouldn't contemplate it too long if you prefer to believe that the CIA machinates ruthlessly in the interests of US imperialism. At the time it seemed more plausible that the CIA was machinating ruthlessly in the interests of revolutionary Cuba. The invasion plan was demented. Even if the Contras had not been stopped cold by Fidel's armour, they would have run out of gas further up the road. The scheme was predicated on the assumption that the people would rise.

Only a fool could have believed they would. If you don't see how a man as smart as Kennedy could have been such an idiot, the only remaining explanation is that the whole enterprise was designed to drive Castro further down the road to Socialism, in order that the eventual lack of consumer goods might serve as an awful warning to the rest of Latin America. If that was the idea, it didn't work with the Nicaraguans. But maybe that's part of the plot too! On my third daiquiri and second cigar, suddenly I saw it all.

I was downing the daiquiri, and mauling the Monte Cristo, back in Havana, where our trip was drawing to an end. At Floridita we got into training for a visit to the Finca Vigia, Hemingway's old house on a hilltop outside the city. This item had not been on the schedule either, but half a day came free when one of our number, a fluent Spanish speaker, fell victim to Cuban paperwork. He wanted to stay on a few extra days, an initiative which would alter his status from Intur invitee to individual foreign visitor. Two different departments being involved in this change of classification, a third department had to be brought in so that the first two

354

could be put in touch with each other. Only narrowly did he avoid having his visa cancelled altogether. I watched him disappear under a hill of paper.

On a hill only slightly larger, Hemingway's villa looked out over the polluted city and back to a less bureaucratic time. But it had been a corrupt time, too – a fact of which Hemingway was well aware. Papa had liked Fidel, and vice versa. With beards interlocked they had given Batista the kiss-off. Fidel has kept the friendship well tended. The villa is in spanking condition. You aren't allowed inside because of weak floorboards, but everything can be seen from the windows. On the walls are the heads of everything he shot except his own. The size of his shoes is a revelation. His custom-made penny loafers are like twin canoes. He couldn't be more present if he was there.

A vivid writer doesn't write vividly, he sees vividly. Hemingway went where he could see life, and lived in Cuba because he thought the Gulf Stream was the great, clean, deep well of truth. He was an awful liar but he knew what the truth was.

That night in the Havana Libre I finished reading the march-of-history manifesto and wondered if Fidel still does. While I read, Fidel was on television, winding up a 20-hour session of the all-Havana assembly in which the delegates addressed themselves to him on those occasions when he did not address himself to them. Several delegates complained of too much paperwork and he promised to look into it. He made a note on a piece of paper, which did not bode well. Criticism was freely expressed but nobody criticised the one-party State. Democracy was dead and buried.

Perhaps it has to be. Revolutionary Cuba has a lot to be proud of. Nobody starves. Everybody goes to school. There is no race prejudice to speak of, or none that is spoken of. Women get equal pay. Old ladies do not get mugged. Though it costs a lot to dress well, it costs little to dress well enough. None of this would have happened under the old system, which would still be there if Fidel had not overthrown it.

If I speak with dewy eyes, it is because the Cuban

355

revolution was the great thrill of my generation. If the tears taste bitter, it is because one's residual admiration for those bearded heroes can't alter the sad fact that no concentration of power can perpetuate itself without ossifying. The horror stories coming out of Fidel's jails are not all of the CIA's invention.

Fidel locks up Cuba's real writers because real writers will agree to lie only selectively, and usually about themselves. For a man of Fidel's mental stature to lie systematically about the whole of modern history is a sorry thing. Because he needs friends among the non-aligned countries he says the Ayatollah Khomeini leads a progressive regime. Because he wants to please the Soviet Union, he calls the rebels in Afghanistan counter-revolutionaries.

It was at this point that I gagged on my last daiquiri and went back on the wagon. What else are the Afghan rebels trying to do except get an interloping giant off their backs? They are doing exactly what Fidel did when *he* was in the mountains. Has he forgotten who he is? But this was too deep a question to tackle on a freebie junket.

For one last time I ventured out along La Rampa and queued for an ice-cream. From far away I watched the cashier accept each customer's money and issue a ticket. Armed with a ticket, each customer queued again in front of the counter behind which a young man delved with a scoop. Nearby hovered a supervisor who had no incentive to sell a ticket or help dig. Elsewhere was an office processing the supervisor's reports. It was full of paper-pushers, who, on a hot evening after an easy day's work, would queue for an ice-cream without too much objection, because that's the system and it has a job for them.

So I didn't object either. It's their country. The girls looked prettier than ever and by now I knew how to chat them up in their own language. 'Ideology,' I said suavely, 'is, above all, consciousness.' They laughed until they cried.

Observer
13 July, 1986

Around the World in One Pair of Shoes

LAST SATURDAY morning when British Airways Concorde Flight 193 for New York taxied out to take off from Heathrow the coveted fourth seat on the flight deck was occupied by myself. My first Concorde flight was starting well. BA, having noted that I would be flying the flag on the opening and closing stages of my planned three-day flight around the world, was unashamedly after a good review.

It was in the bag. For my so-long longed-for, first-ever flight through the sound barrier I would be sitting up there among the lights, dials and digital read-outs. Usually the most glamorous young lady passenger gets the privilege and there were also several self-made British businessmen who had impressed me by their deportment in the Concorde lounge. 'No *way* I'm pain a secrecry nine arf fousand,' one of them had said loudly into the courtesy phone. 'For vat much *I'd* be a secrecry.' Once on board, another tycoon had handed the air hostess a suit-bag saying, 'Can I have this back before we land? On account of I have to make a quick exit.' He was already speaking American.

Twice the speed of sound wasn't fast enough for *him*. Undoubtedly the activities of either of these thrusting entrepreneurs were more essential to the national welfare than my strange mission, about which Captain Massie, as we waited for clearance to take off, frankly confessed himself puzzled. 'Why the whole world in one go?' I gave him the only answer I had ready. 'I just wanted to make sure it was round.'

The young co-pilot's response was something I had always wanted to say. Suave in dark glasses, he said it very well. 'Three, two, one, *now*.' An easy line to overdo. The runway rolled towards us while from a long way behind came an amplified version of the noise an electric train makes crossing Sydney Harbour Bridge. 'Rotate!' The co-pilot was getting all the best lines, but the air-traffic controller's voice through the headphones had a good supporting role. 'Set course direct for the acceleration point.'

With three computers in charge and her 130,000 horse-power on a tight rein, the beautiful aeroplane dawdled upward at only a few hundred knots towards the point, 28,000 feet above the Bristol Channel, where she would be allowed to let rip. 'From up where we cruise you can see the curve after sunset,' said the captain, politely still considering my problem. 'Believe me, it's round.'

Time to pump the lamp. The engineer pushed the four throttles forward with one hand. The pointer on the ana-logue Mach meter moved but almost nothing else did. That was it. Supersonic. After about Mach 1.1 you couldn't even feel her tremble as she went faster and higher all the time towards Mach 2 and 58,000 feet. 'It's a very potent motor,' said the co-pilot, who ought really to have been in movies but was probably too butch. The avuncular Captain Massie smiled tolerantly. It was clear that the Concorde's pilots have a good time. BA pilots who do not get to fly the gracile glamour-puss call her variously the Bionic Toothpick, the Poisoned Dart and the BAC Fuel-Converter, but would probably admit envy if pressed.

Back in my seat, I considered how long it took Magellan, almost half a millennium before, to get started on his pro-posed circumnavigation of the globe. Financed by Charles V, who wanted only 90 per cent of the take, Magellan left Seville with five vessels, having been helped to chart a course by Ruy de Faliero, the astronomer. But Faliero was also an astrologer, and after casting his own horoscope he decided not to go. He foresaw death. It might have been death from boredom, because after five weeks Magellan had still not even got his fleet clear of the river mouth and out to sea. But what Faliero saw was death from danger, of which there was certain to be plenty.

The chief danger I now faced was from too much comfort.

The Concorde is sometimes called cramped but in fact it is just snug. You aren't in it long and anyway it lengthens by ten inches when the racing airstream heats it up. Meanwhile the steak is excellent and the champagne copious. Very aware of the unemployed, I quelled pangs of conscience with the thought that my taxes had been paying the thirsty beast's fuel bills for the previous decade, and that in most respects I was travelling light. Where Magellan had five ships, I had one tote-bag with three shirts, three pairs of underpants, three pairs of socks and a copy of *The Magic Mountain*, this last to be read during any long waits in airport lounges. My portfolio of first-class tickets was just to ensure some sleep, otherwise I would be unable to write up my log at the other end. Magellan never had that problem. He got a sound sleep from exhaustion every night.

Invited back to the flight deck for the landing, I strapped in just as Concorde began a long diving right turn back from the stratosphere and Mach 2 towards a low altitude, 300-knot extended holding pattern that had the pilot muttering imprecations at the Kennedy tower. 'Request longer vectors.' 'Negative, Concorde.' At her least fuel-efficient in such a nose-up attitude, snootily she guzzled gas. 'She doesn't like going slowly,' said the co-pilot, still getting all the best dialogue. 'It's no problem, but it's wasteful.' There were rain clouds but we were signalled down before they broke. The runway swung up and pulled us in. Kennedy was crawling with wide-bodies. We were a needle among haystacks.

Killing two hours and a Silex of coffee in BA's Monarch Lounge, I read half a page of *The Magic Mountain* before picking up the *New York Post* to read about the Miss America disaster. Vanessa Williams, the reigning Miss America, had posed nude for *Penthouse* and forgotten to tell anyone. Now she must resign before the offending pix were published. Pondering the evanescence of fame, I transferred through the rain to the United Airlines terminal for my flight to Hawaii *via* Los Angeles. A short woman with a big behind was shouting at her son, who was called Scart, as in Sir Walter Scart or Scart of the Antarctic. 'Scart! Come here, honey! Come *here*!'

She also shouted at her husband, who was standing right next to her. Praying for a seat near someone else, I trudged on to the aircraft, which I was mildly nervous to discover was a DC-10. Nobody had been killed on a DC-10 for some time but there are an awful lot of seats even up at the front and if you get pinned against a window it can be awkward. Luckily the aisle seat next to me stayed blank. There was a video tape to demonstrate safety. It fouled up. 'Welcome to the friendly sk ... section ... front of ... *blup*.' It started again. 'Welcome to the friendly skies of United.'

For dinner I wisely chose the duck, but I shouldn't have eaten the sourdough roll. The movie started just as we passed over Kansas City. It was *The Bounty*, an excellent film about Captain Bligh's ambition to circumnavigate the globe. For thirty-one days he had tried to round Cape Horn in vain. In vain I tried to suppress the repetition of the sourdough. The movie ended somewhere over California. As we descended over the freeway into LAX, my shoes felt tight. United had not issued the usual enticing little cloth bootees, so I had not taken my shoes off, because getting them back on again can be a problem after the feet swell in the dehydrated air. Another hazard that Magellan never faced.

Nursing an orange juice in the cocktail lounge while waiting for the flight to resume I read another sentence of *The Magic Mountain* before picking up the *National Enquirer*, which had so many stories about the errant Miss America that I was still reading it when I got back on the DC-10. This time the aisle seat beside me was full, and how. At 2 pm local time, or ten at night on my internal clock, I was facing my first big challenge to the successful completion of my voyage. He must have weighed 300 pounds and looked twice that in his black silk Hawaiian shirt writhing with electric-blue flowers. It was Menehune Fats! With a Mai Tai clutched like a thimble in one giant paw he conked straight out. Getting past him to the toilet would take grappling irons.

The movie made things worse. It was *Terms of Endearment*. Before leaving, I had agreed with the Editor that only a movie starring Elliot Gould, or two movies starring Burt Reynolds, would be considered sufficient reason to abandon the expedition, but Shirley MacLaine and Jack Nicholson blending egos was a severe test. Also I had eaten too much papaya, the only fruit on Earth, in my experience, which actually *tastes* yellow. But Magellan, after naming the Pacific, had taken ninety-eight days to cross it with nothing to eat except rotten biscuits. When those ran out, the crew ate oxhides, sawdust and rats. United had treated me a lot better than that and I was duly grateful to arrive in Honolulu safe if swollen.

Until now I had been travelling through an extended day but at last it was night. It was too long before my next plane to hang around the terminal and not long enough to do the town, so I booked a room at a hotel within the airport perimeter. It was fifteen dollars cheaper than the Holiday Inn but it had air-conditioning and a bath. An alarm call woke me at 1 am and I switched on the TV to make sure I stayed alert while repacking my tote-bag. *A Bridge Too Far* was on the Late Show, but just as Sean Connery was landing by glider there was a flickering transition to a porno picture featuring a naked lady practising fellatio on twenty male appendages protruding through a paper screen. From the visual evidence she was not having much success. A chorus of ecstatic groans from her disembodied clients suggested otherwise. I left them all to it and caught a Singapore Airlines 747 bound for Hong Kong.

The seats in the nose of a 747 are arranged in pairs but are so big that you enjoy the pampered solitude of an enthroned boy emperor. Singapore Airlines reinforces this impression by providing twice as many air hostesses as any other airline. For religious reasons they serve you one-handed: hence it takes two of them to do anything. I had always assumed that this was the reason why there are so many of them but apparently it is not so: the real secret is low wages. If they are broke, however, it doesn't stop them being beautiful in their damascene uniforms of hip-hugging sarong plus fitted, waisted jacket. Since cabin service sells the airline, the girls are a big plus. The hot towels they provide are up to JAL standards – i.e., not only hot but wet, so that after steaming your face you can flap them to make them cold.

Bootees being provided, I took off my shoes. This would be the longest stage of the trip – ten hours plus – and the feet would inevitably swell. The rest of my body would swell to match unless I staved off every second meal. The seat reclined to the horizontal. Seven hours of oblivion supervened. When I opened the sliding window shutter it was dawn on the sea of cloud; pink-tinged on the streaked surface, puffs of lavender-blue cream underneath, and the depths shading from turquoise into lapis lazuli. 'Did you have a good sreep?' breathed a lovely face. Oh yes.

Opening *The Magic Mountain* I found Hans Castorp drained of energy, so that each day in the clinic consisted of nothing but meals and the space between. His knees didn't work. Mine still did, but only just. When we landed at Hong Kong I got my left shoe back on all right but the right one popped its stitches at the side.

Hong Kong was my big stop – from dawn to dusk. BA had arranged a press conference in a suite at the Hilton, so that the local media could ask me what I thought I was up to. This promised to be a major embarrassment but there would be several hours before the inquisition started, so I limped down into the Wan Chai district in search of someone who could mend shoes. An ancient man who had been doing nothing else for a century was sitting on a box. He wore sandals, an apron and little more. This was a sensible approach to the torrential humidity. I sat on another box, took off my shoe and handed it over. He took a look and got to work, bodging a fluted spike through the little holes and then threading strong twine through the spike. A dab of polish and the job was done. Five HK dollars. In Britain it would have taken a week and cost more than the shoes.

Once again evenly shod, with my shirt a wet rag, I walked through the fish market, where most of the fish are alive until you point out the one you want. Hong Kong is Computer City but you can still watch a woman gut the fish you will eat for dinner. That was what I told the bright young television man with the American accent and the quiff: that the world had grown smaller without necessarily becoming bland. Just because it was now one world didn't make it all the same place. The young man smiled nicely and told his crew to wrap up. No doubt he was wondering how the philosophical stuff would go over on a channel devoted mainly to the sort of Kung-Fu movies in which the hero wears black flared trousers and the soundtrack makes a noise like a tree being cut down every time he hits someone.

A nice girl called Anita packed up the glasses and the drinks the media had not drunk. For those who want to leave Hong Kong it now costs 400,000 American dollars for the so-called 'investment visa' that will get them safely away. The half-million people who make Hong Kong tick already have their getaway papers. The other five million are stuck. Anita is one of them. For a bad moment I felt like one of those rally drivers who go swerving dustily through an African village. The bad moment recurred at the airport because there were three big pictures of Mark Thatcher up on the wall. Billed as MARK THATCHER: RACING DRIVER, he was modelling Giordano T-shirts and looked dauntless. In the city his father calls Honkers, the same spirit perhaps no longer prevails undiluted.

How nice to have a home to go to. From here on it was a BA 747 all the way. Once again I was asked to the flight deck, for my very first take-off in the cockpit of my favourite heavy. Taking off from Kai Tak can be either interesting or very interesting, according to the wind. If you take off up through the hills it is very interesting because you can look into people's living-rooms. If you take off out to sea it is merely interesting. We took off out to sea through the suddenly dark night but made an immediate 180° climbing turn so as to head back across mainland China. With the turn complete I could see a pool of glowing cloud cupped in the hills of Hong Kong Island and Kowloon. It was shot through with the light coming up from the city, a junket of electric mist.

I had been to Hong Kong before, on the way out of China. It had been like coming back to life. The life was not so much in the glittering shopping malls of the Central district as in the hustling tumult of Wan Chai, where you can see a mechanic squatting on a box as he repairs a Ferrari Dino in a workshop so small that the tail of the car sticks out into the street. There are two-room electronics firms with washing hanging out of the windows. There are men who will repair your shoes. It is all very productive and all very untidy, and one day those mystical pedants from the mainland, who know what history should be like, might get the urge to neaten the place up.

Yes, I had been here before, going the other way. So with a long way left to go I already knew for a moral certainty that the world was round. When Magellan died in the Philippines he had the same certainty for a comfort. He had been there before, and therefore knew the way home. Not that it would have been quite as easy for him as it was for us. The captain dialled the course into the inertial navigation system and the aircraft headed for Abu Dhabi. I went downstairs to my reclining seat for a meal and a movie. The movie was *Footloose* and I watched it half asleep, which was apparently the way it had been made. Then a few words of *The Magic Mountain* put me out completely.

When I woke up and looked through the window I could see fires at the bottom of the dark: oil platforms in the Gulf. Still in my bootees I lurched up the spiral staircase to the flight deck and strapped in just in time for the approach to Abu Dhabi. The lights of the 13,000-foot runway lay on the blacked-out desert like a bejewelled Jugendstil hair-clip. When we touched down I thought there had been a mistake: the 747's cockpit is so high up that you feel there must be another fifty feet to go. 'This is still the only really great people-mover,' said the co-pilot, true to the BA tradition by which the first officer gets better dialogue than the captain as compensation for less seniority.

Topologically speaking, the terminal at Abu Dhabi is a torus – a doughnut of which you inhabit the inside surface. This is completely rendered in mosaic tiles, like a Byzantine particle accelerator transformed into a bathroom. It was here that the retiring captain, who had been even more avuncular than the captain of Concorde, introduced me to his successor, who was more avuncular still, like James Robertson Justice without the beard.

I had a fresh crew for my last leg to London, but in my case they did not have a fresh passenger. Strapping in on the flight deck for the take-off up into the seemingly perpetual dark, I was a hard man to impress or even contact. Nevertheless I was wowed all over again as we rolled like a tall building on castors down the extravagantly long bowling alley of lights. Captain, first officer and engineer all grew six arms each and the sum total of their button-punching sent us up to where, under the dome of the stars, a rim of soft white light ran around us far away, with nothing holding it up except darkness. I thought it might be dawn but the engineer said it was the ozone layer catching the starlight.

The engineer seemed very boyish although no more than the first officer. Nor did the captain, despite a great show of wry eyebrow and booming voice, look anything like what must be his true years. Flying keeps them young. Perhaps if I could work the controls it would do the same for me.

All I could control was my reclining seat. Expertly depressing the lever, I moved smoothly into level flight. The movie was *Splash*, an entertaining nonsense about a mermaid out of her element. On land she grew legs, but had to be back in the sea inside six days. After almost three days in the air I had not grown wings, but got ready to become earthbound again with some regret. To my own satisfaction I had solved the mystery, and in doing so risked disappointment.

On 27 April, 1521, almost two years after Magellan's enterprise began, the only surviving ship came home. She was the *Vittoria*, commanded by Juan Sebastián del Cano. He must have been a world-weary man. I like to think that Ruy de Faliero was waiting on the dock. What a meeting: one of them worn out from having actually been there, the other still excited with the possibility. If Faliero had been less the astrologer and more the astronomer, he would have realised that his science was the true magic and gone in search of adventure.

But he would have found it hard to maintain his enthusiasm. Once the imagined thing is done, it takes more imagination to bring back the excitement. In just my lifetime, long-distance air travel has stopped being an event and started being a cliché. But a miracle is no less miraculous for having become commonplace. Faliero's celestial maps and Magellan's heroic generalship are still there. But they are deep inside the instruments and the computers. One of the things that writers do, I think, is to recapture the old strangeness that lies hidden in the new normality.

Perhaps the price of wanting to do this is a childish nature. After sleeping like a small boy worn out by too much Christmas, I woke somewhere above Frankfurt to be regaled with BA's catering triumph: a jumbo version of the old country's chief culinary treat, the British Railways breakfast. How the ingredients for this had been obtained in Abu Dhabi defied explanation. I ate two lots of everything except the fried tomato, and thereby put the finishing touches to what would be, by the eye's reckoning, a net gain in weight of about ten pounds for the trip. Of the eighteen men who survived Magellan's voyage, few would have had the same complaint.

Back on the flight deck, the windows were alight with the slow dawn of Tuesday morning. We were scheduled for an autolanding but one of the transmitters on the ground got its wires crossed, so the captain took her down hands-on. As we banked over London I could see the *Observer* office where they had a hole in the page waiting for my copy. Then we straightened up, jacked out the flaps, and went in, parking right next to Concorde, which was getting ready for the run to New York. Using my index fingers for shoe-horns I finally got my shoes back on, but spent a lot of time bent double.

Observer
29 July, 1984

Index

367